European Yearbook of International Economic Law

EYIEL Monographs - Studies in European and International Economic Law

Volume 33

EYIEL Monographs is a subseries of the European Yearbook of International Economic Law (EYIEL). It contains scholarly works in the fields of European and international economic law, in particular WTO law, international investment law, international monetary law, law of regional economic integration, external trade law of the EU and EU internal market law. The series does not include edited volumes. EYIEL Monographs are peer-reviewed by the series editors and external reviewers.

Acknowledgments

This book emerged from my doctoral dissertation at Bucerius Law School, which was finalized on 11 October 2021 with *magna cum laude* honors. The dissertation and the resulting book owe their existence to the steadfast support of numerous individuals.

First and foremost, I wish to express my heartfelt gratitude to my doctoral supervisor Professor Michael Fehling at Bucerius Law School, for his exceptional guidance. His help was essential in overcoming the challenges inherent in this comparative research, encompassing four legal spheres. His team at Bucerius Law School provided invaluable help throughout my time in Hamburg.

I extend my thanks to Professor Christian Bumke at Bucerius Law School for meticulously examining my dissertation as the second reviewer and offering constructive feedback. I also wish to express my appreciation to Professor Sedat Çal at Hacettepe University for inspiring me to develop my career in the field of economic regulations and encouraging me to pursue a Ph.D. abroad.

My experience at the Max Planck Institute for Comparative Public Law and International Law in Heidelberg significantly influenced my research. I am grateful to Professor Anne Peters, Professor Armin von Bogdandy, and their team for accommodating me. The multicultural academic environment greatly enriched my thought process.

The German Academic Exchange Service (DAAD) made this work financially possible with their full doctoral support for my time in Germany. I would like to thank their teams in Turkey and Bonn for assisting many Turkish researchers like me to forge scientific and cultural connections between the two countries.

Lastly, I must acknowledge the unwavering support of my family. I am deeply grateful to my mother, Zehra Artantaş, for her unconditional love and dedication throughout my life. My dear wife, Günce Artantaş, has been a constant source of strength and inspiration since we first met. I consider myself truly fortunate to have her by my side.

Milan, Italy
April 2023

Onur Cagdas Artantas

Contents

Chapter 1
Introduction

> Today's great hope for a quick and sweeping transition to renewable energy is fueled mostly by wishful thinking.—Vaclav Smil.[1]

The "energy issue" is a major challenge facing humanity, marked by a triangular relationship between environmental sustainability, affordability, and supply security. When countries try to improve one aspect of this triangle, the other two become harder to achieve. Attempting to address two of these concerns simultaneously makes it almost impossible to reach the third. Unfortunately, this situation reflects the current state of affairs.

Today's technological level adds to the complexity of this triangular problem, as existing solutions often struggle to simultaneously address the three aspects of environmental sustainability, affordability, and supply security. For instance, while environmentally friendly, renewable energy sources like solar and wind power can be intermittent and location-dependent, raising concerns about supply security. Additionally, the current infrastructure and grid systems are primarily designed to accommodate conventional energy sources, posing challenges to the seamless integration of renewable energies. The costs associated with the large-scale deployment of green technologies, such as new investments or retrofitting needs, can be substantial, potentially hindering their widespread adoption. This financial burden, coupled with the relatively slow advancements in energy storage technology and grid modernization, further contributes to the lagging transition towards a greener energy economy. However, several emerging innovations, such as advanced chemical batteries, green hydrogen, highly efficient solar cells, decentralized smart grids, self-sufficient residential neighborhoods, and small-scale nuclear facilities, can potentially change the energy landscape.

Despite the promising nature of these new technologies, their widespread adoption may not happen as quickly as hoped. For some time, stakeholders will have to

[1] Smil (2014), p. 52.

O. Cagdas Artantas, *Promotion of Green Electricity in Germany and Turkey*, EYIEL Monographs - Studies in European and International Economic Law 33,
https://doi.org/10.1007/978-3-031-44760-0_1

work within the limitations of existing technologies. As a result, pursuing more sustainable, affordable, and secure energy systems will require substantial investments in the energy sector. There needs to be more than the private sector's financial resources to support such a large-scale effort. Private companies may not prioritize this transition, even with enough resources, as it may not align with their primary goal of maximizing profits. Furthermore, private actors often do not consider the adverse side effects that result from their operations. These concerns call for the intervention of government actors to (i) oversee and reduce harmful activities (e.g., greenwashing) by private actors and (ii) encourage the shift from the traditional energy economy to a greener approach.

This book focuses on the latter function, looking at the role of government actors in driving this change. It examines various policy tools, regulations, and incentives governments implement to promote the rapid and broad adoption of green electricity. Additionally, the book explores the challenges governments face in balancing the competing demands of environmental sustainability, affordability, and supply security while navigating complex political, legal, and economic landscapes.

Due to size constraints, the scope of this topic has been limited to specific jurisdictions. Green electricity promotion occurs worldwide and is regulated by numerous international and domestic authorities. This work focuses on four distinct jurisdictions.

Firstly, as a forerunner in green electricity promotion, Germany has actively supported green electricity initiatives since the early 1990s and has achieved significant success. Naturally, Germany has encountered a plethora of challenges and unintended consequences related to green electricity promotion. As a result, the German experience in this field is invaluable and serves as the first pillar of this work.

Secondly, as a member of the European Union, German law & policy on green electricity promotion is subject to or influenced by EU law & policy. The EU boasts a comprehensive body of regulations regarding this issue, making examining EU law instrumental in understanding the book's topic. Thus, the EU experience constitutes the second pillar of this work.

Conversely, Turkey is a relatively recent entrant in green electricity promotion. Until the 2000s, the country primarily managed its energy economy through state-owned enterprises, and it was not until 2005 that Turkey launched its green electricity promotion program. Turkey also serves as an excellent example of a developing nation with ambitious green electricity goals. The economic, political, and legal considerations associated with green electricity promotion in Turkey provide valuable discussion points. Turkey also maintains close ties with the EU. In the context of the European Union accession process, Customs Union agreements, and the burgeoning electricity trade with EU member states through the ENTSO-E interconnection, a thorough assessment of Turkey's position with respect to EU legislation offers valuable perspectives. As a result, Turkey emerges as the third pillar of this book. A comparative analysis between Germany and Turkey presents a substantial potential for identifying best practices. Based on this comparison and other international examples, this work seeks to generate policy recommendations for both countries.

The first three pillars—Germany, the EU, and Turkey—are all World Trade Organization members. The WTO plays a crucial role in this work for several reasons. Firstly, the WTO has an extensive body of law on subsidies, and its definitions of subsidies help clarify the notion of promotion. Furthermore, the WTO's dispute resolution arm has adjudicated cases involving green electricity promotion. Additionally, the WTO law is noteworthy due to its relevance to trade barriers on green electricity equipment. Subsidies can influence the trade of these products, making the WTO the fourth and final pillar of this work.

By referring to these four pillars, this book seeks to develop a set of theses on the "law of green electricity promotion." These arguments will be presented in the final chapter. However, the technical and legal background of promotion mechanisms is necessary to support these theses; thus, this background is provided beforehand. The promotion mechanisms examined in this book do not encompass a comprehensive list but instead, represent the most notable examples of promotion.

It is important to note that green electricity promotion is an evolving subject. As such, this book aims to generate broader and more enduring insights on the topic rather than just providing a summary of the status quo.

This book adopts a normative legal research methodology to examine legal regulations and offer insights into their evolution and significance in the realm of governmental entities promoting the transition to a more sustainable energy economy. By employing a variety of normative research techniques, an analysis of legal materials is conducted, reinforcing the book's central argument.

An in-depth exploration of positive law research encompasses applicable international agreements, such as those related to the World Trade Organization and the European Union, as well as case law from diverse entities, including the WTO Dispute Settlement Mechanism, the European Court of Justice, and national courts. Scholarly resources from multiple disciplines are employed to interpret these primary sources, which aids in the identification of key themes, lacunae, and debates within the existing body of knowledge on government-supported green electricity.

Legal principles are scrutinized to clarify the constitutional and administrative law foundations of the jurisdictions under investigation. By employing legal history research, this book seeks to expound on the development of legal domains associated with green electricity. Moreover, the book delves into the harmonization of regulations both vertically and horizontally, proposing potential amendments to address any contradictions that may arise.

Lastly, a comparative analysis explores how different nations, particularly Germany and Turkey, have tackled the challenge of supporting the energy transition. This analysis involves contrasting regulations and underscoring the strengths and weaknesses of various approaches, processes, and institutions in promoting green electricity. The focus remains on problem-solving and comprehending the historical and economic contexts of the examined legal solutions, ensuring a well-rounded understanding of the subject matter for a broader audience.

Reference

Smil V (2014) The long slow rise of solar and wind. Sci Am 310:52–57

Chapter 2
Technological, Economic and Legal Terminology

2.1 Technological Terminology

The topic of "energy transition promotion" is too expansive to cover in a single book adequately. As such, it was necessary to establish several conceptual boundaries. Firstly, the term "energy transition" varies in meaning across the globe. In this work, we adopt the German definition of energy transition (i.e., Energiewende). The energy transition is a multifaceted concept wherein traditional energy systems reliant on carbon-intensive sources are phased out and replaced by environment-friendly, reliable, and affordable alternatives. This concept encompasses the electricity sector and the transition of heating and transportation.

The electricity sector is crucial to the energy transition, as one aspect involves the "electrification" of heating and transportation. This work focuses on the shift from conventional to "green" within the electricity sector. "Green electricity" is a vital term within the context of this study. According to the Cambridge Dictionary, green electricity refers to energy produced in an environmentally protective manner, such as through wind, water, or solar power. Typically, domestic legislation defines green electricity as energy generated from renewable sources and waste.

While "clean electricity" shares some similarities with green electricity, it is a distinct concept. Clean electricity originates from renewable, zero-emission sources that do not contribute to atmospheric pollution when utilized, and it also includes electricity conserved through energy efficiency measures. Consequently, electricity derived from nuclear energy is considered "clean" to some extent. The "greenness" of nuclear electricity remains a subject of debate, particularly after the inclusion of nuclear energy in the EU green taxonomy in 2022. However, for the sake of terminological consistency, this work will not categorize nuclear energy as "green."

Defining "promotion" is another objective addressed in this book. In simple terms, promotion involves incentivizing actions that improve the recipient's position within the market economy. The intricacy of this definition is a subject explored in

O. Cagdas Artantas, *Promotion of Green Electricity in Germany and Turkey*, EYIEL Monographs - Studies in European and International Economic Law 33,
https://doi.org/10.1007/978-3-031-44760-0_2

this work. Nevertheless, for the purposes of this study, the core idea is encapsulated in the phrase: "law of green electricity promotion."

2.2 Economic and Legal Definitions of Promotion

States intervene in the market. To assert otherwise would be to disregard historical evidence, while arguing against such intervention belongs to an entirely separate discussion. Governments generate revenue and allocate it in diverse manners to address a range of objectives, including bolstering national security, promoting social welfare, or safeguarding the environment. At times, states employ their fiscal resources to stimulate economic growth by infusing the market with accessible capital, either through grants or concessional loans. These targeted expenditures are designed to bolster specific industries or private entities, based on the underlying conviction that such support will ultimately yield benefits for the broader economy. Conversely, governments may exercise their regulatory authority to redistribute resources from one set of private actors to another. As explored in the following discussion, this reallocation serves to further various policy objectives and may contribute to the overall well-being of the nation.

The situation where a state offers help to the overall economy, specific sectors, or individual entities has drawn the interest of many economists and legal experts. Various terms are used to describe these situations, such as aid, grant, bounty, incentive, subsidy, promotion, benefit, reward, financial contribution, capital injection, price mechanism, and bail-out. Many attempts have been made to create a standard, universally accepted definition from different perspectives, but without much success. In the following sections, my goal is not to try again to create a perfect definition, but to bring together the existing literature to form a strong theoretical basis for the later chapters. I will start by explaining the term "promotion," which will be used as a general term for all other terminology related to state support in this work, to keep things consistent.

The first section will also include economic definitions of "subsidization," a term that is used quite often in economics. This discussion will connect the concepts of promotion in the legal field and subsidization in the economic sense. After that, two important legal definitions of promotion—subsidies in the context of World Trade Organization (WTO) law and state aid under European Union (EU) law—will be looked at in their respective sections. Also, a comparison of subsidies and state aid will be provided within the state aid section, which will help set the stage for comparing promotion control mechanisms in the two legal spheres in later chapters.

The body of literature on government support for specific sectors and entities is abundant with varied terminology. Numerous scholars utilize different phrasing for a concept that essentially refers to the same subject matter. "Subsidy" is the most prevalent term among others, while "state aid" is crucial within the European legal context. Earlier academic works also encompass terms such as "incentive," "grant," "bounty," and "governmental aid." This wealth of terminology was likely to pose challenges for this work, which addresses the diverse aspects and manifestations of the same subject in distinct legal contexts. Comparative legal studies should at least attempt to adopt a "value-neutral language" to accommodate terms from various legal spheres under the scope of examination.[1]

Therefore, I will employ the term "promotion" as an overarching concept for all types of government support in different forms. This choice alleviates potential confusion for the reader that may arise from using the word "subsidy" in the literature.[2] "Subsidy" could be an all-encompassing term similar to "promotion," without a concrete definition or consensus on its effects, or it may specifically refer to the "subsidy" in the World Trade Organization (WTO) legal context, which has a precise definition and a set of remedies. In this work, the term "promotion" is used to encompass all subsidy, state aid, or incentive types with analogous objectives; and the usage of the literature that favors the general term "subsidy" instead of its WTO meaning is adapted to fit within this "promotion" framework.

Beginning with the current state of the literature, it is readily apparent that an authoritative definition of promotion is lacking. Instead, we encounter a variety of conflicting and overlapping definitions from diverse perspectives, and it should be our endeavor to reconcile these definitions. The methods used to formulate definitions also vary; the literature does not provide a reliable methodology upon which a standard definition of promotion can be established. Consequently, it is important to develop a reconciliatory perspective after considering all available accounts.

With that in mind, I can now proceed to define promotion. Dictionaries typically lack definitions for the term "promotion" as employed in the context of this work. Instead, they offer definitions for the term "subsidy," which is, to some extent, interchangeable with "promotion." Therefore, in this chapter, I will initially discuss the definitions of subsidy.

A widely cited definition of subsidy comes from the Organization for Economic Co-operation and Development (OECD): *". . . any measure that keeps prices for consumers below market levels, or for producers above market levels or that reduces costs for consumers and producers."*[3] The OECD definition does not restrict the concept of promotion to grants or any form of non-repayable monetary injections. "Any measure" in this context may encompass various other means of promotion, such as fiscal measures or regulatory easing, which I will address later. Additionally, the definition does not confine subsidies to government actions, allowing for a debate on the attributability of promotion. As a result, the requirement of governmental intervention is open to question. Finally, it envisions a "market benchmark," as the primary equilibrium factor in this definition is the "price at the market level."

---

[1] Moréteau (2019).

[2] The Kyoto Protocol itself prefers the term "promotion" to avoid the confusion and the political baggage of the term "subsidy": *"Research on, and promotion, development and increased use of, new and renewable forms of energy, of carbon dioxide sequestration technologies and of advanced and innovative environmentally sound technologies. . ."* Article 2.1 (a)(iv). UNFCCC (2005) Kyoto Protocol to the United Nations Framework Convention on Climate Change.

[3] UNEP Economics and Trade Branch (2003); OECD (1998). Cited in Bigdeli (2009), p. 157.

For consumers, promotion materializes as a reduction in the market price, while for producers, it represents an increase. Market benchmarking is a contentious issue in the literature on promotion, as I will illustrate in the subsequent subchapters.

The International Energy Agency (IEA) has formulated a similar definition specifically tailored to the energy sector. It is possible to momentarily remove it from its context and apply the definition to all promotion except energy subsidies in order to compare it with the OECD definition: *"... any government action that primarily concerns the energy sector, lowering the cost of energy production, raising the price received by energy producers, or reducing the price paid by energy consumers."*[4] In this instance, the focus returns to governmental action, moving away from acknowledging the potential role of private actors in providing promotion. This distinction is where the IEA definition diverges from the OECD definition. However, the IEA concurs with the OECD in adopting a more comprehensive definition of promotion by incorporating measures beyond financial grants.

Numerous other attempts to define promotion exist in the literature, both from international organizations and individual scholars. The issues arising from these definitions can be narrowed down to a few main topics. The first would be the scope of promotion or the extent to which it can be interpreted. Does promotion only encompass monetary grants? Or can we include indirect forms of promotion, such as tax credits or border measures? Determining the methodology to adopt when defining promotion is the second crucial question. Finally, it is necessary to explore the economic definition of promotion to assess whether a definitive economic definition is possible and if it could contribute to the descriptive efforts in the legal science domain.

The scope of definitions, as discussed earlier, varies from one to another. Some definitions only acknowledge direct monetary transfers, specifically grants, as subsidies. Others broaden the definition slightly, incorporating the provision of goods and services at a reduced cost. Some go even further, encompassing regulatory measures, such as trade quotas or relaxed environmental standards. Consequently, we can categorize the approaches to the scope of promotion into three groups:

1. The first group encompasses direct transfers to consumers or producers, resulting in direct or potential budgetary expenditure or the use of regulatory power to instruct a private actor to make a transfer, which is then reimbursed. Direct transfers can be exemplified by grants, such as research or investment aid, which provide non-repayable funds to recipients. An example of potential expenditure is the provision of loan guarantees (contingent liability). While the guarantees may never be utilized if the recipient never defaults, they reduce the risks for the recipient and decrease their borrowing costs.
2. In the second group, the government (or the instructed private actor) may offer goods or services at no cost or below-market prices, such as infrastructure, education, or raw materials. These contributions resemble grants but differ in

[4] International Energy Agency (1999). Cited in Morgan (2007), p. 5.

their means, as grants provide financial assistance, while the provision of goods and services are "in-kind" contributions.

3. In the third group, regulatory policies take center stage. This category of hidden promotion is facilitated by the government through regulatory easing for the promoted party—for example, an exemption from environmental standards—or by imposing a higher regulatory burden on competitors, such as border protection measures.[5]

The second challenge in defining promotion stems from the legal approach. A robust method must be adopted to identify promotion, but addressing this need itself is not without difficulties. Four distinct legal methods can be utilized for this purpose:

1. The first method differentiates measures based on their financial or regulatory nature. This measuring involves examining the legal act or contract on a broad or narrow scope. If the legal text characterizes the measure as promotion, it may be considered as such. However, governments often turn to hidden promotion to avoid countermeasures in the international arena.
2. The second legal method pertains to more indirect and concealed forms of promotion, which raise questions of imputability. Governments may act through private actors (e.g., companies, funds, foundations, or non-profit associations) to promote third parties. Definitions may necessitate a causal link or a clear act of direction (i.e., an order) to establish a connection of imputability.
3. The third method addresses the issue of the origin of resources used for promotion. The crux of this matter is whether a cost to the government is required or if it can be financed by private resources, leveraging government prerogative when necessary.
4. The fourth legal method centers on the objectives of the promotion. The rationale behind promotion becomes significant in this method. The aims of the promotion might be examined to categorize promotion types. For instance, "green electricity promotion" is one such classification, as the primary goal of some promotion types is to increase the presence of green electricity in the energy mix.[6]

More than the legal approach is needed to fully explain a complex concept like promotion. The economic approach is equally important and should be incorporated into this work by drawing a parallel between the legal and economic methods and clarifying the economic perspective on promotion. Since it is fundamentally an economic notion, promotion requires evaluation with the assistance of economic theory.

For an economist, the natural benchmark for defining promotion is a hypothetical market equilibrium without any government intervention. Classic economic models of general competitive equilibrium are entirely decentralized and do not include a

---

[5]WTO (2006), pp. 48–49.

[6]Rubini (2009), pp. 98–99.

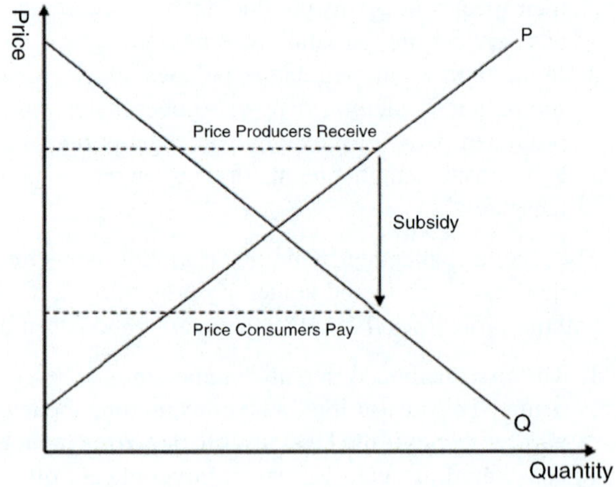

Fig. 2.1 Effect of the consumer subsidy

government sector.[7] Therefore, it is easy to assess promotion in this scenario. Government intervention (i.e., the introduction of promotion) changes the equilibrium. The effects of two main types of promotion in figures should be presented here: promotion of consumption and promotion of production.[8]

Figure 2.1 illustrates the simplified impact of consumer promotion on price and quantity. When a promotion is introduced to stimulate consumption and is offered per consumed quantity, the effect is as depicted. A gap emerges between the price consumers pay and the price producers receive, thus altering the equilibrium.[9] Two price ceilings enable consumers to buy more and producers to sell more, resulting in an increased final output. In the context of green electricity promotion, local content requirements, which will be addressed below, serve as examples of such consumption promotion. In some cases, electricity investors receive higher remuneration if they use locally produced equipment. This type of promotion boosts demand for locally manufactured equipment and increases local output.

In Fig. 2.2, domestic promotion is provided per unit produced. The domestic supply meets the domestic demand at D_0 and S_0; however, the world price (P^*) is lower than the equilibrium. OQ_0 represents domestic production, and Q_0Q_d corresponds to imports. Promotion is introduced per unit produced, causing the supply curve to shift rightward due to increased production (from S_0 to S_1). The domestic price level decreases to P_1, and as a result, imports are reduced by Q_0Q_1. Production promotion is a common method for supporting green electricity. For instance, Feed-in Tariffs typically promote green electricity per kWh of electricity generated.

[7] Sykes (2003).

[8] Other promotion types are examined in the economic literature, e.g., export and import subsidies. Nevertheless, the two mentioned types are more relevant in the context of this book and illustrate a simpler picture of the economic effects.

[9] Skovgaard (2017), pp. 341–343.

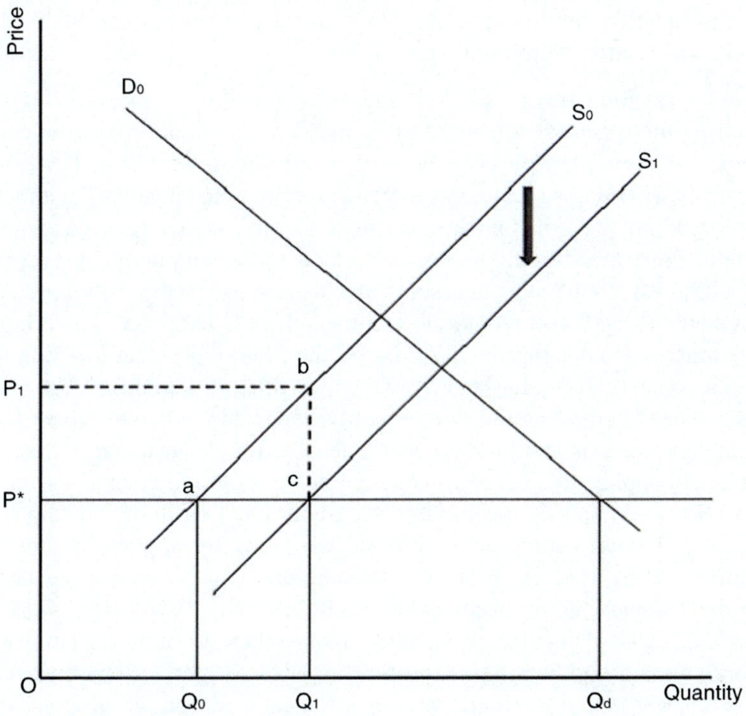

Fig. 2.2 Effect of the production subsidy

Nevertheless, it is crucial to keep in mind that the scenarios mentioned above are purely hypothetical and illustrated for the sake of understanding. In reality, there are no situations where the government is entirely absent and then suddenly enters the frame. Governments are present in every situation and transaction through regulations, taxes, and support. Even when they appear non-interventionist, they still have some services, norms, financial needs, and promotions in play: value-added taxes, public education, highway investments, health, and safety programs, among others. As a result, a hypothetical market equilibrium without government involvement cannot be observed in real-world situations.[10]

Determining the "net" impact of government intervention is even more challenging. With various taxes and regulations in play, it is difficult to determine if a business is "better off" after government measures. The business in the example might receive a grant, tax cut, and employment support, but how heavy are the fiscal and regulatory burdens? Does the business have an advantage over its domestic competition? Is it better off compared to its international competition? Answering these questions is a complex undertaking, and as a result, an economic approach is

[10] Sykes (2003), p. 3.

needed to identify the net situation. Three different methods can be used for the economic assessment of promotion:

1. The first method involves examining each government measure individually, ignoring the offsetting effects of other measures. Promotion may be considered to exist if a program provides benefits to a business or sector. For example, a company receiving a grant may be deemed a "promoted business" without further investigation. While this method is simple and well-suited for legal assessments, it falls short in economic assessments due to its simplicity. It overlooks the offsetting effects of other measures and the competitive situation. As a result, this method may detect promotion in some cases where the business is not truly in a significantly advantageous position, as the promotion identified was merely a partial counterbalance for heavy fiscal and regulatory burdens.[11]
2. The second method assumes a generally applicable situation where fiscal and regulatory burdens and promotions are leveled for all businesses or sectors. If a tax or aid applies to all actors, these can be disregarded when assessing promotion. However, narrowly applicable programs stand out in this method. If some measures benefit certain actors beyond the generally applicable situation, this contrast can be used as a basis for assessing promotion. Regardless, this method has its complexities as well. Sykes describes it as "*little more than deus ex machina*": Calculating the net situation in one sector, let alone the entire domestic economy, is a highly complex process in its own right.[12] Some measures may have unclear benefits or burdens. For instance, a carbon tax program increases costs for polluting industries but benefits cleaner businesses by improving their competitiveness against dirtier technologies.
3. The third method involves comparing the impact of one government in its market with those of other governments in their markets. Suppose most governments offer promotion to a particular sector similarly. In that case, it may be assumed that these supports cancel each other out in international trade, and therefore the promotion can be disregarded in this sector. However, a promotion may be identified if one government offers unique support to an industry without equivalents in other countries. This method is innovative since it treats the issue of promotion as a competitive situation. However, it also has its problems. Governments do not tax and spend similarly; taxation and promotion programs can be quite jurisdiction-specific. Even when a similar program might be found globally (e.g., Feed-in Tariffs, which are widespread), it may be paired with different components such as local content requirements or employment obligations. Thus, all these promotion components will have to be included in the analysis.[13]

In summary, identifying promotion beyond pure economic equilibria is a challenging task. A promotion might be counterbalanced by other burdens within a country,

[11] Martin and Koplow (1998).

[12] Sykes (2003), p. 4.

[13] Ibid., pp. 3–5.

making the assessment of the net situation to detect promotion an incredibly complex endeavor. Comparing programs from different governments offers limited insight, as such measures often have unique aspects in each country. Therefore, the economic methodology can only serve as a starting point for legal assessment and cannot act as a substitute. Attempts to identify promotion solely in economic terms are destined to encounter significant errors.

It is crucial to note that not every transfer made by a government is considered promotion, as governments make transfers for various reasons, such as health insurance, pensions, and distress aid to civilians. Failing to differentiate between transfers and promotion could lead to all transfers being labeled as promotion, resulting in considerable confusion.[14] In the context of this work, only promotions aimed at facilitating the transition to green electricity will be evaluated.

As this part concludes, it is essential to outline the legal and economic terminology referred to in subsequent chapters. Firstly, a "broad understanding" of promotion will be employed in this book rather than a narrow one. The literature that regards fiscal and regulatory measures as forms of promotion beyond direct grants will be followed. Under this perspective, even hidden deficits, contingent liabilities, or border controls may be viewed as promotion.[15] As for the economic method, a straightforward approach that considers promotion as a measure that confers benefit will be preferred for the sake of cohesion in the legal analysis. The other two economic methods will be referenced when necessary, as some debates (e.g., specificity or trade remedies) will require input from these methods.

References

Bigdeli SZ (2009) Incentive schemes to promote renewables and the WTO law of subsidies. In: Nartova O, Bigdeli SZ, Cottier T (eds) International trade regulation and the mitigation of climate change: world trade forum. Cambridge University Press, Cambridge, pp 155–192

Freinkman L, Gyulumyan G, Kyurumyan A (2003) Quasi-fiscal activities, hidden government subsidies, and fiscal adjustment in Armenia. World Bank Working Papers

International Energy Agency (1999) World energy outlook insights: looking at energy subsidies, getting the prices right. OECD Press

Martin A, Koplow D (1998) Fueling global warming: federal subsidies to oil in the United States. Earth Track

Moréteau O (2019) The words of comparative law. J Int Comp Law 6

Morgan T (2007) Energy subsidies: their magnitude, how they affect energy investment and greenhouse gas emissions, and prospects for reform. UNFCCC Secretariat

OECD (1998) Improving the environment through reducing subsidies. Organisation for Economic Co-operation and Development, Paris

Robinson WC (1967) What is a government subsidy? Natl Tax J 20:86–92

[14]Robinson (1967), p. 90.

[15]Freinkman et al. (2003); Noss J, Sowerbutts R, *The Implicit Subsidy of Banks*, ID 2071720, 28 May 2012; Rubini (2009), p. 90.

Rubini L (2009) The definition of subsidy and state aid: WTO and EC law in comparative perspective. Oxford University Press

Skovgaard J (2017) The devil lies in the definition: competing approaches to fossil fuel subsidies at the IMF and the OECD. Int Environ Agreements 17:341–353. https://doi.org/10.1007/s10784-017-9355-z

Sykes A (2003) The Economics of WTO Rules on Subsidies and Countervailing Measures. Law & Economics Working Papers

UNEP Economics and Trade Branch (2003) Energy subsidies:: lessons learned in assessing the impact and designing policy reforms. UNEP

WTO (2006) World Trade Report 2006: exploring the links between subsidies, trade and WTO. WTO Publishing

Chapter 3
Economic and Political Aspects of Green Electricity Promotion

3.1 Historical Context

The initial phase of promoting green electricity can be traced back to the 1970s, in response to the first oil crisis of 1973. The United States implemented the "National Energy Act" in 1978, a comprehensive energy legislation package encompassing several distinct laws, including the Public Utility Regulatory Policies Act (PURPA) and the Energy Tax Act. PURPA mandated that utilities purchase electricity from qualified renewable energy facilities, fostering a market for renewable energy and enticing independent power producers to invest in renewables. The Energy Tax Act introduced tax incentives for renewable energy, offering a federal income tax credit for investments in renewable energy facilities.

However, during this period, the predominant "renewable" sources were primarily hydropower and biomass (wood), and the recession of the early 1980s led to a decrease in energy demand, consequently reducing investments in renewables. Emerging technologies, such as wind and solar power, had to bide their time until the more favorable environment of the 1990s. In the United States, the Energy Policy Act of 1992 broadened the scope of renewable energy support by requiring the federal government to purchase a specified percentage of its electricity from renewable sources. It also introduced tax credits for electricity generated from wind and biomass facilities per kilowatt-hour for the first 10 years of operation. Simultaneously, numerous states began adopting Renewable Portfolio Standards (RPS) during the late 1990s and early 2000s, obliging utilities to generate or procure a certain percentage of their electricity from renewable sources to create demand for renewable energy and stimulate further development in this sector.

Across the Atlantic, the promotion of renewables also gained traction in the 1990s. The inception of renewable electricity subsidization in Germany, the European pioneer in clean electricity, can be traced back to the adoption of the "*Stromeinspeisungsgesetz*" (Electricity Feed-in Act) in 1990. This legislation

O. Cagdas Artantas, *Promotion of Green Electricity in Germany and Turkey*, EYIEL Monographs - Studies in European and International Economic Law 33,
https://doi.org/10.1007/978-3-031-44760-0_3

represented a significant milestone in advancing renewable energy in Germany and established a framework for subsidizing electricity generated from renewable sources. The Act obligated public utilities to connect renewable energy plants to their grids, purchase green electricity, and make payments based on a tariff initially set at a fixed percentage of the market average for electricity.

The Stromeinspeisungsgesetz served as a precursor to the more comprehensive and influential "*Erneuerbare-Energien-Gesetz*" (EEG, Renewable Energy Sources Act) of 2000. The EEG substantially expanded the scope of green electricity promotion in Germany, encompassing a wider range of technologies, implementing a more sophisticated tariff structure, and providing priority grid access for new green investments. Under the EEG, distinct feed-in tariffs were established for various renewable energy technologies, such as wind power, solar power, biomass, hydropower, and geothermal energy. These tariffs were designed to reflect the costs of each technology and provide adequate incentives for their development.

The promotion of green electricity expanded to other parts of the world, with China serving as a notable example. As electricity demand in China grew exponentially, alternative sources such as solar and wind power were advocated through an array of initiatives. In the 2000s, fostering green electricity via renewable energy sources became a national priority in China, driven by escalating concerns regarding air pollution and supply security. Over the years, China has implemented a series of laws and policies to facilitate the development and adoption of renewable energy, including solar and wind power. The first of these acts was enacted in 2006, encompassing grid connection rights, feed-in tariffs, cost-sharing mechanisms, and tax incentives. India followed suit on green electricity subsidization, initiating its efforts with the National Action Plan on Climate Change (NAPCC) in 2008. This plan marked the beginning of India's green electricity development, emphasizing solar, wind, and hydropower sources and providing financial incentives, tax breaks, and regulatory easing to promote new green investments and grid development, aiming to tackle pressing environmental, energy poverty, and grid access challenges.

The EU's dedication to fostering the growth of green electricity began to take shape in the late 1990s with the release of the 1997 White Paper on Renewable Energy and the 2001 Directive on Electricity Production from Renewable Energy Sources (RES-E). Although these early texts were not legally binding, they demonstrated the EU's foresight in recognizing the importance of renewable energy and its potential to address pressing environmental and energy security concerns. While these policies did not prescribe specific measures, allowing member states to tailor their strategies according to their resources and capabilities, they provided a foundation for developing a cohesive strategy to support the renewable energy sector.

It was with the adoption of the Renewable Energy Directive (RED) in 2009 that the European Union (EU) firmly established a binding and ambitious legislative framework for promoting green electricity. The global financial crisis of 2008 played a significant role in driving this policy change, as the EU sought to stimulate economic growth and create new employment opportunities in the renewable energy sector. Additionally, the increasing awareness of energy security and the need for climate protection contributed to adopting a more comprehensive and stringent approach to renewable energy development. This policymaking trend continued with the adoption of the updated Renewable Energy Directive (RED II) in 2018. The RED II raised the renewable energy target, reflecting the EU's commitment to expanding the use of green electricity and reinforcing its position as a global actor in renewable energy.

As the global economic order, characterized by deregulation, international trade, and open competition, began to exhibit signs of a paradigm shift toward the end of President Obama's second term, the United States took steps to counter China's aggressive industrial and trade policies. This shift entailed utilizing legal and diplomatic channels, such as blocking microchip firms from conducting business with their Chinese counterparts and challenging Chinese policies through the World Trade Organization's (WTO) dispute settlement mechanism. The Trump administration escalated this approach to its peak, leading to an increasingly visible Sino-American trade war. Ironically, the United States, the first and most prominent Western power to challenge the global economic order, had been instrumental in constructing this very system following World War II.

The EU initially struggled to respond effectively to this changing landscape. Nevertheless, the "EU Green Deal" was conceived in late 2019 to safeguard the EU economy while pioneering climate and environmental conservation efforts. The EU Green Deal aimed to simultaneously enhance energy efficiency and augment renewable energy generation capacity while shielding the internal market from carbon leakage, i.e., businesses relocating to countries with lax climate and environmental regulations, inexpensive energy and labor, and greater subsidies. A novel "Carbon Border Adjustment Mechanism" (CBAM) was introduced to counteract this, aiming to impose tariffs on imports associated with higher climate and environmental impacts. However, the EU Green Deal encountered challenges in swift implementation, mainly attributable to its comprehensiveness and slow-paced EU decision-making.

As trade issues intensified, the COVID-19 pandemic struck the West in early 2020. The pandemic significantly reduced energy demand and subsequently lowered carbon prices, negatively impacting the momentum behind renewable energy development until early 2022. However, the pandemic also strengthened protectionist sentiment by exposing the fragility of the global supply chain. This vulnerability became evident as the supply chain faltered due to economic fluctuations and national sanctions disguised as pandemic precautions. In the wake of these developments, medium-sized actors, such as Brazil, Turkey, and South Africa, began to distance themselves from the post-war status quo as well.

The evolving global economic landscape, combined with the challenges posed by the COVID-19 pandemic, has highlighted the urgent need for a more resilient and self-sufficient approach to energy production and consumption. This has led to a growing emphasis on developing and expanding green electricity sources. However, the catalyst for this shift toward renewable energy was triggered by a geopolitical crisis in early 2022 when Russia invaded Ukraine. The EU initially responded with diplomatic protests, but as the US intervened in support of Ukraine's survival as an ally, the EU escalated its response to a full-scale sanction regime. As the largest energy supplier to the EU, Russia retaliated by dramatically reducing its gas exports to the region, ultimately reaching near-zero levels by the end of the year.

Consequently, Europe began to experience a so-called "Energy Crisis" in late 2022, with skyrocketing energy prices and significant threats to the security of its energy supply. To avert widespread blackouts during the winter of 2022–2023, the EU was forced to implement stringent energy austerity measures, rapidly expand liquefied natural gas (LNG) imports, and maximize the use of gas storage facilities when needed. The crisis served as a stark reminder of the need to diversify energy sources and reduce dependency on a single supplier, driving the EU to prioritize investments in renewable energy technologies.

The "European Energy Crisis" has served as a stimulus, intensifying the global inclination to underscore the significance of sustainable, diversified, and localized energy portfolios. In light of the persistent risks associated with geopolitical tensions and mounting economic challenges, promoting renewable energy is not only a climate preservation strategy that offers economic benefits anymore but also a geostrategic initiative prioritized by global actors with a few fossil fuel-rich countries remaining as exceptions.

The impact of the war in Ukraine on promoting green electricity became apparent in March 2023 when the REPowerEU plan was provisionally agreed upon, introducing more robust legislation to expedite the renewable energy deployment and increase the EU's binding renewable target. However, it also became apparent that merely raising the renewable share in the energy mix would not be sufficient to construct a sustainable, secure European economy, particularly in light of the US "Inflation Reduction Act" that came into effect in early 2023. At first glance, this comprehensive package seemed to be aimed at alleviating the economic burden on US citizens and businesses. However, upon closer examination, it was apparent that the contents were primarily trade protectionist in nature. The legislation was designed to incentivize US companies to repatriate their production facilities and to encourage foreign entities to invest in the US economy. By offering generous subsidies and imposing trade-limiting measures, the act sought to attract businesses that wanted to capitalize on these benefits or avoid restrictive trade policies.

The only certainty regarding the future of the energy economy is the permeating uncertainty, especially when attempting to predict the long-term trajectory. Escalating open and covert geostrategic tensions contribute to a shift towards onshoring (or reshoring) and friendshoring practices as nations seek to secure their energy interests. Consequently, it should be anticipated that the rapid localization of both energy generation and equipment production will occur, reaching strategically significant levels.

This change in approach necessitates a departure from the multilateral, rule-based international legal framework governing energy generation and equipment production. Instead, plurilateral and more flexible systems serving regional alliances are likely to emerge. The EU's recently adopted "Fit for 55" package, including the Carbon Border Adjustment Mechanism (CBAM), exemplifies this trend from an EU standpoint: The CBAM is crafted to address regional requirements rather than adhere to a broader international order.

Consequently, this book delves into four critical topics: strategies for promoting green electricity, approaches for encouraging the localization of sustainable energy equipment, the legal framework governing promotion, and regulatory policy recommendations based on best practices. Nonetheless, to establish the foundation for these topics, the subsequent section of this chapter scrutinizes the underlying reasons for promoting green electricity and regulating the green electricity promotion schemes.

3.2 Economic and Political Rationales of Green Electricity Promotion

The underlying rationale for promoting green electricity encompass the essential "why" component, which supports the following "what" and "how" aspects. It is crucial to conceive this "why" element to fully comprehend the legal framework, as legal concepts cannot be sufficiently drafted without reference to their economic and policy underpinnings.

The rationale for supporting green electricity can be classified into distinct categories. The initial topic to be addressed is the economic rationale. This rationale is grounded in economic theory and its intersection with the policy realm. The convergence of these fields provides the basis upon which the economic argument for green electricity promotion is built.

The second topic to be explored is the policy rationale, which encompasses the strategic objectives set forth by governments. These policy goals are instrumental in shaping the direction and priorities of green electricity initiatives, ensuring that they align with broader societal and environmental aims.

Lastly, the legal rationales will be examined, wherein the distinctions between traditional command-and-control mechanisms and contemporary regulatory instruments are covered. This analysis sheds light on the legal preferences that facilitate the promotion of green electricity, highlighting the critical role that law plays in shaping and guiding the progression of green electricity policies.

3.2.1 Economic Rationales

The economics literature frequently attempts to explain the efficiency and ramifications of governmental interventions. Inherently a product of governmental action, promotion emerges as an important subject within the purview of economic theory. The underlying causes and consequences of promotion are inseparably intertwined with economic rationality, necessitating that legal research also encompasses the economic dimensions of promotion mechanisms.

Two main inquiries may emerge in relation to the economic aspects of promotion. The first question relates to the rationale underpinning the conferral of economic benefits, such as the provision of financial grants, tax reductions, or concessional loans. The second question relates to the regulatory aspect of promotion: What constitutes the economic reasoning that informs the supervision and oversight of promotional activities by governmental entities or international organizations? Although these two lines of inquiry intersect at numerous junctures, they must be examined independently.

In addressing the initial question concerning the rationale for granting promotion, it is essential to consider the fundamental economic principles upon which it is based. Specifically, welfare economics delves into the issue of promotion (referred to as "subsidy" within the literature) from the standpoint of efficiency.[1] The primary economic justification for promotion lies in its potential to enhance societal welfare.[2]

Promotion can augment economic welfare in two distinct manners: by boosting efficiency and fostering equity.[3] The overarching efficiency of the market may be compromised by market failures, which inhibit the market's ability to yield socially optimal economic outcomes.[4] Various factors contribute to market failures, resulting in suboptimal consequences.[5] Government intervention may bolster the performance of markets when private actors are unlikely to create efficient outcomes with regard to prices, output, and resource allocation. In these instances, governments strive to correct market failures in order to attain the optimal provision of goods or services, which in turn contributes to economic welfare. Nevertheless, governmental involvement should only be pursued when the overall welfare benefits surpass the costs associated with the intervention.[6]

The primary approach to fixing market failure entails introducing or intensifying market competition.[7] If such a course of action is unfeasible or impractical, governments may opt for alternative intervention methods to address the issue.

Within the spectrum of market failures, it is solely the phenomenon of "externalities" that bears a close association with the scope of this study. An externality manifests when economic activity has either a spillover cost or a spillover benefit on a bystander. Externalities can be categorized into two distinct types: When negative externalities occur, it causes social costs that other people must bear, whereas positive externalities generate shared societal advantages that others can capitalize on. In the case of negative externalities, the production expenses incurred by an enterprise are less than the total costs borne by society, whereas the opposite is true for positive externalities.

---

[1] Verouden and Stehman (2016), p. 40.

[2] Morgan (2007), p. 6.

[3] Bacon (2017), p. 7.

[4] WTO (2006), p. 58; Verouden and Stehman (2016), p. 42.

[5] Sweeney and Gillingham (2010), p. 69.

[6] Buccirossi (2008), pp. 632–633.

[7] Micheau (2014), p. 25.

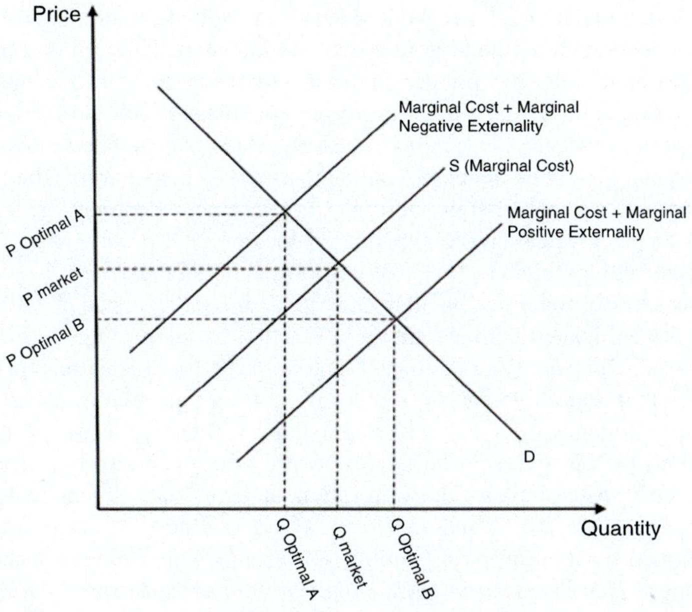

Fig. 3.1 Effects of Negative and Positive Externalities on Price and Quantity

The impacts of negative and positive externalities are illustrated in Fig. 3.1. Negative externalities encompass the adverse cost components generally not accounted for within the market. Consequently, in the presence of a negative externality, the market tends to generate more than the socially optimal quantity (*Q Market* – *Q Optimal A*). In contrast, positive externalities represent the converse scenario: the market is inclined to produce less than the socially optimal amount when a positive externality is present (*Q Optimal B* – *Q Market*). Promotion measures reduce the price level for goods associated with positive externalities (*P Market* – *P Optimal B*), while taxes and other regulatory interventions elevate the price of goods accompanied by negative externalities (*P Market* – *P Optimal A*). By employing such tools, governments strive to correct the imbalances created by externalities and promote a more socially optimal allocation of resources.

The negative externalities associated with electricity generation serve as textbook examples of market failure.[8] Electricity generation from fossil sources (i.e., coal, petroleum, natural gas, oil shale, bitumen, tar sand, and heavy crude oil) results in the emission of greenhouse gases (GHGs). As GHGs accumulate in the atmosphere, temperatures rise, and the climate undergoes significant changes. These alterations in climate are likely to incur both quantifiable and inestimable costs for the global economy, manifested through rising sea levels, crop failures, and the prevalence of diseases. Consequently, climate change can be regarded as a market failure of

[8] Acemoğlu et al. (2016), p. 232.

unprecedented magnitude throughout history.[9] In addition, traditional carbon-based electricity generation methods release toxic pollutants that adversely impact public health.[10] Nonetheless, the pricing of fossil electricity fails to account for these present and potential costs. Such negative externalities are consequently transferred to the national and global economy at large. Markets specifically designated for environmental quality do not exist, leading to a skewed perception of the actual costs associated with various energy sources.[11] For instance, electricity generated from coal may be perceived as an economically viable option; however, when factoring in the negative externalities, its true cost is considerably higher.[12]

Consequently, governments may aim to address the negative environmental externalities associated with electricity production by advocating for the proliferation of sustainable energy generation.[13] The rationale for this approach is grounded in the fact that renewable energy sources do not emit greenhouse gases or release hazardous pollutants. As a result, by endorsing eco-friendly electricity, it is achievable to mitigate the adverse externalities arising from the broader electricity generation process. Alternatively, the imposition of taxes on conventional electricity production could serve to internalize these externalities.[14] This perspective has been affirmed by the European Commission in one of its rulings concerning state aid, stating: *"There is merit in UK's claims that a residual market failure exists in carbon emissions in the long run since there are no long-term price signals for carbon and a lack of a sufficiently precise and stable regulatory framework for carbon reductions in the long term. This argument justifies some sort of government intervention to foster low carbon generation, which includes nuclear."*[15]

An additional adverse externality associated with traditional carbon-based electricity production is the national security risks inherent in this approach. Variability in market prices for petroleum and natural gas, along with supply uncertainties and the dependence on the geopolitically unstable hydrocarbon-producing regions, contribute to the national security risks linked to the promotion of conventional electricity generation.

The third externality associated with conventional electricity generation involves equity considerations. As previously mentioned, equity considerations constitute one of the justifications for promotion, as a more equitable distribution of wealth

---

[9] Stern (2007).

[10] GSI (2021) Air Pollution and the Health Cost of Coal. https://www.iisd.org/gsi/subsidy-watch-blog/air-pollution-and-health-cost-coal.

[11] Fisher and Rothkopf (1989).

[12] Sweeney and Gillingham (2010), p. 73; EIA, Annual Energy Outlook 2022, 2022; IISD, Financial Supports for Coal and Renewables in Indonesia, 2017.

[13] Cosbey and Mavroidis (2014), p. 44.

[14] Owen (2006), p. 632.

[15] Commission Decision (EU) 2015/658 of 8 October 2014 on the aid measure SA.34947 (2013/C) (ex 2013/N) which the United Kingdom is planning to implement for support to the Hinkley Point C nuclear power station. See: Robins and Chakma (2016).

enhances societal welfare.[16] Carbon-based generation is a geographically centralized method of production, with generation concentrated around large power plants. This results in regional welfare disparities and intra-regional urban-rural divides. In contrast, green electricity generation is, to a certain degree, decentralized, potentially fostering welfare and economic cohesion across broader areas, particularly in underdeveloped regions.

The fourth type of externality pertains to the technological and economic barriers faced by green electricity. The market dominance of conventional electricity imposes a negative externality that favors investments in traditional energy sources.[17] Experience with conventional energy forms may engender a "path-dependent" behavior, necessitating diligent policymaking to enact change. Another negative externality accompanying this is the "learning-by-doing" problem, as described in economic literature. The initial inexperience with new technology at the beginning of the supply/price curve results in higher prices for green electricity, followed by a downward slope.[18] Governments, however, may seek to address the learning-by-doing delay through promotion.[19] As the green industry gains experience, promotional efforts for this purpose could be reduced.[20] Germany and Turkey are currently considered to be ahead in the learning curve of green electricity generation. The primary focus for these countries now should be facilitating the transition to "economies of scale" within this sector.

A further notable market failure concerning electricity promotion pertains to the positive externalities accompanying green electricity generation. In contrast to conventional methods, green electricity production necessitates the adoption of innovative technologies, investment in research and development (R&D), and regional development due to decentralized installations and the creation of new employment opportunities. When a company engages in R&D, there may be spillover effects that benefit others through the dissemination of knowledge.[21] In instances of positive externalities, these spillovers are typically not accounted for in the market price of the good.[22] This situation also applies to green electricity. Consequently, promotion may serve to reduce the market price of renewable energy, driving it towards more socially optimal levels.[23]

[16] Verouden and Stehman (2016), p. 82.

[17] Micheau (2014), p. 76.

[18] WTO (2006), p. 60.

[19] Cima (2017), pp. 385–386; Cosbey and Mavroidis (2014), p. 44.

[20] Sweeney and Gillingham (2010), p. 87; Hart and Marcellino (2012), p. 196.

[21] Verouden and Stehman (2016), p. 44.

[22] Mankiw (2017), p. 195.

[23] The EEAG 2014 (Para 35b) explains these positive externalities as follows: *"The fact that part of the benefit from an investment will accrue to market participants other than the investor, will lead undertakings to underinvest. Positive externalities may occur for instance in case of investments in eco-innovation, system stability, new and innovative renewable technologies and innovative demand-response measures or in case of energy infrastructures or generation adequacy measures that benefit many Member States (or a wider number of consumers)."*

Examining the issue from a different angle, climate change exemplifies another market failure. The climate constitutes a public good, as no individual can be excluded from benefiting from the global climate.[24] The world climate is classified as a "common pool resource good," characterized by problems related to open access and depletion through use.[25] One consumer's utilization of the resource diminishes its availability for all others, and no individual can be excluded based on their contribution to the resource pool. Overexploitation of such goods is referred to as "the tragedy of the commons." In the absence of governmental regulation, only some investors would alter their investments to safeguard the climate, as there would be no incentive to do so. At the same time, greenhouse gas emitters and polluters would continue to operate in the market. In theory, polluters should bear the cost of the damages they inflict. This notion is encapsulated in the "Polluter Pays Principle". However, identifying the responsible parties and quantifying the monetary value of the pollution proves to be a challenging task.

Private actors and governments possess distinct approaches to addressing market failures. Private entities may engage in negotiations to achieve optimal outcomes. Such private bargaining can potentially result in an efficient allocation of resources. However, the transaction costs associated with bargaining may be prohibitively high, rendering the process unable to yield optimal results. This argument forms the core of the "Coase Theorem," named after Ronald Coase's argument on social cost: If transaction costs hinder effective bargaining, government intervention in the economy may be deemed necessary.[26]

In cases of market failures, governments may employ two distinct strategies. The first approach involves implementing "command-and-control" policies, wherein the government directly oversees resource allocation, sets prices for goods and services, and prohibits the production of certain commodities. However, command-and-control policies inherently possess certain drawbacks. For instance, they fail to provide adequate incentives for polluting industries to discover cost-effective methods of reducing pollution. The mandated technology or production method might not be the most economically viable solution, potentially leading to inefficiencies. The prevailing economic stance is to avoid command-and-control policies whenever possible.

The second approach adopted by governments is the application of market-based regulatory measures. This method aims to internalize externalities by leveraging market forces. The most prominent regulatory tools include corrective taxes and corrective promotion, collectively called "Pigouvian" measures, named after economist Arthur Cecil Pigou, who advocated for their utilization.[27] Corrective measures can serve to internalize externalities and preserve the stock of public goods.[28]

[24] Stern (2007), p. 25.

[25] Acemoglu et al. (2017), p. 250.

[26] Coase (1960).

[27] Mankiw (2017), p. 196.

[28] Heselhus (2018), p. 27; Cima (2017), p. 387.

Examples of such corrective measures within the energy sector include Feed-In Tariffs and carbon taxes.[29]

Corrective taxes may be employed in instances of negative externalities. By imposing a tax, the price of the good or service can be raised, resulting in output levels that more closely align with socially optimal quantities. Conversely, in cases of positive externalities, corrective taxes may be applied to competing goods or services to reduce competition and encourage the production of more desirable goods or services.

Similarly, corrective promotion can be utilized in both negative and positive externality scenarios. Promoting a desired good or service can bring the output closer to a socially optimal level. Alternatively, promotional efforts may be directed towards alternatives to undesired goods or services with negative externalities, thereby shifting the market equilibrium in favor of those alternatives.[30]

In the context of green electricity, governments employ both corrective taxes and promotional measures. One of the primary arguments presented in this book is that taxes on alternative goods and services can indirectly promote a specific good or service. For instance, a tax on greenhouse gas emissions (such as a carbon tax) may effectively promote green electricity as the market equilibrium shifts in favor of green electricity due to the rising price of conventional electricity. Conversely, the direct promotion of green electricity negatively impacts conventional electricity through an economic mechanism known as the "Merit-Order-Effect." The Merit-Order-Effect describes the decline in power prices at electricity exchanges resulting from an increased renewable power supply. The most cost-effective form of electricity is prioritized for grid integration, effectively displacing more expensive electricity sources from the mix.

The impact of increased utilization of a cost-effective energy source is depicted in Fig. 3.2. The integration of inexpensive wind-generated electricity into the energy mix displaces the more expensive technologies, thereby influencing the market dynamics. Specifically, the average electricity price in the market (referred to as P_1) undergoes a reduction due to the inclusion of low-cost wind electricity, leading to a new lower average price denoted as P_2. Within this particular scenario, the electricity generated from natural gas, nuclear sources, and a segment of solar PV

[29] Barcelona (2012).

[30] Lanneau (2018), p. 321. According to the European Commission the existence of externalities does not justify the promotion measures per se. First, the Member States should implement other measures, suchlike emission trading or carbon taxes. The Commission explains its stance as follows: *"The mere existence of market failures in a certain context is not sufficient to justify State intervention. In particular, other policies and measures may already be in place to address some of the market failures identified. Examples include sectorial regulation, mandatory pollution standards, pricing mechanisms such as the Union Emissions Trading System ('ETS') and carbon taxes. Additional measures including State aid may only be directed at the residual market failure, that is to say the market failure that remains unaddressed by such other policies and measures. It is also important to show how State aid reinforces other policies and measures in place that aim at remedying the same market failure. Therefore, the case for the necessity of State aid is weaker if it counteracts other policies targeted at the same market failure."* (EEAG 2014, Para. 36)

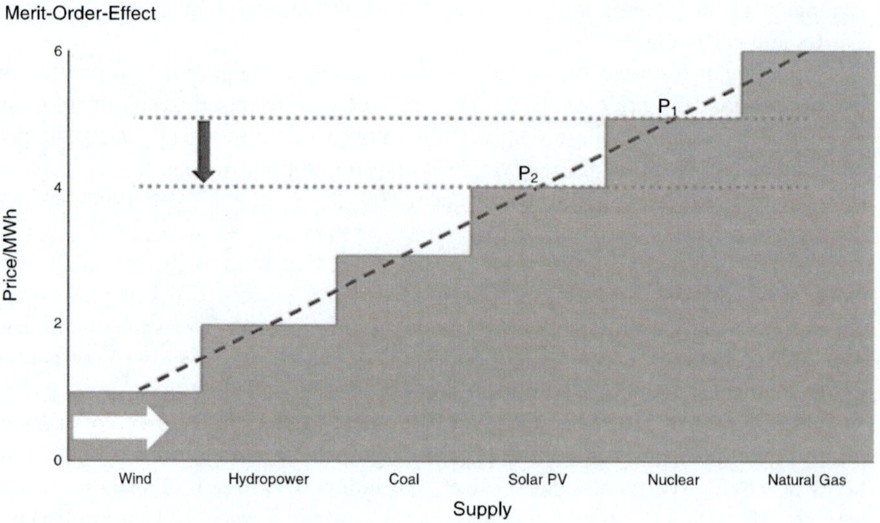

Fig. 3.2 The Merit-Order-Effect on Electricity Mix via Increased Use of Lower Cost Electricity Sources

installations is excluded, while coal electricity output remains in the mix. However, such a situation may not be favorably viewed by policymakers and legislators. Consequently, measures promoting the adoption of green electricity may be implemented to simulate a new regulatory merit-order-effect within the electricity mix.

Figure 3.3 explains the consequences of the heightened utilization of a more cost-efficient energy source as well. However, the cost dynamics of certain source types here are influenced by government intervention. Carbon taxes or cap-and-trade mechanisms led to an increase in the unit cost of electricity derived from coal and natural gas. At the same time, fiscal or regulatory measures promote solar PV output, consequently yielding a reduced cost for this particular source. Similar to Fig. 3.2, low-cost electricity generated from wind power plants is introduced into the equation, displacing the most expensive technologies within the electricity mix. Subsequently, the price equilibrium shifts from P_1 to P_2. Within this hypothetical scenario, the electricity generated from natural gas, coal, and a portion of nuclear power is excluded from the mix, aligning with the objectives of the carbon pricing and green electricity promotion mechanisms.

Although corrective taxes and promotional measures can be used interchangeably, this does not imply that a government should exclusively utilize one method. Many governments employ both taxes and promotional strategies concurrently or sequentially in order to achieve specific economic or policy goals.[31] However, some economists argue for a precedence relationship between corrective taxation and

[31] Meckling et al. (2017), p. 918.

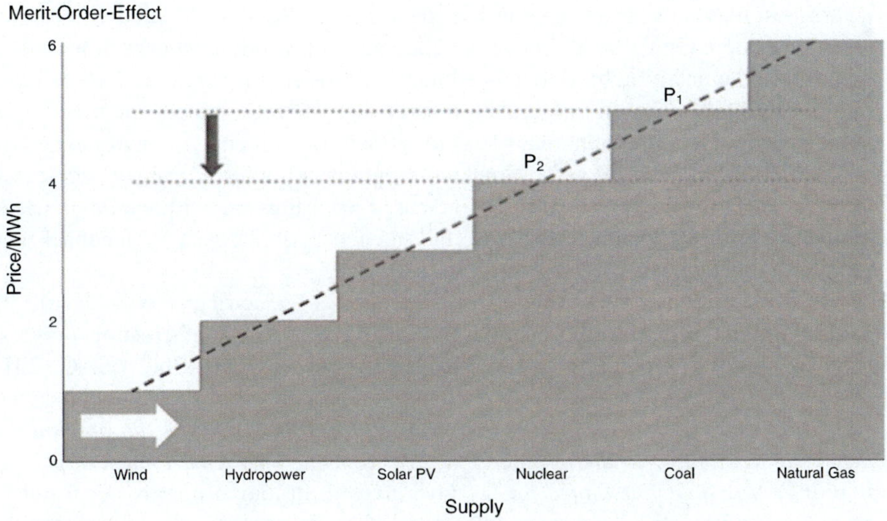

Fig. 3.3 The Merit-Order-Effect on Electricity Mix in a Regulated Market

direct corrective promotion in the realm of decarbonization, a notion referred to as the "Second Best Theory." According to this perspective, promotion diminishes social welfare by deviating from the perfectly competitive equilibrium. While markets are never truly perfectly competitive, the concept serves as a benchmark for evaluating actual markets. Critics contend that promotion may reduce social welfare even in imperfectly competitive markets. Consequently, promotion is considered undesirable and may only be the second-best option compared to corrective taxation. Corrective carbon taxes are viewed as less distortive and, therefore, preferable to economists. The second-best theory posits that if a less distortive measure is unavailable due to technical or political reasons, a more distortive solution might be the second-best alternative. If implementing corrective carbon taxation is not feasible, promotion might serve as the second-best solution.[32]

While significant economic justifications exist for promoting green electricity, several counterarguments exist as well. First, some economists believe that more than promotion being second-best is required to deploy these measures. They argue that promoting green electricity will decrease electricity prices, leading to inefficient usage at taxpayers' expense. This issue may arise in the absence of a "green energy levy" on electricity bills. By transferring the cost of green electricity promotion onto consumers, electricity prices can be maintained at reasonable levels, simultaneously supporting green electricity promotion and energy efficiency.

Second, the potential for regulatory failure always looms in the context of green electricity promotion. Due to political factors or insufficient information, regulatory

[32] See on the "Second Best" approach: Lipsey and Lancaster (1956), p. 11; Hofmann and Micheau (2016), p. 8; Sweeney and Gillingham (2010), p. 71; Atsu (2006), pp. 8–10.

authorities may not make appropriate decisions.[33] Regulatory failure refers to situations where regulators fail to achieve the outcomes stipulated in their mandates or do not adequately adhere to procedural or representative values.[34] Regulatory failure can manifest as under-regulation, over-regulation, or simply incorrect regulation. Naturally, such events can lead to numerous unintended consequences for green electricity promotion.[35] However, regulatory failures can be addressed through specific measures, such as increased coordination within and between regulatory bodies, organizational reform, and the establishment of feedback and monitoring mechanisms.[36]

Thirdly, critics argue that promoting green electricity will result in overinvestment in renewable energy. Indeed, there is a risk of creating perverse incentives while promoting green electricity. For instance, the EEAG 2014 prohibited overinvestment and required that promotion be proportional to objectives: "*Environmental and energy aid is considered proportionate if the aid amount per beneficiary is limited to the minimum needed to achieve the environmental protection or energy objective aimed for*".[37] Overinvestment may primarily occur due to regulatory failures and distorted competition.[38] Governments might overestimate the need for green energy and promote it excessively. Improved coordination, monitoring, and feedback mechanisms can help address this regulatory failure. Moreover, the primary issue concerning green electricity on a global scale is underinvestment rather than overinvestment. While criticisms regarding overinvestment problems in green electricity might be valid for specific regional examples, they do not accurately represent the overall situation.

Lastly, a comprehensive evaluation of the environmental impact of renewable energy and its negative environmental externalities is often advocated. Green electricity generation technologies have some adverse effects on the environment and local communities. For instance, wind turbines are infamous for their detrimental impact on bird migration and local property values. Battery production requires rare metals, which can harm the environment surrounding mines. Additionally, recycling aged solar panels is a problem that has yet to be addressed. However, these issues are generally considered less severe compared to the greenhouse gas emission problem associated with conventional carbon-based electricity, as the global effort for the environment is primarily focused on climate change, in line with the Paris Agreement of 2016. This book cannot provide an authoritative stance on conflicts such as "*climate protection vs. societal needs*" or "*climate protection vs. environmental*

[33] Cosbey and Mavroidis (2014), p. 43.

[34] Baldwin et al. (2011), p. 69.

[35] For instance, Spain had to re-regulate its green electricity promotion schemes due to excessively high subsidies, which became particularly apparent during financial crises. Binnie I (2019) Spain struggles to regulate renewable energy gold rush. Reuters.

[36] Baldwin et al. (2011), p. 78.

[37] Para. 69.

[38] Sweeney and Gillingham (2010), p. 75; Micheau (2014), p. 30.

protection". However, it should be noted that climate benefits alone might not justify a promotion mechanism if societal or environmental adverse effects neutralize these advantages.

3.2.2 Policy Rationales

An additional subject warranting discussion in relation to the justifications for promoting green electricity encompasses the policy objectives. While the previously mentioned economic goals were intimately associated with mitigating the negative externalities of electricity production, policy objectives embody alternative aspirations underlying the encouragement of green electricity. It is not uncommon for economic and political objectives to align. Governments frequently employ promotional strategies to achieve their policy goals. Although policy objectives may occasionally overlap with economic rationales, this is not invariably the case. Policy justifications often serve as the exclusive impetus for promotion. Political-economic structures, such as politicians' re-election motivations, render policy justifications more crucial for green electricity promotion than economic reasoning. Within this book, the intention is to examine the policy objectives associated with green electricity promotion.

Governments have diverse objectives when endorsing green electricity, including environmental protection, economic growth, wealth redistribution, and national security.[39] The policy objectives of green electricity promotion can be classified into three primary categories. The first encompasses "Environment and Climate Protection Objectives", which involve preventing health-hazardous pollution, reducing climate-altering emissions, and ensuring the sustainability of biodiversity and natural resource utilization. The second category, "Industrial and Developmental Objectives", includes economic growth, enhancement of welfare, employment creation, fostering innovation, and, consequently, improved export performance. Lastly, the "Energy Security Objectives" pertain to issues of supply security and national security concerns.

[39] In RED 2018 (Para. 3), diverse policy aims behind renewable energy promotion in the EU were explained as follows: *"The increased use of energy from renewable sources also has a fundamental part to play in promoting the security of energy supply, sustainable energy at affordable prices, technological development and innovation as well as technological and industrial leadership while providing environmental, social and health benefits as well as major opportunities for employment and regional development, especially in rural and isolated areas, in regions or territories with low population density or undergoing partial deindustrialisation"*.

3.2.2.1 Environment and Climate Protection Objectives

Since the 1970s, environmentalism has emerged as a significant movement, attracting a diverse political base. Over the past four decades, numerous states worldwide have implemented various measures to protect their citizens from pollution, natural resources from overexploitation (e.g., excessive deforestation or fishing), and the climate from harmful emissions. Notably, in the past decade, there has been a heightened awareness of climate, pollution, sustainability, clean technology, renewable energy, and energy efficiency. Nevertheless, substantial work remains to be done concerning the environment. Fossil fuel emissions persist in many countries, and emission levels have not yet reached tolerable levels in developed nations. In certain developing countries, natural resources are exploited unsustainably, and air and water pollution continue to pose global health risks.

This chapter will explore why and how green electricity promotion can serve as a beneficial tool for environmental protection, as perceived by numerous governments, will be undertaken. The majority voice in the literature argues that greenhouse argues that the most pressing contemporary environmental challenge is climate change. The GHG emissions contribute to a warming effect on the planet, known as "global warming".[40] This warming, by creating abnormal weather conditions, threatens biodiversity and agricultural capacity and is expected to impact the Global South disproportionately. Mediterranean countries, such as Turkey, will likely suffer more than Northern European nations due to their limited water resources.[41]

Climate change can potentially hinder or even reverse global economic growth. According to the Stern Report, 20% of global GDP could be lost indefinitely due to climate change, and additional factors may ultimately halve global welfare.[42] New migration waves are anticipated from underdeveloped countries in temperate climates to developed, colder regions. As food and water sources diminish, welfare in most countries may decline significantly. The emergence of new disease strains could pose further health risks. Consequently, there is an emerging global consensus to prevent climate change as quickly and effectively as possible.

Among international legal efforts concerning climate protection, the "United Nations Framework Convention on Climate Change" (UNFCCC) stands as a prominent source of law.[43] The UNFCCC aims to "*stabilize greenhouse gas concentrations in the atmosphere at a level that would prevent dangerous anthropogenic interference with the climate system.*"[44] In 2015, the parties to the UNFCCC adopted the "Paris Agreement", which establishes a binding global warming target: "*Holding the increase in the global average temperature to well below 2°C above*

[40] NASA Climate Change Evidence: How Do We Know? https://climate.nasa.gov/evidence.

[41] Tuel and Eltahir (2020).

[42] Stern (2007), p. 144.

[43] United Nations, FCCC/INFORMAL/84 GE.05-62220 (E) 200705, 1992.

[44] UNFCCC Article 2.

pre-industrial levels and pursuing efforts to limit the temperature increase to 1.5°C above pre-industrial levels."[45] Under the UNFCCC framework, parties are expected to submit their emission targets (Intended Nationally Determined Contributions) to contribute to the global objective. For instance, the European Union has submitted a target of reducing emissions by 55% compared to 1990 levels by 2030.[46]

Green electricity generation has been viewed as a significant means to limit GHG emissions, as the electricity sector produces at least one-third of global emissions.[47] Any reductions in emissions from electricity generation processes result in a considerable decrease in national emissions. Green electricity generation emits little to no emissions. Each shift in the electricity industry from conventional forms to green methods equates to avoiding a certain amount of emissions. For example, in 2022, Germany avoided emitting 232 million tons of carbon dioxide equivalent through renewable energy sources; electricity generation from renewables accounting for approximately 78% of all avoided emissions.[48] Consequently, increasing the share of green electricity in the electricity mix is a global policy target to fulfill the Paris Agreement objectives and combat climate change.

The second pressing environmental issue today is air pollution. The release of excessive amounts of pollutants into the atmosphere leads to seven million deaths annually.[49] Poor regions relying on inexpensive lignite coal and developing countries heavily using fossil fuels for electricity and heat generation suffer the most from air pollution. Notably, Asian countries that experienced rapid growth in recent decades (e.g., China and India) have consumed enormous amounts of fossil fuels to meet increasing energy demand. As a result, these countries have faced persistent air pollution issues, especially in their large cities. In these Asian nations, deaths due to air pollution are projected to rise even until 2040.[50] Highly industrialized and populated regions in developed countries exhibit worse air quality than rural areas. For instance, certain areas in Germany experience dangerous levels of air pollution.[51]

Renewable energy generation is perceived as a viable solution to at least partially mitigate air pollution. Green electricity generation, which emits no pollutants, can

---

[45] Paris Agreement of 2016, Article 2.

[46] European Commission (2020) 2030 Climate Target Plan. https://climate.ec.europa.eu/eu-action/european-green-deal/2030-climate-target-plan_en.

[47] Center for Climate and Energy Solutions (2020) Global Emissions. https://www.c2es.org/content/international-emissions/.

[48] Wilke S (2017) Greenhouse gas emissions avoided by renewable energies. In: Umweltbundesamt. https://www.umweltbundesamt.de/en/data/environmental-indicators/indicator-ghg-emissions-avoided-through-the-use-of.

[49] World Health Organization (2023) Air Pollution. https://www.who.int/health-topics/air-pollution.

[50] International Energy Agency World Energy Outlook 2016 – Analysis. In: IEA. https://www.iea.org/reports/world-energy-outlook-2016.

[51] Umweltbundesamt (2020) Luftqualität. https://www.umweltbundesamt.de/daten/luft/luftdaten/luftqualitaet.

help combat air pollution in two ways. First, as impoverished regions without reliable access to the electricity grid depend on electricity and lighting from kerosene or similar fossil sources, microgrids built around renewable sources and storage units may offer a means to avoid air pollution. Second, by transitioning from fossil fuels to green electricity in developing and developed countries, air pollution may be reduced as the introduction of a certain amount of pollutants into the atmosphere will be avoided. Consequently, many governments have prioritized green electricity promotion to address air pollution.[52]

The third environmental issue that green electricity may help to tackle is sustainability. According to the Oxford Dictionary, sustainability in the environmental context refers to *"the avoidance of the depletion of natural resources in order to maintain an ecological balance"*.[53] Sustainability focuses on meeting current needs without jeopardizing the ability of future generations to meet their own needs and may encompass economic, environmental, and social aspects. This concept calls for inter-generational (inter-temporal) equity, requiring consideration of future generations' welfare when making investment decisions to preserve the world's natural resources and biodiversity.[54] At present, humanity requires the resources of 1.7 Earths with the planet's biological and mineral capacity to sustain consumption levels.[55]

Green electricity generation may also contribute to addressing the sustainability issue. First, since green electricity emits fewer greenhouse gas emissions and pollutants, it is less detrimental to global biodiversity. Second, green electricity generation is less resource-intensive than conventional methods. Activities such as petroleum or coal extraction, which harm land, seas, and oceans, will be needed less with the transition to green electricity. However, the extraction of minerals and rare metals for renewable energy generation and energy storage equipment production will still be required. Third, and most importantly, green electricity generation relies on practically infinite sources. For instance, the Sun will continue to shine on Earth for another 5 billion years, the wind will blow as long as the Earth has an atmosphere, and rivers will persist in flowing. This is why the term "renewable" is used. Nevertheless, some renewable energy installations, such as dams, have finite lifespans. Additionally, the life cycles of wind and solar installations (alongside storage system installations) will continually create a demand for minerals and rare metals.

---

[52] International Energy Agency (2020) Energy and Air Pollution. https://webstore.iea.org/weo-2016-special-report-energy-and-air-pollution.

[53] Oxford Lexico Sustainability | Definition of Sustainability by Oxford Dictionary. In: Lexico Dictionaries | English. https://www.lexico.com/en/definition/sustainability.

[54] UN Sustainable Development Platform (2011) Transition to a Green Economy: Benefits, Challenges and Risks from a Sustainable Development Perspective. https://sustainabledevelopment.un.org/index.php?page=view&type=400&nr=131&menu=1515.

[55] Nace T Humanity Has Officially Consumed More Than Earth Can Produce This Year. In: Forbes. https://www.forbes.com/sites/trevornace/2017/08/03/humanity-officially-consumed-more-earth-produce-year/.

Bearing all these factors in mind, green electricity can still be considered more sustainable than conventional carbon-sourced generation methods, as it does not create a constant demand for mining and land use as the primary generation source. Therefore, governments aiming to foster a more environmentally sustainable economy prioritize renewable energy and promote green electricity generation.

3.2.2.2 Industrial and Developmental Objectives

Promoting green electricity constitutes a facet of industrial policy, specifically, a "green industrial policy"—a sector-targeted policy that influences the economic production structure with a secondary intention of generating environmental benefits.[56] Addressing this issue necessitates examining economic objectives alongside environmental aims, as industrial policies are inherently long-term economic plans.

The economic advantages of green electricity promotion have gradually become evident over the past decade. Until the late 2000s, renewable energy production was a costly method. Since then, the cost of green electricity generation has significantly decreased. In the 2010s, it became evident that green electricity generation can substantially benefit other aspects of the economy with the new cost levels. An increased share of green electricity in the electricity mix could positively affect economic growth. Naturally, in the initial phase, the increasing share of green electricity will diminish the economic performance of the conventional energy sector. However, two developments might occur after this point. First, a new wave of economic actors specializing in green electricity generation will emerge. Second, conventional energy sector actors will adapt to the new market situation and begin to invest in green electricity. For instance, in Germany, established energy firms (e.g., RWE AG through sister firm Innogy SE or E.ON SE) became significant investors in renewable energy. In the long term, the transition to green electricity generation is a process that generates new domestic investments and economic activity.[57]

Promoting green electricity may facilitate domestic investments in green electricity, at least during the "infant industry" phase. The EU, for example, emphasizes its focus on clean technology, such as green energy generation, as a source of growth.[58] Green industries were identified as an investment field to boost stimulus spending following the global financial crisis of 2008–2009.[59] According to the OECD, investment in modern, smart, and clean infrastructure in the subsequent decade was a crucial factor for sustainable economic growth, especially since infrastructure generally suffered from chronic underinvestment during the financial crisis.[60]

---

[56] Hallegatte et al. (2013).

[57] Khobai and Roux (2018); Marinaş et al. (2018).

[58] European Commission (2020) 2030 Climate Target Plan. https://climate.ec.europa.eu/eu-action/european-green-deal/2030-climate-target-plan_en.

[59] Omri et al. (2015); Mazzucato M, The Green Entrepreneurial State, October 2015.

[60] OECD, Investing in Climate, Investing in Growth, 2017.

Investments in new green electricity capacity and innovative electrical grids not only stimulate domestic investment but also attract foreign direct investment (FDI). Numerous direct investments originate from capital-rich countries targeting developing nations with high green energy potential. For instance, between 2007 and 2017, Turkey's renewable energy sector garnered USD 15.7 billion in FDI, with a significant portion allocated to green electricity.[61]

In previous decades, FDI in the energy sector was primarily concentrated on fossil fuel-rich countries. The recent shift in FDI towards the green electricity sector reveals unique opportunities for countries such as Turkey and Tunisia, which lack substantial fossil fuel resources but possess significant renewable energy potential. This emerging wave of investments may potentially foster economic growth in economically disadvantaged regions that are also scarce in fossil resources, thus alleviating poverty. By becoming net electricity importers through a surge of green electricity investments alongside a concurrent grid expansion, developing nations may reap the benefits of the energy transition by supplying developed regions with green electricity. However, as cross-border transmission infrastructure is currently unavailable in many parts of the world to facilitate electricity trade from developing to developed countries, foreign investment in the global green electricity sector predominantly targets domestic consumption. Nevertheless, it is plausible to anticipate developments in this area, particularly within the Mediterranean basin, facilitated by the ENTSO-E connections to North Africa and West Asia.

Green electricity generation inherently establishes a new market for green electricity and energy storage equipment. In addition to addressing the lifecycle needs of aging green electricity plants, an escalating demand for photovoltaic panels, turbine blades, and lithium-ion batteries is anticipated for new green electricity installations. This equipment demand may be met through either exports or domestic production. When exported, green electricity equipment procurement contributes to global trade and growth. Governments may promote green electricity equipment exports to expedite the development of green electricity capacity within their country.

Conversely, when domestically produced, which numerous governments prefer, this emerging green electricity equipment market bolsters domestic economic growth. Once a domestic green electricity equipment industry is established, it may start generating export revenue, yielding trade surpluses and additional tax income. Governments may integrate their promotion schemes with local content requirements to develop the national green electricity equipment industry swiftly.

An increased share of green electricity in the energy mix also enhances employment. In 2022, the renewable energy sector employed 12.7 million people globally.[62] It is worth noting that renewable energy is more employment-intensive than conventional energy.[63] Moreover, the decentralized and modular nature of green electricity ensures a more equitable distribution of employment, which benefits rural

[61] TÜİK (2023) Veri Portalı. https://data.tuik.gov.tr/.

[62] IRENA, Renewable Energy and Jobs - Annual Review 2022, 20 September 2022.

[63] ILO, Green Jobs: Towards Decent Work in a Sustainable, Low-Carbon World, 2008.

development.[64] However, it is also acknowledged that the transition to green electricity will likely result in unemployment due to the contraction of the conventional electricity industry. The OECD and World Bank urge governments to provide transitional education programs for workers in the carbon industry, advocating for a "just and inclusive transition" to the green sector. Transition assistance may also be allocated to areas impacted by such changes (e.g., aid program proposals for the "Coal Regions" affected by environmental policies in Germany).[65]

In summary, when paired with transition policies to mitigate adverse effects, the green electricity transition holds the potential to create additional employment across various job fields, including engineering, research, logistics, office personnel, design, and legal work, and manual labor. Consequently, governments often promote green electricity transition to stimulate employment. According to IRENA, the green energy transition may increase global employment by up to 0.1% and global welfare by up to 15% by 2050.[66]

Green electricity generation presents new opportunities for regions grappling with chronic "energy poverty." Energy-poor regions or households suffer from inadequate energy access or unaffordable energy costs. Affordable and accessible energy is essential for rural development. Green electricity generation, combined with microgrids and storage capacities, offers a viable solution for providing electricity to energy-poor regions. Clean energy reduces household pollution, conserves time spent on fuel collection, and enhances working conditions. Consequently, governments may promote green electricity to address energy poverty and potentially provide electricity to some households for the first time.[67]

Green electricity also holds benefits for welfare redistribution. As mentioned, the decentralized nature of green electricity distributes employment and investments across the country more evenly. With conventional methods of electricity generation, investments are concentrated in carbon-rich or industrialized regions. However, green electricity unlocks new possibilities for rural, underdeveloped regions with high green electricity potential. Investment and employment may shift from conventional electricity-producing developed regions to underdeveloped areas. Governments may expedite this process by implementing regional promotion schemes for green electricity.

Welfare redistribution due to green electricity expansion is not limited to the domestic level. Although expected only in the long term, with advancing cross-border transmission lines, electricity trade will become more feasible in many regions. This process might involve transferring investment and employment from

---

[64] Bhattacharyya (2011), p. 257.

[65] Bundesministerium für Wirtschaft und Klimaschutz, Wachstum, Strukturwandel und Beschäftigung für ein Strukturstärkungsgesetz Kohleregionen, 2019.

[66] IRENA, Global energy transformation: A roadmap to 2050, 2019.

[67] Daly H, Walton M, Energy Access Outlook: from Poverty to Prosperity, World Energy Outlook, 2017; Bhattacharyya (2011), p. 257; Beaton C, Moernhout T, A Literature Review on Subsidies to Electricity From Renewable Energy Sources, 2011.

developed countries to their underdeveloped neighbors or even poorer, distant regions. As such, expanding green electricity may create, for example, intra-EU redistribution of welfare.

Naturally, the movement of capital and employment domestically or cross-border will pose economic challenges for previously electricity-producing regions. The coal-producing regions in the EU are renowned for their escalating issues. As mentioned earlier, educational and social aid programs may be introduced to counterbalance the adverse effects of green electricity promotion.

A potential positive externality of promoting green electricity may be observed in the domain of innovation. Green electricity generation, being a comparatively novel approach, is amenable to ongoing research and innovative developments. Consequently, the expansion of green electricity stimulates innovation. Governments might choose to concentrate their efforts on promoting R&D within the green electricity sector in order to augment the overall innovation capacity. By promoting R&D in new technologies, governments can indirectly foster the growth of green electricity in the long run.[68] Emerging sustainable technologies, backed by the demand resulting from promoting green electricity, can be adapted to other industries in subsequent phases. For instance, as investments in green electricity increase, battery technologies may attract more R&D funding, pushing the transportation sector forward through battery-based e-mobility in return.

The promotion of green electricity may also address efficiency and regulatory capture concerns. Regulatory capture, a pervasive issue in industries characterized by dominant players, is common in countries with a dominant conventional energy sector. In cases of regulatory capture, interest groups within the regulated sector exert excessive influence over the regulatory agenda.[69] Governments may therefore favor green electricity generation over conventional methods to create a more diverse energy market, safeguarding regulatory watchdogs against capture. Nonetheless, monopolistic or oligopolistic energy market structures may impede this development for an extended period in many countries lacking ambitious transition targets. A considerable shift towards green electricity could take decades without robust policies and effective promotion in place. However, promoting green electricity with effective measures can create a more competitive electricity sector, as the number of firms operating in this area would likely grow. Smaller, regional generation firms could compete in tariff auctions (given that these auctions are held equitably), resulting in a more efficient electricity market. New market actors may emerge since the required start-up capital for green electricity generation is substantially lower than for conventional carbon-based electricity generation.

The final aspect of the economic rationale for promoting green energy pertains to path dependency in certain countries. Specifically, countries rich in fossil resources tend to rely heavily on these resources for their energy needs, leading to lock-ins

---

[68] Acemoglu et al. (2012); Hallegatte et al. (2013).

[69] On regulatory capture: Stigler (1971).

with conventional energy technologies.[70] Some fossil resource-rich countries, such as Saudi Arabia and the United Arab Emirates, endeavor to diversify their energy mixes since promoting green electricity can potentially reduce their economies' dependence on global petroleum prices.[71] Furthermore, industrialized nations have made substantial investments in conventional energy and possess extensive experience in this mode of generation, contributing to conventional energy lock-ins. Overcoming path dependency on conventional energy sources may constitute one of the economic objectives underpinning the promotion of green electricity.

3.2.2.3 Energy Security Objectives

From one standpoint, energy security objectives can be perceived as components of economic development goals, especially considering the term's narrow definition. In this limited sense, energy security refers to the uninterrupted energy supply. However, such a narrow definition fails to capture the complex underlying connotations of the term. Broadly speaking, energy security encompasses key concepts such as security of supply, resource availability, energy accessibility, resource diversity, supplier diversity, and affordability.[72]

Fossil energy resources are distributed unevenly among countries, with some being oil-rich (Saudi Arabia), natural gas-rich (Russia), or coal-rich (South Africa), while many countries lack fossil fuel resources to meet domestic demand (Germany and Turkey). Consequently, fossil resource-poor countries must import energy or fuel. Civilian, industrial, and military activities in these countries rely heavily on imported fossil energy sources, and even brief disruptions in supply can cause significant harm to welfare and national security.

Although nuclear energy necessitates dependence on enriched nuclear fuel and, by extension, a limited number of economies that extract and enrich these fuels, this has not posed a problem, as the nuclear fuel supply chain (such as Australia and the USA for mining, and France and Japan for enriching) is considered more stable and reliable than some fossil resource producers. In contrast, the Organization of the Petroleum Exporting Countries (OPEC) comprises 14 members that account for 40% of global crude oil production and possess 80.4% of known reserves.[73] Supply cuts or sharp price increases by OPEC and non-OPEC members pose threats to oil-importing countries. Natural gas creates even greater dependencies on gas-producing countries, as production fields and distribution lines are far more

---

[70] Fouquet (2018); Stein (2017).

[71] However, most fossil resource-rich countries (e.g., Russia and Iran) encourage domestic use of fossil resources via subsidized tariffs, rendering significant transitions to green electricity impractical.

[72] Jonsson et al. (2015), pp. 48–49.

[73] OPEC (2023) Annual Statistical Bulletin 2022. https://asb.opec.org/. Adding the "plus" members of the OPEC+ (Russia, Kazakhstan, Azerbaijan, Mexico, and Oman), this shares drastically increase.

limited than those for oil. For instance, 40% of the gas consumed by European Union (EU) members was imported from Russia before the invasion of Ukraine.[74] European industries relied heavily on natural gas or electricity from natural gas for their economic activities, generating political vulnerability for the EU.

Similarly, some nations exhibit a high dependence on energy imports. For instance, Turkey's import reliance exceeds 90% for oil and 98% for natural gas.[75] For such economies, diversification of the import portfolio is crucial. Primarily, they aim to diversify the countries from which they import resources. Importing oil or natural gas from as many countries and regions as possible is generally import-dependent countries' primary energy security goal. Secondly, from an energy security perspective, diversifying the resources utilized for energy generation is equally important.

Fossil resources may be substituted for one another to avoid excessive dependence on a single resource. For example, Turkey's aspiration to generate more electricity from local coal to reduce reliance on imported natural gas illustrates this strategy. Alternatively, nuclear energy and renewables can be employed as alternative technologies to address the energy security problem. However, nuclear energy will create new dependencies for nations without nuclear fuel extraction capacities or nuclear technology competencies. Consequently, renewable energy emerges as a more feasible solution for these actors to tackle the energy security problem as a national security issue.

Advancements in storage technologies will be a driving force behind the geopolitical effects of the ongoing green electricity expansion, as the intermittency problem still constrains this expansion's capacity. However, storage technologies have yet to experience the rapid advancements anticipated in optimistic projections. Furthermore, the need for rare materials or intermediate goods for storage expansion will give rise to new dependencies, particularly to China, due to their (often aggressive) success in dominating the global storage equipment market.[76]

Among other renewable energy modes, green electricity generation contributes to the resource diversification of import-dependent countries and resilience against supply cuts and sudden price increases. Setting aside (intra-day and seasonal) intermittency problems, electricity generated from renewable sources can replace electricity generation from natural gas. Green electricity may also supplant petroleum in the transportation sector through electric mobility. In the long term, heating and cooking needs could also be met with electric heaters and stoves powered by green electricity, thereby reducing the demand for natural gas and coal. However, this transition is challenging and likely to occur only over the long term.

Another advantage of green electricity is its localized mode of generation, which contributes to protecting the energy supply from external shocks. Moreover, green electricity is often available in the form of flows rather than stocks, making it more

---

[74] EUROSTAT, EU Imports of Energy Products - Recent Developments, 2020.

[75] EPDK, Doğalgaz İstatistikleri, 2020.

[76] On equipment dependencies: Vakulchuk et al. (2020).

difficult to disrupt.[77] Due to its localization and diversification potential, green electricity is a viable option for enhancing energy security.[78] Consequently, governments may promote green electricity. For instance, the European Commission has repeatedly emphasized the role of renewable energy in improving the Union's energy security.[79]

However, green electricity generation creates demand for green electricity equipment often imported by developing countries from more developed nations. This demand may not create energy dependency but can nonetheless result in import dependency. Sudden supply shocks or extreme price increases in green electricity equipment could indirectly affect the electricity supply negatively and jeopardize energy security. Alongside economic reasons (e.g., creating new export markets), energy security considerations underlie the "local content requirements" that many governments employ to promote local energy equipment production.

The objectives of localizing and diversifying energy sources address only the "short-term" aspect of energy security. The more far-reaching implication of the concept of energy security concerns the sustainability of natural resources. Oil, natural gas, and coal resources are finite and non-renewable. In contrast, green electricity generation does not face the issue of resource depletion. As a result, a robust green electricity capacity strengthens long-term energy security at both national and global levels. However, the materials used to produce green electricity equipment are not renewable; they are finite and require ongoing extraction. Recycling aged green electricity installations and redesigning green electricity equipment to incorporate recycled materials represent new frontiers for green technology innovation. Governments may, therefore, promote green electricity and green technology R&D to enhance long-term energy security.

3.3 Rationales of Regulating Promotion Activities

Promotion is a matter that the WTO and EU heavily regulate for legitimate reasons. Unchecked promotion can introduce new distortions to the economy as much as it eliminates them. This section aims to describe the adverse effects of promotion, which form the basis for the rationales behind controlling green electricity promotion. As mentioned earlier, there is a risk of regulatory failure associated with promotion. The occurrence of regulatory failures may be a reason for advocating for phasing out promotion or tighter control over it.

Promotion can be harmful in two ways. Firstly, a promotion measure may be distortive by itself and can be evaluated individually, in isolation. The second way of

[77] IRENA, A New World: The Geopolitics of the Energy Transformation, 2019.

[78] Koulouri and Mouraviev (2018).

[79] Crossley (2017); European Commission (2018) Security of electricity supply. https://ec.europa.eu/energy/topics/energy-security/security-electricity-supply_en.

examining the adverse effects of promotion is that it may create a promotion race between governments. This second approach entails a political-economic aspect. It should be noted that, in the EU, this political-economic aspect gains a legal framework and forms the basis of promotion control in EU law. Therefore, for the EU, this cross-boundary effect will be addressed. However, aside from the EU, this second aspect will be disregarded in the remainder of this book since examining promotion competition at a global level would be beyond its scope. The focus will rather be primarily on individual promotion measures and their effects in specific countries, as the cross-boundary political effects of promotion are still less relevant in the electricity sector.

First and foremost, the economic rationale behind the WTO's promotion control regime must be addressed. The WTO's rationale for promotion control aligns with its ultimate aim, which is to protect multilateral trade liberalization and drive it further.[80] WTO law control promotion to protect liberalized market access from trade-distorting promotion measures. The underlying logic for WTO control of promotion is that promotion, i.e., "subsidies", has effects similar to import tariffs. Through promotion, the costs of promotion recipients decrease, making their products more competitive *vis-à-vis* competing imported products. Thus, promotion represents a government-induced obstacle to international trade, akin to import tariffs.[81]

In parallel, promotion may increase export performance in the global market, distorting international trade in favor of inefficient companies. Promotion reduces welfare in both the promoting country and the competing countries. The welfare of the promoting country falls because the promotion is financed by public sources collected from citizens. The welfare of competing countries does not initially decline. At first, cheaper imported products raise welfare. However, over time, the industry of the competing country will be displaced or subjected to increased price pressure, which in turn reduces welfare as unemployment increases and the current account deficit widens.

There is also a risk of predatory pricing: the prices of promoted products may increase to excessive levels once they dominate the international market and eliminate competition. The excessive pricing of imported products with no domestic competition will have a substantial adverse effect on social welfare. With these concerns in mind, the negotiators of the WTO rules sought to control promotion at the international level through multilateral and unilateral measures. The "most-favored-nation" and "national treatment" principles are applied to ensure non-discrimination at the WTO level.[82]

---

[80] Micheau (2014), p. 32.

[81] Müller (2017), p. 5.

[82] The preamble of the GATT 1947 explains the aims of the WTO as follows: "*Recognizing that their relations in the field of trade and economic endeavour should be conducted with a view to raising standards of living, ensuring full employment and a large and steadily growing volume of real income and effective demand, developing the full use of the resources of the world and expanding the production and exchange of goods...*".

In the EU system, the control aspect of promotion is dominated by another concern: internal market integration. The EU's promotion control law is considered a subtopic of their competition law. TFEU Article 107(1) sets the goal of ensuring the compatibility of national policies with the EU's objective of achieving an internal market. As a result, promotion within the EU should conform with TFEU rules governing free movement. Distortions to competition in the internal market may counteract the effects of removing trade barriers. Thus, the primary aim of EU promotion control is to ensure that no new trade barriers are created through promotion. As a secondary aim, EU promotion control strives to prevent wasteful promotion races between Member States. These states may engage in competing promotion measures to influence the location decisions of existing and new investments. Thus, it can be emphasized that promotion control in the EU has a "harmonization" objective. As highlighted in the Communication for state aid modernization, a robust promotion control is essential for ensuring a well-functioning single market.

In conclusion, it can be asserted that the WTO and EU rationales for "subsidization - state aid" control are similar. Both systems aim to protect competition and trade, albeit on different geographical scales. The WTO focuses on preventing trade distortions and ensuring a level playing field in the global market, while the EU aims to maintain a well-functioning internal market, preserve the free movement of goods, services, and capital, and avoid wasteful promotion races among its Member States. Despite their different scopes, both institutions share the common (often unrealistic) goal of fostering sustainable economic growth and development, and their promotion control mechanisms contribute to creating a more stable, efficient, and equitable international trade system.

Building upon these arguments, the economic rationale behind the control of green electricity promotion can now be addressed. Similar to the general theoretical stance, the primary argument for controlling green electricity promotion lies in the market distortions it generates. While remedying market failures inherent to the energy market, green electricity promotion may introduce regulatory failures. Firstly, green electricity promotion may be excessive due to mismanagement and a lack of economic feedback mechanisms. Feed-in Tariff systems are particularly susceptible to this type of failure, while Feed-in Premium schemes reflect some market signals, as will be discussed later. The excessive promotion of green electricity may result in overinvestment in a few or all green electricity technologies. For instance, an excessively high solar electricity generation tariff may create a solar generation boom.

At first glance, overinvestment in green electricity may appear as a positive development. However, the technical characteristics of the electricity market should not be disregarded. Electricity demand, supply, storage, and trade must always be coordinated. Since electricity storage technology and cross-border trade are still not at desired levels, the intermittency of renewable sources may create risky grid congestion (over-supply) and power outages. Until storage and export become more viable, overinvestment in green electricity will remain an undesirable consequence. Limiting grid access to renewable energy projects may address the electricity congestion problem. However, in a congestion scenario, the promotion received by some projects will be wasted, which signifies the waste of public funds or foregone tax revenue.

Secondly, green electricity promotion may result in a lock-in on low energy efficiency. Promoted electricity may reduce electricity prices via the merit-order effect. Lower energy prices will diminish the incentive for transitioning to high energy efficiency. Inefficient technologies may persist at the expense of public welfare. This problem may be tackled through two measures. The first measure would involve promoting energy efficiency alongside green electricity. However, the effort to eliminate the adverse effects of one promotion measure with another may lead to a "promotion spiral", considered a distortive cycle that should be avoided. Nevertheless, governments may prefer to promote both domains so as to accelerate the sustainability transition.

Alternatively, as mentioned previously, electricity prices may be increased with a "green electricity fee" levied per electricity consumption. Increased electricity prices will incentivize energy efficiency investments, and the collected revenue could, in turn, finance further green electricity or energy efficiency promotion. This green electricity fee should cover the difference between the price of green electricity after the promotion and the market equilibrium.

However, due to the intermittency of renewable sources and fluctuations in demand, the price of green electricity after the promotion may exceed the market equilibrium price for some periods while being lower than the so-called "market clearing price" for the remaining days. This condition is inherent to green electricity. The first two market distortions caused by green electricity promotion mentioned above (overinvestment in green electricity and underinvestment in energy efficiency) may not exist in situations where green electricity remains more expensive than the market price of electricity, even after promotion.

However, in the third instance, promoting a particular green electricity generation technology may lead to a lock-in effect.[83] The promoted technology may become inefficient over time as new technologies emerge or customer needs change. Consequently, the promoted technology may persist for a longer duration than economically feasible, distorting the market. Some (tariff-based) promotion designs block price signals, while these signals also reflect the technological shift requirements. Other "market-oriented" designs might provide a limited but steady reflection of these signals, thereby reducing the possibility of a lock-in effect.

Fourth, promoting green electricity may aggravate development disparities at the EU level. Economically developed Member States might excessively promote green electricity to expedite the transition to new technologies, enabling them to overcome the learning-by-doing curve faster than less developed Member States. Technology disparities could negatively impact energy integration through the ENTSO-E. European electricity grid sections vary in age and technology, and promoting smart grids, for example, may create additional challenges in connecting national

[83] Meckling et al. (2017), p. 1.

grids at the European level. In this context, harmonizing grid-related promotion schemes might also be crucial.

Fifth, local content requirements associated with green electricity promotion can disrupt international trade as they function as non-tariff trade barriers. Although local content requirements are not mandatory elements of green electricity promotion schemes, they are prevalent worldwide. These requirements hinder the use of imported green electricity equipment in domestic projects. In response, competing states may also introduce local content requirements bundled with green electricity promotion, leading to a spiral of trade obstructions.

Finally, green electricity promotion can disrupt the international market through electricity trade. While still limited in volume worldwide, cross-border trade has become viable in interconnected regions, such as the Nordpool members. Promoted electricity may displace competing domestic electricity generation in the importing country, causing adverse effects. This outcome is prohibited under WTO law and challengeable in EU law. However, due to the current state of electricity trade, transnational trade disruptions related to green electricity promotion are not considered a significant issue.

References

Acemoglu D, Aghion P, Bursztyn L, Hemous D (2012) The environment and directed technical change. Am Econ Rev 102:131–166

Acemoğlu D, Laibson D, List JA (2016) Macroeconomics. Pearson

Acemoglu D, Laibson D, List J (2017) Microeconomics. Global Edition, Harlow

Atsu A (2006) The economics of subsidies. Crossroads 6

Bacon K (2017) European Union law of state aid, 3rd edn. Oxford University Press, Oxford

Baldwin R, Cave M, Lodge M (2011) Understanding regulation: theory, strategy, and practice, 2nd edn. Oxford University Press, Oxford

Barcelona RG (2012) Failed with subsidies?— try CO 2 tax! Renewable Energy Law Policy Rev 3: 121–130

Bhattacharyya SC (2011) Energy economics: concepts, issues, markets and governance. Springer

Buccirossi P (ed) (2008) Handbook of antitrust economics. The MIT Press

Cima E (2017) Caught between WTO rules and climate change: the economic rationale of 'green' subsidies. In: Klaus M, Huber BR (eds) Environmental law and economics. Springer International Publishing, pp 379–404

Coase RH (1960) The problem of social cost. J Law Econ 3:1–44

Cosbey A, Mavroidis P (2014) A turquoise mess: green subsidies, blue industrial policy and renewable energy: the case for redrafting the subsidies agreement of the WTO. J Int Econ Law 17

Crossley P (2017) The role of renewable energy law and policy in meeting the EU's energy security challenges. In: Leal-Arcas R, Wouters J (eds) Research handbook on EU energy law and policy. Edward Elgar Publishing

Fisher AC, Rothkopf MH (1989) Market failure and energy policy a rationale for selective conservation. Energy Policy 17:397–406

Fouquet D (2018) Germany. In: Fouquet D (ed) Renewable energy in the member states of the EU, 2nd edn. Claeys & Casteels

Hallegatte S, Fay M, Vogt-Schilb A (2013) Green industrial policies: when and how. The World Bank

Hart C, Marcellino D (2012) Subsidies or free markets to promote renewables? Renewable Energy Law Policy Rev 3:196–204

Heselhus S (2018) Energy transition law and economics. In: Mathis K, Huber BR (eds) Energy law and economics. Springer

Hofmann HCH, Micheau C (eds) (2016) State aid law of the European Union. Oxford University Press, Oxford

Jonsson DK, Johansson B, Månsson A et al (2015) Energy security matters in the EU energy roadmap. Energ Strat Rev 6:48–56

Khobai H, Roux PL (2018) Does renewable energy consumption drive economic growth: evidence from granger-causality technique. Int J Energy Econ Policy 8:205–212

Koulouri A, Mouraviev N (2018) Energy security through the lens of renewable energy sources and resource efficiency. In: Energy security: policy challenges and solutions for resource efficiency. Palgrave Macmillan, pp 9–35

Lanneau R (2018) Promoting renewable energies through state aid, a reform is required. In: Mathis K, Huber BR (eds) Energy law and economics. Springer International Publishing, pp 303–330

Lipsey RG, Lancaster K (1956) The general theory of second best. Rev Econ Stud 24:11–32

Mankiw NG (2017) Principles of microeconomics, 8th edn. Cengage Learning, Australia, Boston, MA

Marinaș M-C, Dinu M, Socol A-G, Socol C (2018) Renewable energy consumption and economic growth. Causality relationship in central and eastern European countries. PLoS One 13. https://doi.org/10.1371/journal.pone.0202951

Meckling J, Sterner T, Wagner G (2017) Policy sequencing toward decarbonization. Nat Energy 2: 918–922. https://doi.org/10.1038/s41560-017-0025-8

Micheau C (2014) State aid, subsidy and tax incentives under EU and WTO law. Wolters Kluwer

Morgan T (2007) Energy subsidies: their magnitude, how they affect energy investment and greenhouse gas emissions, and prospects for reform. UNFCCC Secretariat

Müller W (2017) WTO agreement on subsidies and countervailing measures: a commentary. Cambridge University Press

Omri E, Chtourou N, Bazin D (2015) Rethinking the green recovery through renewable energy expansion. Int J Sustain Dev 18:59–76

Owen AD (2006) Renewable energy: externality costs as market barriers. Energy Policy 34:632–642. https://doi.org/10.1016/j.enpol.2005.11.017

Robins N, Chakma T (2016) State aid in energy under the spotlight: the implications of the Hinkley point decision. Eur State Aid Law Q 15:247–257

Stein A (2017) Breaking energy path dependencies. Brooklyn Law Rev 82

Stern N (2007) The economics of climate change: the Stern review. Cambridge University Press

Stigler GJ (1971) The theory of economic regulation. Bell J Econ Manage Sci 2:3–21. https://doi.org/10.2307/3003160

Sweeney J, Gillingham K (2010) Market failure and the structure of externalities. In: Padilla J, Schmalensee R (eds) Harnessing renewable energy. RFF Press

Tuel A, Eltahir EAB (2020) Why is the Mediterranean a climate change hot spot? J Clim 33:5829–5843. https://doi.org/10.1175/JCLI-D-19-0910.1

Vakulchuk R, Overland I, Scholten D (2020) Renewable energy and geopolitics: a review. Renew Sust Energ Rev 122:109547. https://doi.org/10.1016/j.rser.2019.109547

Verouden V, Stehman O (2016) Economics of state aid control. In: Pesaresi N, van de Castelle K, Flynn L, Siaterli C (eds) EU competition law: state aid, Book One, 2nd edn

WTO (2006) World Trade Report 2006: Exploring the Links Between Subsidies, Trade and WTO. WTO Publishing

Chapter 4
Theoretical Issues of Green Electricity Promotion

4.1 WTO Subsidies Law

4.1.1 Definition

The regime of the World Trade Organization (WTO) on subsidies is distinguished as a significant framework for defining "subsidy" and its corresponding remedies. Consequently, an examination of promotion cannot disregard the WTO's subsidy regime and the associated literature. The objective is to encompass this literature to the extent necessary for establishing a foundation for subsequent discussions. Initially, it is essential to address a particular issue: The concept of "subsidy" within the WTO context encompasses merely a fraction of "promotion," as previously explicated. Thus, not all promotional measures are considered subsidies in the WTO's interpretation. However, all subsidies are regarded as promotion in the context of this study.

Prior to delving into the concept of subsidy, familiarity with the historical background and its evolution is required. The "General Agreement on Tariffs and Trade" (GATT) of 1947 incorporated multiple provisions on subsidies and countervailing measures within Articles II, III, VI, and most notably XVI, which directly addressed subsidies. Article II acknowledged the potential for countervailing duties, while Article VI stipulated the conditions for their implementation. GATT's Article III (8)(b) introduced an exception to the "National Treatment" principle, permitting the utilization of subsidies for domestic producers as an instrument.

Article XVI, as the central provision in the GATT concerning subsidies, does not provide a definition. Instead, it merely acknowledges the possibility of subsidies while imposing a notification obligation on the subsidy provider. The subsidy provider is also required to discuss the potential limitations of the subsidy with other members. However, Article XVI accepts that a subsidy may exist "in any form

O. Cagdas Artantas, *Promotion of Green Electricity in Germany and Turkey*, EYIEL Monographs - Studies in European and International Economic Law 33,
https://doi.org/10.1007/978-3-031-44760-0_4

of income or price support," indicating that even the original GATT favored a broad understanding of promotion. The Tokyo Round negotiations of 1973–1979 witnessed an effort to define the notion of subsidy and establish a complex subsidy control regime. Negotiations for a "Subsidies Code" emerged from this effort; however, they were not fruitful as only some developing countries ratified the code.[1] It was only following the Uruguay Round of 1986–1994 that the "Agreement on Subsidies and Countervailing Measures" (SCM) of 1995 was established. The SCM serves as the primary text regulating subsidies, while the "Agreement on Agriculture" (AoA) governs agricultural subsidies. A crucial aspect of the SCM is its application solely to subsidies on goods, while services are regulated by the "General Agreement on Trade in Services" (GATS) of 1995. Given that the subject of this work falls outside the realm of agriculture and electricity has been recognized as a good, the focus will be on the SCM.[2]

According to the SCM Article 1.1, a subsidy is deemed to exist if a financial contribution is made by a government or any public body within the territory of a Member State. [3] Three aspects of this definition are prominent. First, the phrase "contribution by a government or any public body" identifies the subsidy provider or promoter and requires initial scrutiny. Second, the types of "financial contribution" are enumerated in Article 1.1 (a) (1) and (2). The list from (a)(1)(i) to (iv) is not exhaustive, as (a)(2) introduces a new category: Any form of income or price support in the sense of Article XVI of GATT may be considered a financial contribution. Lastly, according to Article 1.1(b), a subsidy is deemed to exist only if the financial contribution by the public body confers a benefit. This third aspect will also be examined in this book.

Additionally, "specificity" is often considered part of the definition of the subsidy concept in the literature. However, specificity is more about remedying the subsidy rather than defining it. Subsidies that are specific may be countervailed or taken to the dispute settlement mechanism, but even when they are not specific, subsidies still exist.

---

[1] Krämer and Krajewski (2011), pp. 408–409.

[2] Para. 9, WTO Council for Trade for Services, Energy Services: Background Note by the Secretariat, 1998.

[3] *"... a subsidy shall be deemed to exist if: (a)(1) there is a financial contribution by a government or any public body within the territory of a Member ... i.e. where: (i) a government practice involves a direct transfer of funds ..., potential direct transfers of funds or liabilities ...; (ii) government revenue that is otherwise due is foregone or not collected ...; (iii) a government provides goods or services other than general infrastructure, or purchases goods; (iv) a government makes payments to a funding mechanism, or entrusts or directs a private body to carry out one or more of the type of functions illustrated in (i) to (iii) above which would normally be vested in the government and the practice, in no real sense, differs from practices normally followed by governments; or (a)(2) there is any form of income or price support in the sense of Article XVI of GATT 1994 and (b) a benefit is thereby conferred."*

4.1.1.1 Government or Public Body

The terms "public body" or "government," collectively referred to by the SCM, serve as the starting point of the SCM subsidies regime. Private entities may only confer subsidies if entrusted or directed by the government (Article 1.1(a)(1)(iv)). The government or public body can be situated at the national, regional, or municipal level.[4] The scope of the term "public body" encompasses sub-national public entities, such as state-controlled agencies, institutions, or financial bodies.[5] However, neither the GATT nor the SCM provide a definition for "public body." Alternatively, the GATS Annex on Financial Services offers a definition for "public entity": *"...a government, a central bank, or a monetary authority of a Member, or an entity owned or controlled by a Member, that is principally engaged in carrying out governmental functions or activities for governmental purposes, not including an entity principally engaged in supplying financial services on commercial terms."*

In the *US – Anti-Dumping and Countervailing Duties (China)* case, the Appellate Body addressed the issue of the public body.[6] They concluded that contrary to the Panel's findings, the term "public body" within the context of Article 1.1. (a) (1) encompasses only those entities possessing, exercising, or vested with governmental authority. In *Canada – Dairy, the Appellate Body* determined that the essence of a government is its prerogative to regulate, control, and supervise individuals or otherwise restrain their conduct through the exercise of lawful authority.[7]

A government agency is defined as an entity that exercises powers conferred upon it by a government to perform functions of a governmental nature. In certain instances, a statute or legal instrument may explicitly vest authority. However, in other cases, assessing such authority is not straightforward.[8] The Appellate Body asserts that the absence of an express statutory delegation does not preclude the determination that a specific entity is a public body. Evidence of an entity exercising governmental functions may demonstrate that it possesses a sustained and systematic practice. The Panel on *Korea – Commercial Vessels* assessed that a "public body" is an entity controlled by the government but not necessarily owned by it.[9] Thus, any entity carrying out governmental functions can be considered a public body in the context of SCM Article 1.1.

In *US – DRAMS*, the Panel emphasized that while not decisive, hundred percent public ownership would be a contributing factor when determining if a body is

[4] Müller (2017), p. 66.

[5] Stoll and Koebele (2008), p. 429.

[6] Appellate Body Report, WT/DS379/AB/R of 11 March 2011, United States - Definitive Anti-Dumping and Countervailing Duties on Certain Products from China.

[7] Appellate Body Report, WT/DS103/AB/R - WT/DS113/AB/R of 13 October 1999, Canada - Measures Affecting the Importation of Milk and the Exportation of Dairy Products.

[8] den Bossche and Zdouc (2021), p. 840.

[9] Para. 7.50, Panel Report, WT/DS273/R of 7 March 2005, Korea – Measures Affecting Trade in Commercial Vessels.

public.[10] Government or public bodies may also "entrust or direct" a private body to provide financial contributions according to Article 1.1(a)(1)(iv). The Panel in *EC – Countervailing Measures on DRAM Chips* argued that for the "entrust" or "direct" tests to be met, an entity must be acting "on behalf of" a government.[11] The Panel held that there must be "probative and compelling evidence" that these tests are met.

The Appellate Body in *US – Countervailing Duty Investigation on DRAMs* decided that the private body's actions must be attributable to a government to characterize its support as a financial contribution.[12] According to the Appellate Body, the terms "entrustment and direction" require a significant degree of command and control from the government. To meet the paragraph's standard, the attribution of responsibility should (1) constitute an explicit and affirmative action, (2) be addressed to a specific party, and (3) have a particular task or duty as its objective. The refusal of function by the entity does not imply that the private body was not entrusted or directed. However, this state of command and control is insufficient on its own. According to Article 1.1. (a)(1)(iv), firstly, the conduct should typically be vested in the government. Secondly, the practice should not significantly differ from practices generally followed by governments. The language of these two provisos is ambiguous, and there are not enough cases to provide clarity. The provisos may refer to governmental functions of, *inter alia*; revenue expenditure, public revenue policy, tax collection, or regulatory powers.[13]

Devising a uniform, overarching definition of the "public body" is challenging. The Appellate Body in *US – Carbon Steel (India)* emphasizes that the determination of whether an entity's conduct constitutes that of a public body must be made on a case-by-case basis, considering the core characteristics and functions of the relevant entity, its relationship with the government, and the legal and economic environment in the country where the investigated entity operates.[14] Following this logic, the identification of a public body may be based on a different set of facts in each case. One approach is to evaluate the promoting entity's objectives. According to this teleological view, if the entity's aims align with the public benefit or public good, the entity can be considered a public body. Another option, as previously discussed, is the application of the "governmental authority" criterion.[15] The "public body" discourse in WTO law literature is crucial for understanding trade law issues surrounding green electricity promotion.

---

[10] Panel Report, WT/DS99/R of 29 January 1999, United States - Anti-Dumping Duty on Dynamic Random Access Memory Semiconductors (DRAMs) of One Megabyte or Above from Korea.

[11] Panel Report, WT/DS299/R of 17 June 2005, European Communities - Countervailing Measures on Dynamic Random Access Memory Chips from Korea.

[12] Appellate Body Report, WT/DS296/AB/R of 25 June 2005, United States - Countervailing Duty Investigation on Dynamic Random Access Memory Semiconductors (DRAMs) from Korea.

[13] See: Mavroidis (2016), p. 207; Matsushita et al. (2015), p. 313; Stoll and Koebele (2008), p. 442.

[14] Appellate Body Report, WT/DS436/AB/R of 8 December 2014, United States — Countervailing Measures on Certain Hot-Rolled Carbon Steel Flat Products from India.

[15] Messenger (2017), p. 60.

Green electricity promotion is provided by various entities in each country. Examples include direct promotion from the state treasury, soft loans from state-owned banks, and market regulation to secure funds for green energy investors (e.g., Feed-in Tariffs). Consequently, the first question is how to define the "public body" in cases of green electricity promotion. There can be four instances of green electricity promotion concerning the promoting entity:

1. Promotion directly by the government or any other part of the state's legal personality.
2. Promotion by a public body other than the state's legal personality, such as a municipality or an independent administrative authority.
3. Promotion by a state-owned or publicly controlled private legal person, such as a state-owned bank or a national wealth fund.
4. Promotion by a state-supported or regulated entity, such as a privately-owned bank, an NGO, or a transmission system operator.

The first and second instances are relatively easier to identify, as they would typically be included in the official budgets of the government or public body. However, the third and fourth instances are more challenging to detect and assess, as they may be concealed in the records of private companies, which may not be publicly available in some countries. In such cases, the flexibility of WTO subsidy law comes into play. To recall the Panel on *Korea – Commercial Vessels*, a "public body" is an entity controlled by the government but not necessarily owned by it. The *Korea – Commercial Vessels* case addresses the third instance mentioned above. If the promotion goes through a publicly owned or controlled entity, it would be covered by SCM Agreement Article 1.1. (a)(1). On the other hand, Article 1.1. (a)(1)(iv) addresses the issue raised by the last instance. Recognizing a subsidy through an entrusted or directed private body limits the possibility of circumventing subsidy rules with the assistance of private actors.[16] A Feed-in Tariff program for green electricity would fall into this category and be covered below.

4.1.1.2 Financial Contribution

The second constituent of the subsidy concept within the WTO legal framework is the financial contribution. The term "financial contribution" is substantially delineated in the SCM, as well as in WTO dispute settlement cases and academic literature. According to the panels and Appellate Body, not all government or public body measures that confer a benefit can be deemed subsidies, as they require the element of financial contribution.[17] Article 1.1(a)(1) enumerates various types of financial contributions that constitute a subsidy when they confer a benefit and are provided by the government, public bodies, or entrusted-directed private entities.

---

[16] Stoll and Schorkopf (2006), p. 149; Mavroidis (2016), p. 204.

[17] Stoll and Koebele (2008), p. 428.

Firstly, subparagraph (i) encompasses direct or potential transfers of funds or liabilities. The SCM provides examples of direct financial contributions, such as grants, loans, and equity infusions, while loan guarantees exemplify potential transfers of liabilities. Secondly, subparagraph (ii) incorporates fiscal contributions, specifically the foregoing of public revenue otherwise due. Thirdly, subparagraph (iii) includes the provision of goods or services other than general infrastructure or government purchase of goods, which may be interpreted as "in-kind contributions." The fourth subparagraph (iv) does not define another type of financial contribution but includes contributions via a private entity or a funding mechanism.

In *Canada – Renewable Energy & Feed-In Tariff Program* (*Canada – RE*), the AB ruled that a measure could fall under multiple types of financial contributions.[18] Additionally, it should not be overlooked that the list in Article 1.1(a)(1) is non-exhaustive. Article 1.1(a)(2) encompasses "*any form of income or price support in the sense of Article XVI of GATT 1994*" in the definition, paving the way for broader interpretations. The negotiators of the SCM may have intended for panels and the AB to primarily assess cases within the scope of Article 1.1(a)(1) and resort to Article 1.1(a)(2) as a failsafe mechanism to prevent circumvention by innovative promotional measures.

A financial contribution entails transferring economic value from the government to the recipient. In the context of subparagraph (i), direct financial contributions imply that the government, public body, payment mechanism, or directed-entrusted private entity directly provides funds to the recipient. Fund provision can manifest in various forms, including grants, soft loans and low-cost credits, interest rate support, capital or equity infusion, corporate bond purchases, debt-to-equity swaps, investments, and corporate debt forgiveness.[19]

For instance, in *Canada – Aircraft Credits and Guarantees*, the Panel determined that measures such as loan guarantees, interest rate support, equity guarantees, residual value guarantees, and "first loss deficiency guarantees" constituted subsidies under Article 1.1(a)(1)(i).[20] The AB in *EC and Certain Member States – Large Civil Aircraft* contended that equity infusions create a similar effect to lenient loans.[21] The capital was provided to the recipient even though the company's future performance remained uncertain. Consequently, the Panel classified the measure under subparagraph (i) purview.

A crucial aspect of Article 1.1(a)(1)(i) is that the transfer of funds or liabilities can be actual or potential. Consequently, both the real payment of a grant and a debt guarantee fall within the scope of Article 1.1(a)(1)(i) simultaneously. For example,

---

[18] Appellate Body Report, WT/DS412/AB/R; WT/DS426/AB/R of 6 May 2013, Canada - Certain Measures Affecting the Renewable Energy Generation Sector - Canada - Measures Relating to the Feed-In Tariff Program.

[19] Stoll and Koebele (2008), p. 430.

[20] Panel Report, WT/DS222/10 of 17 February 2003, Canada - Export Credits and Loan Guarantees for Regional Aircraft.

[21] Para 616. Appellate Body Report, WT/DS316/AB/R of 18 May 2011, European Communities and Certain Member States - Measures Affecting Trade in Large Civil Aircraft.

in *Korea – Commercial Vessels*, the panel acknowledged that advance payment refund guarantees supplied by the Korean public body constituted a potential direct transfer of funds, as they were effectively equivalent to cash grants.[22]

Subparagraph Article 1.1(a)(1)(ii) encompasses fiscal subsidy measures, which refer to government revenue that is otherwise due but is forgone or uncollected. The subparagraph provides tax credits as an example of these fiscal measures. The central case regarding this subparagraph, *US – FSC*, demonstrates that the "otherwise due" test is challenging to satisfy and requires careful consideration of differing tax regulations in each country.[23] In *Canada – Autos*, the AB concluded that the duty exemption aimed to support the domestic industry.[24] In *US – Large Civil Aircraft (Second Complaint),* the AB deemed that the panel's evaluation of the tax treatment generally applicable in Washington State to businesses in specific sectors was satisfactory, as the panel employed a benchmark comparing the general tax rates and the lower tax rates at the heart of the case.[25] The case established a three-step test: (1) Identify the tax treatment of subsidy recipients. (2) Determine the tax treatment for the comparable income of comparably situated taxpayers and establish the benchmark. (3) Compare the two models.[26]

Subparagraph Article 1.1(a)(1)(iii) addresses the provision of goods or services other than general infrastructure or the purchase of goods. In *US – Softwood Lumber IV*, the AB determined that this type of transaction possesses the capacity to artificially inflate the revenues derived from selling the product.[27]

The issue of financial benefit is pivotal for green electricity promotion cases. For a green electricity promotion measure to be contested under WTO Dispute Resolution provisions, it must align with Article 1.1(a)(1) classifications of financial contribution. First, a grant or a soft loan for a green electricity investment could fall under Article 1.1(a)(1)(i). A tax concession program for green electricity projects might be classified under Article 1.1(a)(1)(ii). Feed-in Tariff mechanisms, which are regulatory measures by nature, may be categorized under Article 1.1(a)(1)(iv). These three types of financial contributions are relatively straightforward to identify.

In contrast, measures that could fall under Article 1.1(a)(1)(iii) are more complex. The provision of goods or services other than general infrastructure or purchase of goods can manifest in various forms within green electricity promotion. Firstly, grid-related promotion would be encompassed by the "provision of goods or services other than general infrastructure. . ." clause. Secondly, the government may directly

---

[22] Paras 7.408–7.413.

[23] Appellate Body Report, WT/DS108/AB/R of 24 February 2000, United States - Tax Treatment for "Foreign Sales Corporations".

[24] Appellate Body Report, WT/DS139/AB/R; WT/DS142/AB/R of 31 May 2000, Canada - Certain Measures Affecting the Automotive Industry.

[25] Appellate Body Report, WT/DS353/AB/R of 12 March 2012, United States - Measures Affecting Trade in Large Civil Aircraft (Second Complaint).

[26] See: Lester et al. (2018), p. 322; Stoll and Koebele (2008), p. 432; Müller (2017), p. 92.

[27] Para. 53, Appellate Body Report, WT/DS257/AB/R of 19 January 2004, United States - Final Countervailing Duty Determination with Respect to Certain Softwood Lumber from Canada.

purchase electricity generated by the installation rather than having private companies buy it, as is the case with Feed-in Tariff schemes. This situation would fall under the "purchase of goods" provision.

4.1.1.3 Benefit

The benefit is the third component of the notion of subsidy within the WTO legal sphere. As previously mentioned in the context of *US – Export Restraints*, benefit and financial contribution are two distinct components that panels and the Appellate Body consider when determining whether a measure is a subsidy. A financial contribution by a government, public body, or a directed-entrusted private body may be deemed a subsidy only if it confers a benefit to the recipient. Benefit, on the other hand, is a more elusive concept than financial contribution. It can be identified by its effect: Benefit makes the recipient better off.[28] *US – Lead and Bismuth II* offers a definition for benefit, with the panel in the case defining "benefit" as the portion of a financial contribution that the recipient receives *gratis* compared to a market benchmark.[29]

In *Canada – Aircraft*, the Appellate Body introduces a benchmark: the private investor test (or the commercial benchmark).[30] According to this, benefit can only be determined by analyzing market conditions and typical market practices. For instance, if the issue involves a loan, panels and the AB must identify an undue advantage on the debtor's side. If the issue concerns privatization, they must assess whether the privatization occurred at arm's length. The mentioned benchmark appears in SCM Article 14. Article 14(a) requires applying the "usual investment practice" benchmark in evaluating benefit in equity capital provision cases. In *EC and Certain Member States – Large Civil Aircraft*, the Appellate Body defined "usual investment practice" as private investors' ordinary or customary conduct regarding equity investment.[31] Article 14(b) and (c) address benefit assessment in loans and loan guarantees, introducing the "comparable commercial loan" benchmark for government loans and loan guarantees. The economic difference between the provided loan or loan guarantee and the comparable commercial loan forms the basis of the benchmark. If a measure fails this test, it will be deemed a financial contribution that confers a benefit.

Article 14(d) parallels Article 1.1(a)(1)(iii), as it covers the provision of goods and services and purchases of goods. This paragraph establishes the "adequate

[28] Matsushita et al. (2015), p. 316.

[29] Footnote 80 to Para 6.70. Panel Report, WT/DS138/AB/R of 23 December 1999, United States - Imposition of Countervailing Duties on Certain Hot-Rolled Lead and Bismuth Carbon Steel Products Originating in the United Kingdom.

[30] Appellate Body Report, WT/DS70/AB/R of 2 August 1999, Canada - Measures Affecting the Export of Civilian Aircraft.

[31] Appellate Body Report, WT/DS316/AB/R of 18 May 2011, European Communities and Certain member States — Measures Affecting Trade in Large Civil Aircraft.

remuneration" test, where the provision of goods or services or the purchase of goods is compared to economically equivalent market transactions. If the provision of goods and services occurs at less than adequate market-equivalent fees or the purchases of goods at a higher price, it will be determined that the measure confers a benefit. The market conditions for all these benchmarks are the conditions of the country where the measures were offered, as confirmed by the Appellate Body in the *US – Carbon Steel (India)* case.

In *US – Softwood Lumber IV* and *US – Anti-Dumping and Countervailing Duties (China)*, the Appellate Body determined that out-of-country prices may be used to establish a benefit benchmark when the government distorts in-country prices. If the government also sets prices in equivalent commercial transactions within the country, panels and the Appellate Body must seek comparable data from global examples.[32] This approach was extended in *Canada – RE*, where the Appellate Body argued that the relevant market, the renewable energy market, was non-existent and solely created by the government. They acknowledged that governments have the prerogative to regulate the energy mix and suggested that the only viable benchmark for benefit analysis in such situations is the use of "price-discovery mechanisms" like tenders.[33]

Another issue is benefit pass-through and the extinction of benefit. When the benefit is conferred on a processed input product, the question arises whether the processed product is subsidized. Privatization also presents a problem, as it raises the question of whether the privatization of a public entity might confer a benefit. In both cases, the Appellate Body's solution is that transactions must be conducted "at arm's length," i.e., in a commercially adequate manner. In *US – Lead and Bismuth* and *US – Countervailing Measures on Certain EC Products*, the AB found that if privatization transactions were conducted "at arm's length" and "for fair market value," it could be assumed that the benefit had become "extinct" after privatization.[34]

Challenges related to the concept of benefit in green electricity promotion schemes arise in various forms. Firstly, if the promotion measure is linked to the price of electricity, it becomes evident that a "free market price" for electricity does not exist due to the heavy regulation of electricity markets worldwide. Secondly, soft loans from state-owned or state-controlled banks, or investments by national wealth funds, may invite WTO scrutiny if they do not conform to the scope of usual investment practices. Lastly, the privatization of publicly owned green electricity installations, may attract WTO scrutiny if not conducted "at arm's length."

[32] See: Bossche and Zdouc (2021), p. 790; Lester et al. (2018), p. 322; Matsushita et al. (2015), p. 319.

[33] Asmelash (2014); Condon (2017).

[34] Appellate Body Report, WT/DS138/AB/R of 5 May 2000, United States - Imposition of Countervailing Duties on Certain Hot-Rolled Lead and Bismuth Carbon Steel Products Originating in the United Kingdom.; Appellate Body Report, WT/DS212/AB/R of 9 December 2002, United States - Countervailing Measures Concerning Certain Products from the European Communities.

4.1.2 *Subsidy Control Law*

As previously mentioned, the innovation of the SCM system lies in the introduction of control mechanisms to global trade, which was largely absent in the GATT system, aside from a notification obligation for subsidies. Nonetheless, as understood by the WTO, not every subsidy is subject to enforcement in WTO dispute resolution or countervailing measures. Per SCM Article 2, a subsidy must be "specific" to fall under the purview of subsidy control within the WTO legal framework. Consequently, the first topic within this subchapter will address the specificity of subsidies.

Certain subsidies are considered inherently specific, namely "prohibited subsidies," which will constitute the second topic of discussion. The other category, "actionable subsidies," will be examined as the third topic, with the WTO dispute resolution system integrated into both the second and third topics. The fourth topic will briefly explore the issue of countervailing measures. Lastly, the environmental exception delineated in GATT Article XX will be scrutinized as the fifth topic to examine whether green electricity subsidies can potentially benefit from this provision by discovering policy space.

4.1.2.1 Specificity

WTO rules do not encompass all subsidies. Even when a measure is identified as a subsidy according to SCM Article 1, it is not inherently actionable. The distinguishing factor for subsidies subject to WTO control regulation is "specificity." Specificity serves as a prerequisite for both unilateral and multilateral actions against subsidies.[35] SCM Article 2 outlines the categories of specificity. Article 2.1 applies to enterprise or industry-specific measures. The rules of the paragraph are as follows:

1. Subsidies explicitly limited to certain enterprises will be deemed specific.
2. Measures for which the granting authority has not established objective criteria or eligibility conditions will be considered specific.
3. In some cases, even if the measure in question appears non-specific, it may be deemed specific if there is evidence of *"use of a subsidy program by a limited number of certain enterprises, predominant use by certain enterprises, granting of disproportionately large amounts of subsidy to certain enterprises, and the manner in which the granting authority has exercised discretion in the decision to grant a subsidy".*

SCM Article 2.2 addresses regionally specific subsidies: "A subsidy which is limited to certain enterprises located within a designated geographical region within the jurisdiction of the granting authority shall be specific." Lastly, SCM Article 2.3

[35] SCM Article 1.2.

establishes the principle for "prohibited subsidies," addressed in Article 3's chapeau. These subsidies will be considered *per se* specific.

4.1.2.2 Prohibited Subsidies

Two norms govern prohibited subsidies. Article 2.3 refers to subsidies falling under Article 3's chapeau as inherently specific, while Article 3 defines these types of subsidies.[36] There are two categories of prohibited subsidies: The first encompasses subsidies contingent upon export performance, while the second targets subsidies aimed at substituting imports.

The Appellate Body (AB) in *US – Upland Cotton* explains export contingency as a situation in which the "*granting of a subsidy should be tied to export performance*".[37] Annex I of the SCM contains an illustrative list of export subsidies, including, *inter alia*: Direct export subsidies, fiscal measures tied to export performance, and exemption from social welfare charges. In the *Brazil – Aircraft* case, the AB emphasized that a subsidy falling under Annex I is *ipso facto* prohibited without demonstrating general compliance with Article 3.1.[38]

Footnote 4 of the SCM establishes de facto contingency; even when a subsidy is not legally contingent upon export performance, it can still be tied to export performance or anticipation. Analyzing de facto export contingency requires careful examination of the internal characteristics of the measure. In the Canada – Aircraft case, the AB elucidated the difficulty of inferring de facto contingency: "*...There is no single legal document which will demonstrate, on its face, that a subsidy is contingent...in fact...upon export performance. Instead, the existence of this relationship of contingency between the subsidy and export performance must be inferred from the total configuration of the facts constituting and surrounding the granting of the subsidy, none of which on its own is likely to be decisive in any given case...*".[39] The primary test developed by the Appellate Body for evaluating export subsidies involves assessing whether the measure in question is designed to induce the promotion of future export performance by the recipient, as explained in *EC and Certain Member States – Large Civil Aircraft*.[40]

The second type of prohibited subsidies is more significant for the scope of this book. Subsidies contingent upon the use of domestic goods over imported goods are

[36] Article 3 lays down its definitions as follows: "*(a) subsidies contingent, in law or in fact, whether solely or as one of several other conditions, upon export performance, including those illustrated in Annex I5; (b) subsidies contingent, whether solely or as one of several other conditions, upon the use of domestic over imported goods.*"

[37] Para. 572. Appellate Body Report, WT/DS267/AB/R of 3 March 2005, United States - Subsidies on Upland Cotton.

[38] Paras 59 ff. Appellate Body Report, WT/DS46/AB/R of 2 August 1999, Brazil - Export Financing Programme for Aircraft.

[39] Paras 167–169.

[40] Para. 1050.

inherently specific and prohibited.[41] Consequently, local content requirements attached to Feed-in Tariffs and Premium systems are considered inherently specific and prohibited. A key case for this work in this context, *Canada – RE*, will be examined below.

SCM Article 4 outlines the principles for multilateral remedies for prohibited subsidies. According to Article 4.1, members may request consultations with other members regarding prohibited subsidies. If consultations fail, as a second step, members may bring the issue to the "Dispute Settlement Body" (DSB) as per Article 4.4. Subsequently, a panel will be established and review the case. If the panel determines that the measure in question is a prohibited subsidy, it will demand the withdrawal of the measure without delay. Parties may appeal to the panel in the Appellate Body, which will review the issue as the final instance. The "Dispute Settlement Understanding" (DSU) serves as another principal text for this process.

4.1.2.3 Actionable Subsidies

Actionable subsidies represent the second and final type of subsidies under the SCM, as the category of non-actionable subsidies (i.e., Green Light Subsidies) expired in 2000. Article 8 of the SCM, the non-actionable subsidies clause, included several exceptions protected from multilateral or unilateral remedies; however, the article's application lapsed, and no arrangement was made to extend its validity.[42] Consequently, a subsidy is now either prohibited or actionable under WTO law.

Actionable subsidies are not inherently prohibited; however, they can be challenged if they are specific and have adverse effects on another member's interests. Article 5.1 of the SCM enumerates three types of adverse effects: "(a) injury to the domestic industry of another Member; (b) nullification or impairment of benefits accruing directly or indirectly to other Members under GATT 1994, particularly the benefits of concessions bound under Article II of GATT 1994; (c) serious prejudice to the interests of another Member." The multilateral remedies for actionable subsidies are similar to those of prohibited subsidies. Members may request a consultation in cases of alleged injury, nullification or impairment, or serious prejudice, as per Article 7. The main topic of the consultations will be removing the adverse effects or withdrawing the subsidy. If consultations fail, the Member party may bring the issue to the Dispute Settlement Body to establish a panel (Article 7.4). The Appellate Body will review the issue as the ultimate authority (Article 7.6 and 7.7).

---

[41] See: Bossche and Zdouc (2021), p. 807.

[42] Bigdeli (2011).

4.1.2.4 Countervailing Measures

Members may challenge prohibited and actionable subsidies in the Dispute Settlement Body or confront them directly with unilateral measures, specifically "countervailing measures." First, they must conduct a domestic investigation procedure governed by the relevant rules of the SCM. Article II(2)(b) provides the competence for applying countervailing measures as long as it is consistent with Article VI. A countervailing duty is an offsetting measure that aims to counterbalance the effects of subsidization by another Member.

According to the GATT and SCM (Article 10), Members may impose countervailing duties if the criteria are fulfilled: First, there must be subsidized imports, with the subsidization being specific in the context of Article 2 of the SCM. Secondly, there must be an injury as defined by Articles 15 and 16 of the SCM. Finally, a causal link must exist between the subsidized imports and the injury to the domestic industry, with the injury caused by other factors not attributed to the subsidized imports.

Countervailing duty investigations should be conducted transparently, allowing all interested parties the opportunity to defend their interests, and investigating authorities must explain the grounds for their decisions.[43]

4.1.3 GATT Article XX Exceptions

The final consideration under this subchapter will be the issue of applying GATT Article XX to the SCM. GATT Article XX is a primary norm of the treaty containing an exhaustive list of exceptions to the GATT. However, neither the GATT nor the SCM provide any remarks on the application of GATT Article XX to the SCM. In the absence of such a clause, and with the lapse of "non-actionable subsidies" under the SCM, the policy space for so-called "green subsidies" or environmentally concerned promotions is diminished.

The relevant subparagraphs in the context of this work are (b), (g), and (j) of Article XX.[44] Subparagraph (b) is prominent in trade and environment debates. It

[43] Bossche and Zdouc (2021), p. 847.

[44] Together with the chapeau, these subparagraphs are as follows: *"Subject to the requirement that such measures are not applied in a manner which would constitute a means of arbitrary or unjustifiable discrimination between countries where the same conditions prevail, or a disguised restriction on international trade, nothing in this Agreement shall be construed to prevent the adoption or enforcement by any contracting party of measures: . . . b) necessary to protect human, animal or plant life or health; . . . g) relating to the conservation of exhaustible natural resources if such measures are made effective in conjunction with restrictions on domestic production or consumption, . . . j) essential to the acquisition or distribution of products in general or local short supply; Provided that any such measures shall be consistent with the principle that all contracting parties are entitled to an equitable share of the international supply of such products,*

asserts that GATT rules will not prevent members from protecting human, animal, or plant life or health. The Panel in *US – Gasoline* envisions a three-fold test for Article XX(b): 1) The measure in question must aim to protect human, animal, or plant life or health; 2) The measure in question must be proportionate, as in being necessary to fulfill the policy objective; 3) The measure in question must be applied in conformity with the requirements of the chapeau of Article XX.[45] Subparagraph (b) is generally perceived as a measure closely connected with the health standards of goods and, therefore, with the "WTO Agreement on the Application of Sanitary and Phytosanitary Measures" (SPS).

For energy issues, subparagraph (g) is deemed more critical. Article XX (g) provides an exception for states to develop policies addressing exhaustible natural resource problems. Animal species may be easily included in the definition, as demonstrated in the *Canada – Herring and Salmon* and *US – Shrimp cases*.[46] The *US – Gasoline* case goes further, defining "clean air" as an "exhaustible natural resource". *US – Gasoline* is notable as it paves the way for the future use of GATT Article XX(g) for climate protection measures. Following the same logic, the climate may be defined as an exhaustible natural resource.[47]

Subparagraph (j) governs the issue of supply shortages of goods. During a shortage, members may take precautions to ensure a steady flow of goods using discriminatory measures, which would otherwise be inconsistent with the GATT. Some countries have claimed that their subsidies to local producers and exporters of manufactured goods were in line with Article XX(j) and, therefore, justified.[48] Subparagraph (j) may serve as a basis for circumventing the WTO subsidy control system by states claiming supply shortages on "green products," such as wind turbines, photovoltaic panels, or batteries.

However, one central problem remains when assessing the possibility of circumventing WTO rules in the question of energy subsidies. There is no reference in GATT on the application of GATT Article XX to SCM, nor is there any mention in the SCM regarding the application of GATT Article XX on itself. For example, the SPS makes a strict reference to the application of Article XX(b), but the SCM lacks such a clause. The WTO case law has not addressed the issue yet. The now lapsed "non-actionable subsidies" category of the SCM can be considered grounds against the application of GATT Article XX to the SCM. The existence of such an exemption in the SCM might indicate that the negotiators had no intention of applying GATT Article XX to the SCM. Furthermore, the chapeau of Article XX

and that any such measures, which are inconsistent with the other provisions of the Agreement shall be discontinued as soon as the conditions giving rise to them have ceased to exist..."

[45] Panel Report, WT/DS2/R of 29 January 1996, United States - Standards for Reformulated and Conventional Gasoline. See: Stoll and Strack (2009).

[46] Panel Report, 22 March 1988, Canada — Measures Affecting Exports of Unprocessed Herring and Salmon.; Appellate Body Report, WT/DS58/AB/R of 12 October 1998, United States - Import Prohibition of Certain Shrimp and Shrimp Products.

[47] Wolfrum and Matz-Lück (2009).

[48] Aidelojie and Makuch (2008).

forbids the use of the exception clause for discriminatory measures; therefore, the negotiators would not wish to have discriminatory subsidy measures allowed by the language of the GATT.[49]

However, arguments for such an application may also be developed. First, the GATT may be treated as the *lex generalis* in trade-related matters, filling the gaps of the *lex specialis*, the SCM. The second argument for applying GATT to the SCM is that the GATT has its environmental exception for more trade-distortive measures than subsidies, e.g., bans and quotas. In this case, would it not be more logical to claim that the GATT exception should also apply to the SCM?[50] Lastly, there is the fact that the AB applied GATT Article XX to the Protocol of Accession of China in *China – Publications and Audiovisual Products*.[51] Following this example, it is possible to argue that the AB can apply GATT Article XX to SCM.

To fulfill the criteria of Article XX, green electricity promotion measures should, in the first instance, be reasonably related to reducing emissions and other climate-altering interventions.[52] In *Brazil – Retreaded Tyres*, the AB emphasized that: "*... the results obtained from certain actions—for instance, measures adopted in order to attenuate global warming and climate change, or certain preventive actions to reduce the incidence of diseases that may manifest themselves only after a certain period of time—can only be evaluated with the benefit of time. ... a panel might conclude that an import ban is necessary on the basis of a demonstration that the import ban at issue is apt to produce a material contribution to the achievement of its objective. This demonstration could consist of quantitative projections in the future, or qualitative reasoning based on a set of hypotheses that are tested and supported by sufficient evidence.*"[53] The logic in *Brazil – Retreaded Tyres* requires the demonstration of definite facts establishing the measure in question as scientifically necessary to fulfill the criteria of GATT Article XX concerning import bans per Article XX(b). The same reasoning can be followed for subparagraphs (g) and (j). Measures aiming to protect exhaustible resources, or the security of domestic supply must be supported by scientific facts that include future projections of exhaustible resource demand or supply problems.

In the case of green electricity promotion measures, it is possible to argue that they might fit into three subparagraphs of GATT Article XX using different argumentations. However, the discriminatory nature of local content requirements could make it difficult to meet the "non-discriminatory" criterion of the chapeau of Article

---

[49] Cosbey and Mavroidis (2014).

[50] Farah and Cima (2015).

[51] Appellate Body Report, WT/DS363/AB/R of 21 December 2009, China - Measures Affecting Trading Rights and Distribution Services for Certain Publications and Audiovisual Entertainment Products.

[52] Espa and Marín Durán (2018).

[53] Para. 151, Appellate Body Report, WT/DS332/AB/R of 3 December 2007, Brazil - Measures Affecting Imports of Retreaded Tyres.

XX.[54] Applying GATT Article XX exceptions to green electricity promotion schemes may be an alternative to the often-suggested "resurrection" of the green-lit environmental subsidies of the SCM Agreement. Still, it would shift the responsibility of environmental and climate-friendly action from WTO members to the Dispute Resolution Body, which may only be a temporary solution.

Combating climate change and environmental degradation requires a more robust response to the challenges surrounding "green" subsidies. Firstly, WTO members should address the problem of local content requirements, which are currently prohibited under WTO law. In line with the fight against climate change, the WTO members should decide whether developing countries have a "right to green industry," considering the challenges in local economies and deficiencies in global supply chains.

Secondly, as the cross-border electricity trade gains impetus, the free trade disrupting properties of green electricity promotion schemes will become more visible. As a preemptive action, WTO members should decide whether to strengthen GATT Article XX exceptions or resurrect green-lit subsidies. This decision would be crucial in fostering a more sustainable and cooperative global environment for promoting green electricity and tackling climate change issues while maintaining a balance with international trade rules.

4.2 EU State Aid Law

4.2.1 Definition

The EU law encompasses one of the most extensive regulatory frameworks for promotion, both in terms of definition and control, potentially rendering it the strictest. The state aid rules of the EU were initially incorporated into the 1958 "Treaty of Rome" as "Aids granted by the States," governed by Articles 92 and 93. These rules remained predominantly unaltered by subsequent amendments. The contemporary system for state aid regulation within the EU is dictated by Articles 107 and 108 of the "Treaty on the Functioning of the European Union" (TFEU).[55] In addition to these articles, a collection of secondary regulations, soft law, and European jurisprudence further presides over the issue.

Nonetheless, the primary norm concerning the definition of state aid is enshrined in the first paragraph of Article 107 TFEU.[56] Four key components underpin this norm. So as to identify a measure as state aid:

---

[54] Espa and Marín Durán (2018).

[55] Ex. Articles 92 and 93.

[56] *"Save as otherwise provided in the Treaties, any aid granted by a Member State or through State resources in any form whatsoever which distorts or threatens to distort competition by favouring*

1. An advantage must be conferred upon the recipient.
2. The advantage must be granted by a Member State or through state resources.
3. The aid must distort or threaten to distort competition within the EU.
4. It must impact inter-state trade.

4.2.1.1 Advantage on the Recipient

The first tenet of Article 107(1) TFEU posits that an advantage must be conferred upon the aid recipient. This advantage may manifest in positive aid, including grants and land aid, or negative aid, such as fiscal measures or reductions in social security conditions. While the advantage in cases of grants is readily apparent, a more subtle, negative form of state aid may arise in instances of public sector capital investments. Should the investment not possess an economic nature, for example, by lacking a long-term interest in profitability, an advantage conferred upon the recipient could be deemed present.[57] In this context, the "market investor test" (or "market economy operator test"), which is also employed for benefit analysis within the WTO domain, emerges.[58] The distinction between state aid and conventional commercial measures might solely rely on the market investor benchmark.

As per the *SFEI* ruling, "it is necessary to establish whether the recipient undertaking receives an economic advantage which it would not have obtained under normal market conditions…".[59] The test's crux lies in determining whether a specific undertaking is favored and granted an advantage compared to its competitors. Any benefit that could not have been procured under identical conditions constitutes an advantage and may potentially be classified as aid.[60] The comparison subject of this test is a private market actor; however, locating a suitable example may not always be possible.

EDF exemplifies the application of the market investor test in the scenario of a publicly owned company, as the member state's fiscal measures to support EDF, a French electricity firm, were found to be in accordance with the EU law.[61] The Court maintained that an economic advantage must be evaluated under the private investor test, even when granted through fiscal measures.

In the context of capital investments, the Market Economy Investor Principle (MEIP) emerges as an extension of the market investor test. State capital injections or those from public sources cannot be considered state aid if a private investor,

---

certain undertakings or the production of certain goods shall, in so far as it affects trade between Member States, be incompatible with the internal market".

[57] Craig and de Búrca (2020), p. 1164.

[58] Säcker and Montag (2016), p. 108.

[59] Case C-39/94 Syndicat français de l'Express international (SFEI) et al. v La Poste et al. [1996] ECR I-3547.

[60] Hofmann and Micheau (2016), p. 84; Heidenhain (2010), p. 24.

[61] Case T-156/04 EDF v Commission [2009] ECR II-04503.

operating under normal market conditions, would have made the same investment.[62] The central question is whether the beneficiary entity obtained an advantage from the investment it could not have secured in the private market. The MEIP is frequently applied to cases involving loans and loan guarantees.[63]

As demonstrated in *GEMO*, positive or negative, direct or indirect, advantages of any type may constitute state aid.[64] The *Steenkolenmijnen* ruling further elucidates this point by defining state aid as a concept broader than subsidy, encompassing interventions in various forms.[65] Ultimately, the form of aid in EU law is immaterial. Many court rulings provide examples of aid, including state guarantees, tax exemptions, privatizations, emission trading schemes, and green electricity purchase obligations.[66]

To further delineate economic advantage, the recipient must also be aptly described. The term "undertaking" within TFEU encompasses any entity engaged in economic activity, irrespective of its public or private law status. Activities involving the provision of goods or services in the market are considered economic activities. Public sector assistance to the private sector to offset the burdens of public service obligations (or services of general economic interest, SGEI) will not be recognized as state aid. The *Altmark* case is notable in this area, as the Court determined that if a state measure is considered compensation for services provided by recipient undertakings in order to fulfill public service obligations, and if those undertakings do not gain a real financial advantage, the measure does not place them in a more favorable competitive position than competing undertakings.[67] Consequently, such a measure does not fall under Article 92(1) of the Treaty. However, *Altmark* established criteria for this exemption:

1. The recipient undertaking must perform a service of general economic interest with clearly defined obligations;
2. The parameters for calculating the compensation must be established beforehand in an objective and transparent manner;
3. The compensation should not exceed what is necessary to cover all or part of the costs incurred, including a reasonable profit;

[62] Plender (2004).

[63] Bacon (2017), pp. 38–43.

[64] Case C-126/01 Ministre de l'Économie, des Finances et de l'Industrie v GEMO SA [2003] ECR I-13769.

[65] Case 30/59 Steenkolenmijnen v High Authority [1961] ECR 1.

[66] E.g., Case T-154/10 France v Commission [2012]; Case C-387/92 Banco Exterior de Espana [1994] ECR I-877; Case T-268/08 Land Burgenland v Commission [2012]; Case T-279/08 P Commission v Netherlands [2011]; 2007/580/EC Slovenian green electricity scheme [2007] OJ L219/9. See: Bacon (2017), pp. 23–24.

[67] Case C-280/00 Altmark Trans GmbH and Regierungspräsidium Magdeburg v Nahverkehrsgesellschaft Altmark GmbH [2003] ECR I-7747.

4. If the undertaking was not selected through a public procurement procedure, the compensation must be calculated in accordance with the economic realities of services of general economic interest, including a reasonable profit.[68]

The *Chronopost* cases confirm these findings by accepting that an advantage may be conferred upon a private postal company as long as it is responsible for providing universal postal service.[69] The Commission adopted the fundamentals of *Altmark* as the "SGEI Package" and "SGEI II" (i.e., Altmark I and II) in 2005 and 2011, respectively.[70]

Within the scope of this book, it is crucial to determine whether green energy generation and associated services constitute services of general economic interest. Firstly, a distinction must be made between energy generation, a good, and services related to green electricity. For instance, transmission and distribution phases are primarily services, while green energy generation resembles the production of a good. Nevertheless, in the *Slovenia Energy Producers* decision, the Commission acknowledged that energy generation could be viewed as a public service to the extent that it aims to ensure supply security.[71] The Commission applied the Altmark test to the case at hand and concluded that the measure in question met the Altmark criteria, and thus was not state aid. Moreover, "SGEI Communication" clarifies that public authorities in Member States, at the national, regional, or local levels, have considerable discretion in defining what they consider as services of general economic interest, depending on the allocation of powers under national law.[72]

This leads to a conclusion regarding energy goods: akin to the conventional energy plant in *Slovenia Energy Producers*, green electricity installations may be entrusted with public service obligations. The extent of these public service obligations will be defined by public authorities and be subjected to SGEI II limitations. The possibility of services related to green electricity generation falling under the scope of the SGEI Package must be examined at the second level. The mentioned services may be within the de minimis thresholds. If the service exceeds these thresholds, it will be assessed according to the four Altmark case criteria, as previously outlined. If the measure satisfies the Altmark test, no aid is present. Another possibility is that the measure may have no effect on trade and may not

[68] Paras. 89–93. See: Klasse (2013).

[69] Cases C-341-342/06 P Chronopost v Ufex [2008] ECR 1-4777.

[70] Commission Decision 2005/842/EC of 28 November 2005 on the Application of Article 86(2) of the EC Treaty to State Aid in the Form of Public Service Compensation Granted to Certain Undertakings Entrusted with the Operation of Services of General Economic Interest.; Commission Decision of 20 December 2011 on the Application of Article 106(2) of the TFEU to State Aid in the Form of Public Service Compensation Granted to Certain Undertakings Entrusted with the Operation of SGEI, OJ 2012, L7/3.

[71] Commission Decision of 24 April 2007 on the State aid scheme implemented by Slovenia in the framework of its legislation on qualified energy producers (2007) 2007/580/EC Case No C 7/2005 (notified under document number C(2007) 1181).

[72] Communication from the Commission of 11 January 2012 — European Union framework for State aid in the form of public service compensation (2011), 2012/C 8/03.

be deemed aid. Indeed, if the grid is not interconnected with foreign grids, green electricity-related measures may not impact trade. However, given the substantial interconnectivity of European transmission grids, it may be challenging to disregard such a measure's trade effects.

At the third level, if a measure promoting services related to green electricity does not meet the Altmark criteria, it will be examined according to the SGEI Package and SGEI II exemptions. One relevant criterion is that the compensation should be below 15 million EUR. This may be a possibility with green electricity services. Even in this case, the measure must comply with all conditions of the Decision. At the fourth level, measures without significant competition distortions may conform to EU law if they satisfy the conditions of SGEI II (overcompensation test, compliance with public procurement rules, efficiency incentives).[73] Services related to green electricity may also find room within the framework by adhering to its criteria.

Privatization, carried out through legislative acts, administrative acts, or agreements, may also be considered state aid if the privatization occurs below market price levels. If a tender for privatization is conducted, the highest bid corresponds to the market price. In the absence of a tender, the Commission may accept scrutiny by a monitoring trustee entrusted with ensuring that the sale of assets takes place at market prices. In the case of purchasing works, goods, and services, the highest bid in a tender would be accepted as the market-level price. If no such tender has occurred, it will be necessary to compare the sale to comparable private commercial agreements.[74] Privatizations in the green energy sector remain relevant in some Member States (e.g., France), which continue to hold tenders to privatize green electricity installations, such as hydroelectric plants.

4.2.1.2 Transfer by Member State or through State Resources

The second pillar of the EU definition of state aid concerns the imputability or origin of the advantage. Article 107(1) applies to aid "granted by a Member State or through State resources." This criterion may be examined at two levels. The first level involves the imputability of the measure, i.e., being granted directly by the Member State. For instance, as per the *Stardust Marine* ruling, attribution to the State is a requirement for a measure to be considered state aid.[75] The second level pertains to the origin of the funds for the measure, i.e., being granted through state resources. Both levels of examination have their challenges.

The first level, aid by the Member State, has a specific issue: in every case, it is not always clear whether the State grants the aid. Indeed, resources of a fund financed by parafiscal duties are considered State resources as long as the State

[73] Hofmann and Micheau (2016), p. 99.

[74] Ibid., p. 52.

[75] European Court of Justice Judgement, C-482/99 Aid granted to the French Republic to Stardust Marine [2002] ECR 1-4397.

controls the fund allocation.[76] However, in *Van der Kooy,* the Court held that even though the State owns 50% of the gas company Gasunie and appoints board members, state aid cannot be presumed.[77] The attribution to the State may only be proved by assessing the control of the State over the company.

At the second level, there are narrow and broader views on utilizing private resources as state aid. The narrow view, as presented in *Van Tiggele*, states that there must be a burden on public finances through either expenditure or reduced revenue.[78] Therefore, it does not consider financing through private sources using State power as state aid. The broader view perceives financing through private undertakings using State power as similar to financing from the State budget or resources. According to the latter view, Member States may circumvent state aid rules via funding by private undertakings.[79]

The Court sided with the narrow view in the landmark *PreussenElektra* decision of 2001.[80] The case revolved around Germany's renewable energy feed-in tariff act, which required private distribution companies to purchase a portion of their mix from renewable sources at prices higher than the market level for electricity. Ultimately, the cost of support for renewables was passed down to the final consumer. The overall scheme involved Germany obligating the funding of the green electricity sector by the private sector, using their private resources, through legislative force. The critical question was whether the German Feed-in Tariff scheme satisfied the imputability or origin of advantage criteria of TFEU Article 107(1).

The General Advocate (GA) opined that it did not, arguing that the tax losses due to the German Feed-in Tariff scheme could not (in itself) justify treating that system as aid. According to the opinion, the funds raised by the German Feed-in Tariff scheme did not come from a loss in tax revenue but rather from the undertakings subject to a legislative act and ultimately from consumers. The GA also emphasized that the funds in question stayed in the private sphere, away from state control. In the end, the opinion argued that state control of the tariff did not coincide with funding through state resources.[81] Following a similar logic, the Court held that the measure did not involve a direct or indirect transfer of State resources and, therefore, did not amount to State aid: *"... allocation of the financial burden arising from that obligation for those private electricity supply undertakings as between them and other private undertakings cannot constitute a direct or indirect transfer of State resources ... the fact that the purchase obligation is imposed by statute and confers*

[76] See: Heidenhain (2010), p. 36.

[77] European Court of Justice Judgement, C-67/85 Van der Kooy v Commission [1988] ECR 1988, 219.

[78] European Court of Justice Judgement, Case 82/77 Openbaar Ministerie (Public Prosecutor) of the Kingdom of the v Jacobus Philippus van Tiggele [1978] ECLI:EU:C:1978:10.

[79] Bacon (2017), pp. 61–62.

[80] European Court of Justice Judgement, C-379/98 PreussenElektra AG v Schleswag AG, in the presence of Windpark Reußenköge III GmbH and Land Schleswig-Holstein. [2001] ECR 1-2099.

[81] Paras. 162–177.

an undeniable advantage on certain undertakings is not capable of conferring upon it the character of State aid...".[82]

PreussenElektra gave Member States a larger policy field for green electricity promotion, since the ECJ approved Feed-in Tariff schemes at least in principle.[83] However, some argued that the decision enabled the circumvention of State aid rules, and the use of resources of private entities under private law should be treated no differently than resources stemming from parafiscal duties and taxes.

Contradicting *PreussenElektra*, the Court held in *GEMO* that requiring private undertakings to supply animal waste and carcasses to farmers and slaughterhouses in return for a tax concession, which was ultimately financed by a levy on supermarkets, constituted State aid. In this case, the resources in question were of the private sector, indicating that the Court's state resources test was inconsistent. In *Essent Netwerk*, the Court reapplied its test, deeming the payment of a surcharge by private companies to a private company as state aid since it was subject to the legislature's decision.[84] The Court clarified that the case differed from *PreussenElektra* because *"In the latter case, the undertakings had not been appointed by the State to manage a state resource, but were bound by an obligation to purchase by means of their own financial resources". Essent Netwerk* was criticized for this vague differentiation between two cases.[85] In *Vent de Colere*, the green electricity surcharge was collected by the State.[86] According to the Court, since the intermediary body that collects funds and compensates green electricity investors was designated by the Member State, the mechanism in question amounted to a transfer by a Member State or through state resources.

If the concept of State aid hinges upon the State and its resources, it is imperative to define these terms. Firstly, the term "State" encompasses all bodies and entities within a Member State, extending beyond federal or central authorities to include regional and local bodies as well as State undertakings. Likewise, State resources encompass all government funds and assets, incorporating those of regional and local bodies. The determining factor lies in whether the funds in question fall under State control and are thus accessible to public authorities.[87]

[82] Paras 59–61.

[83] Hofmann and Micheau (2016), p. 70; Bacon (2017), p. 381; Talus (2015), p. 130; Biondi and Eeckhout (2004); Struckmann (2017); Könings (2002); Koenig and Kühling (2002); Kingston (2011), p. 385; Roggenkamp et al. (2016), p. 322.

[84] European Court of Justice Judgement, C-206/06 Essent Netwerk Noord BV supported by Nederlands Elektriciteit Administratiekantoor BV v Aluminium Delfzijl BV,. [2008] ECR I-5497.

[85] Struckmann (2017).

[86] European Court of Justice Judgement, C-262/12 Association Vent De Colère! Fédération nationale and Others v Ministre de l'Écologie, du Développement durable, des Transports et du Logement and Ministre de l'Économie, des Finances et de l'Industrie. [2013] ECLI:EU:C:2013:851.

[87] Clayton and Catalan (2015).

ENEA is a case that sheds light on the "state resources" debate.[88] This case revolved around a Polish measure that mandated electricity suppliers to purchase a portion of their portfolio from heat/electricity cogeneration plants. The Court ultimately ruled that the measure did not constitute state aid, as the portfolio obligation did not correspond with the utilization of state resources.[89]

In *EEG 2012*, the focus was on the Erneuerbare-Energien-Gesetz (EEG, Renewable Energy Act), Germany's renewable energy legislation amended in 2012.[90] While EEG and its previous iterations will be discussed in a later chapter, this analysis aims to address the primary aspects of this case about feed-in tariffs. The EEG 2012 imposed a hybrid Feed-in Tariff/Feed-in Premium system, in which a surcharge was imposed on suppliers and subsequently passed onto final consumers. This surcharge provided funding for green electricity producers. Additionally, the surcharge incorporated varying reference points based on consumer type.

In 2014, the Commission adopted a decision on the EEG 2012 scheme, deeming the mechanism incompatible with the internal market for two reasons. Firstly, the support for electricity production from renewable energy sources and mine gas, which guaranteed EEG electricity producers a price for electricity above the market price through feed-in tariffs and market premiums. Secondly, the special compensation scheme allowed for a reduction of the EEG surcharge for energy-intensive users.

Germany appealed this decision to the General Court, which rejected the appeal despite identifying some errors in the Commission's analysis.[91] The General Court concluded that the Commission's assessment of state resource usage was accurate.[92] Germany then appealed this judgment to the ECJ.

Germany's appeal focused on four main arguments:

1. EEG 2012 mechanism relied on the duties of Transmission System Operators (TSOs), and funding for green electricity producers did not impact state resources.
2. The State's regulatory function did not equate to control over EEG resources.
3. The EEG surcharge was not equivalent to a public levy.
4. The sole difference between the two schemes was that electricity suppliers in the EEG 2012 system purchased not the physical electricity but its renewable

---

[88] European Court of Justice Judgement, C-329/15, ENEA S.A. v Prezes Urzędu Regulacji Energetyki. [2019] ECLI:EU:C:2017:671.

[89] See: Bouchagiar (2020).

[90] European Court of Justice Judgement, C-405/16 P, Federal Republic of Germany v European Commission. [2019] ECLI:EU:C:2019:268.

[91] Judgement of the General Court, Case T-47/15, Federal Republic of Germany v European Commission, Aid Granted by Certain provisions of the Amended German Law Concerning Renewable Energy Sources (EEG 2012), 10 May 2016.

[92] Paras. 127–128.

character (i.e., its greenness) at a fixed price, similar to the *PreussenElektra* precedent.[93]

The ECJ deemed the case admissible and proceeded to evaluate the merits. Addressing Germany's non-imputability argument, the ECJ noted that Germany failed to contest the General Court's arguments concerning the role of TSOs in the German Feed-in Tariff system. The ECJ also emphasized that the prohibition of state aid "by Member State" and "through state resources" does not permit Member States to circumvent TFEU Article 107(1) by establishing "autonomous institutions charged with allocating aid". Subsequently, the ECJ introduced a "state control-centered" approach, asserting that constant public control over resources is the primary determinant of the "state resources" category. Consequently, even when a separate entity manages resources for aid, the aid may fall within the scope of TFEU Article 107(1). However, the ECJ determined that the General Court's findings were insufficient to classify the EEG 2012 surcharge mechanism as aid through state resources.[94]

Subsequently, the ECJ elucidated the distinction between "public control of resources" and the "effect of general interests on the resource-controlling entity." It concluded that the General Court failed to demonstrate that TSOs remained indefinitely under public control. The ECJ sought to explain how the present case differed from *Vent De Colere*. In *Vent De Colere*, the Court argued that resource control belonged to the State, which funded green electricity investors. In contrast, in EEG 2012, these responsibilities were delegated to TSOs, except for the electricity regulator's supervisory duties. Consequently, the ECJ determined that the EEG surcharge in this case did not constitute a public levy, claiming that the EEG 2012 system did not involve the use of State resources. The decision of the General Court was ultimately overturned.[95]

The EEG 2014 was also brought before the European Commission.[96] This legislation included numerous novelties, which will be detailed later. This section focuses solely on the primary functions of the EEG 2014 and the Commission's approach to them. The EEG 2014 was a hybrid of Feed-in Tariff (FIT), Feed-in Premium (FIP), and tendering for capacity schemes. TSOs were required to purchase electricity from Distribution System Operators (DSOs), who were in turn obliged to buy from local green producers. The system was financed by a green electricity surcharge ("*EEG Umlage*").

Initially, the Commission argued that the EEG 2014 conferred an advantage.[97] They then assessed the other components of the state aid test, concluding that it was

---

[93] Paras. 27, 34–37.

[94] Paras. 57, 71–73.

[95] See: Alija (2016).

[96] European Commission Letter to the Member State, 25.11.2014, C(2014) 8786 Final. SA.33995 (2013/C) (ex 2013/NN).

[97] Para. 149.

selective, likely to distort competition and affect trade between Member States.[98] The Commission imputed the designation and monitoring process of the EEG surcharge to the State.[99] Moreover, they contended that the scheme in question diverged from the *PreussenElektra* case, as the State exercised greater control over the EEG resources.[100] The Commission ultimately determined that the EEG 2014 system was based on State resources within the meaning of TFEU Article 107(1).[101]

Having established the presence of state aid, the Commission proceeded to examine its compatibility with the internal market.[102] They found that the EEG 2014 scheme pursued an objective of common interest, and that state intervention was necessary to address market failures in the renewable energy sector.[103] They also determined that distortions of competition and effects on trade were limited. In conclusion, they decided that the state aid mechanism in the EEG 2014 was compatible with the internal market.[104]

The Commission also assessed the EEG 2014 in the context of TFEU Articles 30 and 110. They discovered no discrimination based on guarantees of origin, and the EEG 2014 complied with TFEU Articles 30 and 110.[105] Ultimately, after these considerations, the Commission approved the EEG 2014, avoiding a legal dispute similar to the one surrounding the EEG 2012, creating a "green policy space" for FIT/FIP schemes.

Germany took a different approach with the EEG 2017 by obtaining the Commission's approval before adopting the amendment.[106] In its decision, the Commission maintained that the EEG 2017 constituted state aid for reasons identical to the EEG 2014 decision.[107] However, as in the previous decision, they determined that the EEG 2017 passed the compatibility test. The Commission found that the compatibility criteria, i.e., the objective of common interest, need for state intervention, appropriateness, incentive effect, and proportionality, were fulfilled. Consequently, they decided not to raise objections against the EEG 2017. The Commission approved the EEG 2021 and EEG 2023 without raising objections, using similar arguments, in 2021 and 2022, respectively.[108]

---

[98] Paras. 151–152.

[99] Para. 174.

[100] Para. 198.

[101] Para. 218.

[102] Para. 227.

[103] Paras. 231, 232.

[104] Para. 273.

[105] Para. 337.

[106] Frenz (2018), p. 53.

[107] European Commission Letter to the Member State, C(2016) 8789 final, State Aid SA.45461 (2016/N) – Germany EEG 2017 – Reform of the Renewable Energy Law.

[108] European Commission SA.57779 EEG 2021 - Erneuerbare Energien Gesetz. In: State Aid Registrar. https://ec.europa.eu/competition-policy/index_en; European Commission SA.102084 EEG 2023 - Erneuerbare Energien Gesetz. In: State Aid Registrar. https://ec.europa.eu/competition-policy/index_en.

The final case to be examined in this context is *Achema*.[109] In *Achema*, the subject pertained to the Lithuanian measure of considering electricity generation from certain green electricity installations as a SGEI. In return, the government paid compensation for the electricity generation. This compensation was financed by a levy which was passed on to the end consumer. The Court concluded that the measure in question amounted to using state resources for two reasons: funding by an obligatory levy on the end-consumer and the state's control over the funds raised by the levy.[110]

The ECJ judgments provide solutions for two distinct situations regarding the use of state resources. In the first situation, the state imposes a levy that finances a publicly controlled initiative. The *Essent Netwerk*, *Vent de Colere*, and *Achema* cases pertain to this type of situation. For this scenario, the legal precedent of the ECJ is to recognize the measure as state aid. In the second situation, the state assumes only the role of a regulator. In this situation, the state may introduce a levy for funding green electricity promotion; however, it does not exercise any control over it. The electricity sector actors merely transfer the resource among themselves, ultimately financing the green electricity installation. The *PreussenElektra*, *EEG 2012*, and *ENEA* cases represent this second situation.

In a general evaluation, it appears that the legal precedent of the ECJ concerning the use of state resources in green electricity-related cases has found its appropriate course. By excluding the *PreussenElektra* line of measures from state aid consideration, they created policy space for green electricity promotion across the EU. The outcomes of this precedent benefit the green electricity and climate protection objectives of the Union.

4.2.1.3 Effect on Competition and Inter-State Trade

The final aspect of the definition of State aid under Article 107(1) is that state aid measures should distort or threaten to distort competition and have an effect on inter-state trade. To be prohibited, a measure must fulfill these two criteria. Due to its selective nature, state aid is presumed to be more distortive than mergers and contractual agreements.[111] Distortions in competition manifest themselves as an advantage for one undertaking over its competitors. The distortion arises through favoring, or selectivity, as per the "by favoring certain undertakings or the production of certain goods" language of TFEU Article 107(1).[112]

A measure is selective if it exclusively provides advantages for certain undertakings or certain sectors. According to TFEU Article 107(1), preferential treatment of

[109] European Court of Justice Judgement, C-706/17, Achema AB and Others v Valstybinė kainų ir energetikos kontrolės komisija (VKEKK). [2019] ECLI:EU:C:2019:407.

[110] See: Bouchagiar (2020).

[111] Medghoul (2016).

[112] Heidenhain (2010), p. 43.

certain undertakings or the production of certain goods falls under the "favoring" (or selectivity) criterion. A grant to an individual private actor is *prima facie* selective and constitutes favoring. However, not all aid schemes are as straightforward as individual grants. Most aid schemes have a broader base and complex criteria, requiring more detailed analysis. In such cases, the position of the recipient undertakings must be compared to others in a comparable legal and factual situation.[113]

How does selectivity distort competition? The Court held in *Philip Morris that "when State financial aid strengthens the position of an undertaking compared with other undertakings competing in intra-Union trade, the latter must be regarded as affected by that aid"*.[114] Even small amounts of aid may distort competition. Thus, the condition of distortion of competition is not dependent on the quantity of aid.[115] However, as discussed below, the Commission has implemented block-exemptions to exclude *de minimis* aid from the control process.

As the language of TFEU Article 107(1) also encompasses potential distortions of competition, measures do not need to show actual effects or distort competition. The effect on inter-State trade is another component of this final aspect of the State aid concept and is closely related to the "distortion of competition" criterion. To establish a State aid claim, it is necessary to demonstrate that the measure affects inter-State trade. This condition is inherently fulfilled if the recipient engages in cross-border trade within the Union. However, undertakings not engaging in cross-border operations may also affect trade by increasing domestic production and reducing demand for exporting competitors. Aid may also enable the recipient to become an exporter with new, more competition-distorting pricing. Even trade with non-Member States may affect trade between the Member States due to market interdependence: the recipient might change strategy at any time and begin to supply the Common Market.[116]

The Commission is not required to demonstrate the actual effects of State aid on inter-State trade, as establishing the potential for adverse consequences is sufficient. Even when State aid is provided to counterbalance aid in competing Member States, the measure is considered State aid that impacts inter-State trade.[117]

Consequently, how does the promotion of green electricity relate to the subject matter of this subchapter? Firstly, it must be acknowledged that green electricity promotion schemes typically do not distort competition. For instance, feed-in tariff conditions generally apply universally, while tenders are customarily open to all participants. However, upon closer examination, one may identify certain competition-distorting elements, such as regionally biased measures,

[113] Säcker and Montag (2016), p. 188.

[114] Para. 11. European Court of Justice Judgement, C-730/79 Philip Morris Holland BV v Commission [1980] ECR 209.

[115] Medghoul (2016), pp. 355–356.

[116] Hofmann and Micheau (2016), pp. 154–155; Säcker and Montag (2016), p. 239.

[117] Heidenhain (2010), p. 157.

technology-specific tenders, or local content requirements. Therefore, the Commission's vigilance in addressing energy aid is understandable.

Secondly, it may be posited that intra-EU trade in electricity remains limited, if not virtually nonexistent. As a result, the trade-affecting characteristics of green electricity aid are nearly unnoticeable. While presenting this perspective, it should also be emphasized that, with the continued development of the EU-wide electricity super-grid in the future, the aforementioned trade-impacting properties will become increasingly evident.

4.2.2 State Aid Control Law

The second concern within EU state aid law, after defining the notion, is the control of Member State mechanisms. State aid control encompasses a series of provisions that dictate the congruence of state aid measures with the EU acquis, as stipulated in the TFEU, directives, and guidelines. The TFEU contains pivotal rules concerning control. Within the TFEU, two control mechanisms have been devised: "automatic compatibility," which exempts certain measures from the control process, and "discretionary compatibility," which essentially entails a permitting procedure. Additional compatibility rules, often sector-specific, are also being enforced. However, those relevant to the scope of this book are to be addressed in the following section.

4.2.2.1 Automatic Compatibility

Article 107(2) of the TFEU governs automatic (*de jure*) compatibility, which is *per se* exempt from the state aid control process. The Commission lacks discretion when applying measures conforming to TFEU 107(2)(a) to (c). The rule states: *"The following shall be compatible with the internal market: (a) aid having a social character, granted to individual consumers, provided that such aid is granted without discrimination related to the origin of the products concerned; (b) aid to make good the damage caused by natural disasters or exceptional occurrences; (c) aid granted to the economy of certain areas of the Federal Republic of Germany affected by the division of Germany, in so far as such aid is required in order to compensate for the economic disadvantages caused by that division..."* The language of the Article is unambiguous, as "shall" is employed instead of "may" in Article 107(3). Nonetheless, the Commission may still scrutinize the measure to assess whether it aligns with the prerequisites of Article 107(2). If the measure in question adheres to Article 107(2), the Commission will be devoid of discretion. However, if it is determined that the requirements of Article 107(2) are unfulfilled, the derogation cannot be approved, and the Commission will proceed to the scope of Article 107(3).

In the context of this book, emphasis must be placed on subparagraph (a), as the provision of certain aid to consumers could pertain to green electricity issues. Article 107(2)(a) stipulates that aid with a social character, provided the measure does not depend on the origin of production, is exempt from Commission control. Subparagraph (a) encompasses three conditions. Firstly, the measure must possess a social character, meaning the aid should be restricted to specific categories of consumers whose circumstances justify social intervention. Secondly, the recipients must be individual consumers, thereby limiting the subparagraph's coverage solely to final consumers. Lastly, the aid must be granted without discrimination based on the product's origin. Discrimination related to the product's origin may target particular undertakings or sectors and, as a result, would be noncompliant with the subparagraph. This subparagraph could readily encompass the promotion of green electricity installations in impoverished regions with limited access to electricity.

4.2.2.2 Discretionary Compatibility

Article 107(3) of the TFEU addresses discretionary compatibility concerning state aid, granting the Commission the authority to determine whether a measure in question aligns with EU law without being obligated to do so. According to this provision, the Commission may deem the following categories of aid compatible:

1. Aid promoting the economic development of areas with abnormally low living standards or significant underemployment,
2. Aid supporting the implementation of an "important project of common European interest" (IPCEI) or to remedy a serious disturbance in the economy of a Member State,
3. Aid facilitating the development of specific economic activities or areas provided it does not negatively impact trading conditions contrary to the common interest,
4. Aid advancing culture and heritage conservation, as long as it does not affect trading conditions and competition in the Union to an extent contrary to the common interest,
5. Any other categories of aid specified by a decision of the Council upon a proposal from the Commission.

The Commission has restricted its discretion stemming from TFEU 107(3) through various texts, including block exemptions and guidelines. When applicable, these limiting texts will be employed, and the Commission will decide accordingly. In the absence of such a legal source, the Commission must directly apply TFEU 107(3).

A critical aid category under TFEU 107(3) is regional aid, governed by subparagraphs (a) and (c). Regional aid is distinguished from other aid types by its geographical dimension, as it pertains to regions economically underdeveloped compared to the EU average. However, energy is excluded from the regional aid scope, as per the Regional Aid Guidelines, due to the existence of a common internal market for energy in the EU.

TFEU 107(3)(b) is crucial for environmental and energy-related matters. Under paragraph (b), measures against a common threat, such as air pollution, may be taken. However, fulfilling the conditions of this paragraph is challenging, as it necessitates a significant, demonstrable contribution to an IPCEI.[118] TFEU 107(3)(b) projects, particularly in the energy sector, often materialize as joint grid-related investments, such as the construction of an EU super-grid (under the TEN-E umbrella).[119]

Lastly, specific aid measures may not surpass the Union's de minimis threshold.[120] The "De Minimis Regulation" governs this issue and encompasses green electricity promotion measures.[121] *De minimis* aid measures are considered not to meet all the criteria in TFEU Article 107(1) and are therefore exempt from the notification requirement in Article 108(3).[122] The threshold for *de minimis* aid is set at 200,000 Euros over any period of three fiscal years.[123] This compliance threshold may benefit low-budget programs supporting green electricity projects, for example, at the municipal or energy cooperative (i.e., community) level.

4.2.3 Compatibility Rules for Green Electricity

In terms of compatibility, the "General Block Exemption Regulation" (GBER) will be examined as a legal document that prescribes a range of exemptions from the discretionary compatibility process. The "Energy Tax Directive," a significant text for fiscal matters, will be explored. Then, the new "Guidelines on State aid for Climate, Environmental Protection and Energy" (CEEAG) and the revised "Renewable Energy Directive" (RED II), which has undergone multiple amendments, will be discussed as the primary regulatory texts concerning green energy. Finally, the Temporary Crisis and Transition Framework (TCTF), a direct result of the recent geopolitical turbulences, will be covered.

---

[118] de Sadeleer (2014), p. 454.

[119] European Commission Press Release, "New energy Projects of Common Interest for the Energy Union built on European solidarity." 31 October 2019. https://ec.europa.eu/commission/presscorner/detail/en/IP_19_6203.

[120] Grozea-Knuth (2016), p. 375.

[121] Commission Regulation (EU) No 1407/2013 of 18 December 2013 on the application of Articles 107 and 108 of the Treaty on the Functioning of the European Union to de minimis aid.

[122] Article 3(1).

[123] Article 3(2).

4.2.3.1 General Block Exemption Regulation (GBER)

The objective of the GBER is to designate certain aid types as compatible with the internal market and exempt them from the notification requirement stipulated in TFEU Article 108(3). The initial version of GBER, GBER 2008, consolidated prior block exemption systems into a single instrument.[124] In 2014, the GBER was amended, and this work will focus on the revised GBER. The GBER prescribes various maximum aid intensities depending on the investment's objective, regional coverage, and type of recipient. According to the GBER, state aid for "environmental protection" may be granted.

Paragraph 101 of the GBER defines environmental protection as any action designed to remedy or prevent damage to physical surroundings or natural resources caused by a beneficiary's own activities, to reduce the risk of such damage, or to promote a more efficient use of natural resources. This includes energy-saving measures and the utilization of renewable sources of energy. Consequently, it can be asserted that aid promoting the more efficient use of natural resources, energy conservation, and the utilization of renewable energy sources falls under GBER's scope.[125]

GBER outlines key principles governing investment and operating aids for energy projects, particularly those focusing on efficiency, high-efficiency cogeneration, and renewable sources. Articles 41–43 are pivotal in this regard, each addressing a specific aspect of energy promotion and regulation.

Article 41(1) of the GBER stipulates that investment aid for renewable energy is compatible with the internal market, as defined in Article 107(3) of the Treaty on the Functioning of the European Union (TFEU) and is exempt from the notification requirement under TFEU Article 108(3), provided that GBER's conditions are met. The investment aid applies only to new installations for green electricity generation, with eligible costs covering additional investment for promoting renewable energy. Aid intensity ceilings are flexible, ranging from 30% to 100%.

Article 42 provides guidelines for operating aid for electricity from renewable sources. This aid must be granted through a competitive bidding process with clear, transparent, and non-discriminatory criteria. GBER Article 42(3) acknowledges the potential for technology limitations and permits the bidding process to be limited to specific technologies under certain circumstances, such as the need for diversification, network constraints, or the longer-term potential of new technology.

Article 42(4) stipulates that a maximum of 5% of the annual projected new renewable electricity capacity can be allocated to innovative technologies through a competitive bidding process. Article 42(5) indicates that aid should be given as a premium supplementary to the market price, with generators selling their electricity directly within the market. Other provisions in Article 42 stipulate the conditions for

[124] Commission Regulation (EC) No 800/2008 of 6 August 2008.

[125] Grozea-Knuth et al. (2016), p. 603.

providing aid without a competitive process for small-scale projects and the obligation to subtract any previously received investment aid from the operating aid.

Article 43 covers operating aid for small-scale renewable energy installations. It dictates that aid should be granted exclusively to installations below specific capacity thresholds. The aid per energy unit should not exceed the difference between the total levelized costs of producing energy from the renewable source and the market price of the corresponding energy form.

In essence, Articles 42 and 43 of the GBER set out a comprehensive policy framework for promoting green electricity generation, particularly for small-scale installations and the deployment of innovative technology. They establish a tendering system as the primary allocation mechanism for green energy support but allow aid to be granted without tendering for small installations. The Feed-in Premium schemes appear to be legitimate operating aid for small installations under Article 43.

These GBER articles facilitate streamlining regulations around small green electricity investments, which is instrumental in achieving climate and renewable energy targets. In turn, they reflect the European Union's political prioritization of green energy, underscoring the EU's commitment to a sustainable future.

4.2.3.2 Energy Tax Directive

The seminal document concerning fiscal state aid within the European Union is the "Energy Tax Directive", enacted in 2003. As stipulated by this directive, Member States are granted the prerogative to implement, under fiscal oversight, comprehensive or partial exemptions or reductions in the tax level applicable to electricity derived from renewable sources. Furthermore, it is permissible for Member States to reimburse producers for a portion or the entirety of the tax amount that consumers have paid for electricity generated from renewable sources.

The directive also provides for the application of tax reductions on electricity that favor energy-intensive enterprises or in circumstances where agreements have been established with enterprises or associations thereof. Similarly, reductions may apply where tradable permit schemes or comparable arrangements are put into operation, provided they contribute to attaining environmental protection goals or enhancing energy efficiency. Various fiscal measures, such as tax exemptions, reductions, differentiation, and refunds, as defined within the context of this directive, might be construed as state aid. In such instances, these measures must be officially communicated to the Commission in accordance with Article 108(3) of the Treaty. A minimum tax rate for electricity has been established, set at 0.5 Euros per MWh for business consumption and 1 Euro per MWh for non-business use.

4.2.3.3 Guidelines on State Aid for Climate, Environmental Protection and Energy (CEEAG)

Before the "Guidelines on State aid for Climate, Environmental Protection and Energy" (CEEAG) entered into force in 2022, the "Guidelines on State Aid for Environmental Protection and Energy 2014-2020" (EEAG) functioned as the secondary legislation aimed at promoting renewable energy and environmental protection through incentives such as market premiums, tenders, and certificate schemes.

The EEAG laid the groundwork for achieving the objectives of the 2030 Framework, despite its application ending in 2022. It covered various forms of aid, from energy efficiency measures to infrastructure support, but it had no binding legal obligations. Instead, it established a self-assessment procedure for Member States, encouraging them to balance the benefits of environmental aid with potential trade and competition implications. Although it granted exemptions for certain projects, the EEAG had strict assessment principles to ensure that state aid contributed to common interests and maintained minimal viable aid without undue negative impacts on competition and trade among Member States.

Part of the EEAG's goal was to empower Member States to self-assess their needs while collaborating towards shared energy goals. It acknowledged that promoting green energy could affect competition and trade but also noted that these negative effects could be offset by positive outcomes such as achieving the EU's climate and energy targets.

A significant part of the EEAG's policy focused on promoting renewable energy, suggesting a transition from fixed tariff systems to price-sensitive mechanisms. It also emphasized the importance of market instruments such as auctions and competitive bidding processes. The EEAG advocated for operating aid to be offered as a premium on the market price, with generators selling electricity directly in the market. It also aimed to discourage the generation of electricity under negative price conditions, particularly in wind-rich areas. Nonetheless, there were exceptions for smaller installations and demonstration projects.

EEAG stipulated that aid must be provided via competitive bidding, characterized by transparent and non-discriminatory criteria. Exceptions could be made under certain circumstances, such as limited project eligibility or risks of inflated support levels due to strategic bidding or low project realization rates from underbidding. While the rule was technology-neutrality, it allowed for technology-specific tenders based on the longer-term potential of innovative technologies or the need for diversification and grid stability. A significant aspect of the EEAG was transitioning from fixed-tariff systems to market-oriented mechanisms. However, it again allowed exemptions for specific scenarios, such as overbidding or underbidding, and small-scale installations or demonstration projects. These exemptions, particularly for smaller installations, facilitated aid for local, decentralized projects by simplifying regulations. Finally, the EEAG only allowed aid until a plant's full depreciation according to standard accounting rules, with any previous investment aid deducted from the operating aid.

In 2019, the European Commission reinforced its ambitions for climate action and sustainable growth by introducing the European Green Deal Communication, a strategy aiming to achieving net-zero by 2050 and restoring the dynamism of the Union economy.[126] The realization of objectives such as climate neutrality, climate change adaptation, and resource and energy efficiency, among other environmental goals, necessitates substantial effort and well-designed promotional mechanisms. Addressing this investment challenge requires the strategic mobilization of private and public financial resources in an "economically optimal" manner, influencing all sectors. In this context, State aid law assumes a pivotal role, functioning as the enabler of the Green Deal policy objectives. Nonetheless, establishing certain guiding principles and regulations is imperative to prevent state aid from introducing distortions in the internal market competition and adversely impacting trade among Member States.

In this regard, the amendment of the EEAG and the regulation of state aid exemptions were crucial to safeguard the interests of the European Union. The "Guidelines on State Aid for Climate, Environmental Protection and Energy" (CEEAG), published in February 2022, establish the principles for the compatibility of investment aid and operating aid.[127] The introduction of the CEEAG has provided much-needed clarity on the Commission's approach toward assessing the compatibility of environmental protection and energy aid measures in the coming years.

While markets can yield efficient results, State intervention may also be required to bolster certain economic activities that would otherwise lag in their development without adequate support. This condition is particularly relevant during the implementation of the Green Deal Industrial Plan, where state intervention may serve to prevent "Carbon Leakage" (the offshoring of carbon-intensive activities) or incentivize onshoring.[128] Consequently, the interplay of market mechanisms and State interventions is essential for the successful execution of the Green Deal objectives.

CEEAG Sect. 4.1 outlines the compatibility criteria for decarbonization-oriented interventions. Such measures encapsulate promotion of renewables, energy efficiency, and a set of technologies that may contribute to reaching climate objectives. Promotion measures ought to be designed to incorporate all technologies capable of contributing to reducing or removing greenhouse gas emissions from the environment. A measure may be justified based on, for instance, the requirement to achieve a specific technology target established in Union law, as is the case for renewable energy and energy efficiency, the necessity for diversification, or the long-term potential of innovative technologies.

---

[126] Communication from the Commission to the European Parliament, the European Council, the Council, the European Economic and Social Committee and the Committee of the Regions the European Green Deal COM/2019/640, 11.12.2019.

[127] Communication from the Commission – Guidelines on State Aid for Climate, Environmental Protection and Energy 2022 (2022/C 80/01).

[128] Communication from the Commission to the European Parliament, the European Council, the Council, the European Economic and Social Committee and the Committee of the Regions: A Green Deal Industrial Plan for the Net-Zero Age, COM/2023/62, 1.2.2023.

To facilitate a cost-effective allocation of aid and minimize competition distortions, aid for reducing emissions should generally be allocated through a competitive bidding process open to all eligible beneficiaries. CEEAG Point 49 stipulates that a bidding process should fulfill the following conditions cumulatively:

- It should be open, clear, transparent, and non-discriminatory, based on objective criteria, defined ex-ante in accordance with the objective of the measure, while minimizing the risk of strategic bidding,
- The process should be based on criteria published sufficiently in advance of the deadline for submitting applications to enable effective competition,
- The process should have a budget or volume as a binding constraint, such that it can be expected that not all bidders will receive aid. The expected number of bidders should be sufficient to ensure effective competition, and the design of undersubscribed bidding processes should be corrected to restore effective competition,
- The process should prevent any ex-post adjustment to the bidding process outcome.

In principle, the bidding process should be open to all technologies that can contribute to reducing or removing greenhouse gas emissions. However, the process can be limited to one or more specific categories of beneficiaries where there is a deviation of more than 10% between the bid level that different categories of beneficiaries are expected to offer or where the objective of the measure might be better achieved by limiting the bidding process to certain categories of beneficiaries, in line with CEEAG point 96.

The selection criteria employed in the allocation of aid through the competitive bidding process should correlate the contribution to the primary objective of the measure with the amount of aid requested by the applicant. Selection criteria that are not directly or indirectly related to the main objective of the measure may account for up to 30% of the total weight of all selection criteria.

Exceptions to the mandate of allocating aid and determining the aid level through a competitive bidding process may be justified under certain conditions. These include scenarios where the expected number of potential bidders is insufficient to ensure competition, where the beneficiaries qualify as small projects per point 107 (b) of the CEEAG, and where individual projects employing innovative technologies have been selected in an open call to be a part of a large integrated cross-border project collectively designed by several Member States, as per point 107(c).

In situations where aid is not allocated through a competitive bidding process, the Commission deems its amount to be proportionate if it is restricted to the net extra cost (i.e., finance gap) required to achieve the objective of the measure compared to a realistic counterfactual scenario. The net extra cost is determined by the differential between the economic revenues and costs, including the investment and operation of the aided project and those of the alternative project the aid beneficiary would credibly undertake in the absence of aid.

In certain circumstances, fund recall provisions may be mandated to ensure proportionality and mitigate the risk of overcompensation in cases where the supported projects prove more profitable than anticipated, aligning with CEEAG point 90. This precaution applies particularly to future market developments with operation cost or profit fluctuations.

It should be noted that where aid is granted through competitive bidding, an estimation of the finance gap for one or more reference (equivalent) projects supported might be required to assess the necessity of the promotion and its effect.

For operation aid, Member States should design the measure to prevent undue distortion to the efficient functioning of markets. Consequently, aid beneficiaries should not be incentivized to offer their output below their marginal costs. They must not receive aid for production in any period wherein the market value of that production is negative. Furthermore, incentives should not be provided to generate energy that would displace less polluting forms of energy.

Per point 116, the aid must result in an overall reduction in emissions, and it should not merely shift the emissions from one sector to another, such as from the industrial production sector to the energy sector. This rule implies that decreases in direct emissions from the supported activity should not be offset by simultaneous increases in other sectors caused by the aided. This condition bears particular relevance for projects aiming to reduce greenhouse gas emissions from industrial activities through electrification or hydrogen-based technologies.

Furthermore, aligning with point 117 of the CEEAG, aid designated for the decarbonization of industrial activities must reduce the emissions directly resulting from that industrial activity, and aid intended for improvements in the energy efficiency of industrial activities must enhance the energy efficiency of the beneficiaries' activities.

Aid for decarbonization should positively contribute to the reduction or removal of greenhouse gas emissions and aid in the achievement of the Union's climate targets. In this context, the Commission asserts that measures incentivizing new investments in energy or industrial production based on the most polluting fossil fuels, such as coal, diesel, lignite, oil, peat, and oil shale, do not yield any positive environmental effects.

Likewise, measures that incentivize new investments in energy or industrial production based on natural gas may exacerbate negative environmental externalities in the long run. Therefore, for investments in natural gas to be perceived as having a positive environmental effect, Member States must present how energy and industry lock-in with gas-based technologies will be evaded. The position of nuclear energy is nonetheless unclear.

Finally, for measures designed commencing from July 2023, Member States will be mandated to publicly consult on the competition effects and proportionality of measures to be notified under Sect. 4.1 of the CEEAG under the circumstances delineated in section 17 4.1.3.4. Moreover, Member States will be required to calculate the subsidy per tonne of CO2 equivalent emissions avoided for each project or reference project supported.[129]

4.2.3.4 Renewable Energy Directive (RED)

The Renewable Energy Directive (RED) represents the EU's paramount "secondary law" text concerning green electricity matters. While the GBER addresses block aid exemptions, and CEEAG focuses on self-assessment processes and policy structures in the environmental and energy sectors, the RED deals explicitly with renewable energy promotion. The original documents of 2001 and 2009 underpinned numerous practices throughout the Union. Following its most recent amendment in 2018, the RED II has been in force. To delineate the contrast between these three documents, it is necessary first to elucidate the frameworks of the RES and RED.

Per the RES, the first attempt, the Member States were required to establish national indicative targets for generation from renewable energy sources, ensuring their compatibility with climate change commitments.[130] These targets were to be reported every 5 years, along with measures taken to achieve them. Member States also had to evaluate and report their progress biennially. It mandated the Commission to evaluate the promotion mechanisms used in Member States that provided direct or indirect support to electricity producers. The directive introduced the "guarantee of origin" for electricity produced from renewable sources, with Member States required to ensure the authenticity of these guarantees. It obliged Member States to evaluate existing legislation and regulatory frameworks, aiming to reduce barriers and streamline procedures for renewable energy production. The directive further addressed grid system issues, requiring Member States to ensure that operators guaranteed the transmission and distribution of electricity produced from renewable energy sources. It also called for transparent and non-discriminatory rules for bearing the costs of technical adaptations necessary for integrating new renewable energy producers into the grid. Lastly, the Commission was required to present summary reports on implementation every 5 years.

The RED (of 2009) established mandatory national targets for 2020 for the overall share of energy from renewable sources in the gross final consumption of energy and the share of energy from renewable sources in transport.[131] Additionally, it laid down rules relating to statistical transfers between the Member States, joint

---

[129] See on CEEAG energy law provisions: European Commission, Guiding template: Investment/operating aid for the reduction and removal of greenhouse gas emissions including through support for renewable energy and energy efficiency, 2023.

[130] Directive 2001/77/EC of the European Parliament and of the Council of 27 September 2001 on the promotion of electricity produced from renewable energy sources in the internal electricity market.

[131] Directive 2009/28/EC of the European Parliament and of the Council of 23 April 2009 on the promotion of the use of energy from renewable sources and amending and subsequently repealing Directives 2001/77/EC and 2003/30/EC.

projects between the Member States and with third countries, guarantees of origin, administrative procedures, information and training, and access to the electricity grid for energy from renewable sources. It also established sustainability criteria for biofuels and bioliquids. The RED distinguished itself from the RES by shifting from electricity mix-share targeting to energy mix targeting, thereby broadening the inclusion of all energy types, and contributing to the Commission's renewable energy targets. To reach these targets, Member States could, among other measures, implement support schemes and measures of cooperation between different Member States and with third countries.

Each Member State was obligated to adopt a national renewable energy action plan that outlined national targets for the share of energy from renewable sources consumed in transport, electricity, and heating and cooling by 2020. The Commission was tasked with evaluating these national renewable energy action plans and could issue a recommendation. This "bottom-up approach" aligns with the target-centered orientation of the Paris Agreement and EU climate policy.

The RED introduced a set of rules on calculating the share of renewable energy in the energy mix, including the effect of intra-Union transfers, joint projects, and projects with third states. It also set targets concerning the coordination of Member States and intra-State bodies, streamlining procedures related to aid, transparency of governing rules, and bureaucratic simplification. Nevertheless, the RED did not detail approaches regarding how Member States could[132] foster renewable energy initiatives. Instead, it deferred this to their competence.

Member States were required to explicitly define any technical specifications that renewable energy equipment and systems must meet to benefit from support schemes. They were also urged to ensure that information on support measures was available to all relevant actors and that information on the net benefits, cost, and energy efficiency of equipment and systems for the use of heating, cooling, and electricity from renewable energy sources was made accessible either by the supplier of the equipment or system or by the competent national authorities.

According to the 2009 RED, Member States had to guarantee that the origin of electricity produced from renewable energy sources could be verified in accordance with objective, transparent, and non-discriminatory criteria. As such, Member States were required to issue a guarantee of origin in response to a request from a producer of electricity from renewable energy sources.

One of the objectives was to encourage Member States to develop transmission and distribution grid infrastructure, intelligent networks, storage facilities, and the electricity system. This objective reflected the Commission's vision for the future of the energy sector. It is often argued that grid development should proceed concurrently with renewable energy generation to manage congestions and evenly distribute the benefits and burdens of the green economy across the EU.

Member States were also mandated to expedite authorization procedures for grid infrastructure and synchronize the approval of such infrastructure with

[132] Ide (2017), p. 81.

administrative and planning procedures.[133] Furthermore, they were to guarantee that the imposition of transmission and distribution tariffs does not discriminate against electricity derived from renewable energy sources, particularly electricity generated in peripheral areas such as island regions and sparsely populated areas.

Each Member State was obliged to submit a report to the Commission detailing their progress in promoting and utilizing energy from renewable sources by 31 December 2011 and biennially thereafter. The sixth report, due by 31 December 2021, was stipulated as the final required report. These reports were to encompass, among other things, the sectoral (electricity, heating and cooling, and transport) and overall shares of energy from renewable sources, the establishment and operation of support schemes, and other measures to promote energy from renewable sources. Moreover, where applicable, these reports were to demonstrate how the Member State has structured its support schemes to take into consideration renewable energy applications that yield additional benefits compared to other comparable applications, albeit potentially at a higher cost. They were also to describe the functioning of the system of guarantees of origin for electricity.

The RED 2018 introduced several key changes compared to the RED 2009.[134] Firstly, it revised the renewable energy targets, setting a binding goal of a 32% renewable energy share across the EU by 2030. This target is set to be reevaluated in 2023 by the Commission and may be increased should there be further cost reductions in renewable energy generation or a decrease in demand. As with the RED, Member States have national contribution targets under the RED II.

New Article 4 of the RED II allows Member States to implement support schemes to promote renewable energy. These schemes must be market-based and responsive to ensure that renewable energy producers react to market price signals and maximize their market revenues.[135] This provision is similar to the RED approach, while the RED II places a particular emphasis on market premiums awarded as a result of open, transparent, competitive, non-discriminatory, and cost-effective tenders as the primary tool in promoting renewable energy, except for small-scale installations and demonstration projects.[136] This framework aligns with the CEEAG, but while the CEEAG was not legally binding, RED II enshrines these policies in hard law, significantly limiting the policy options of Member States for promoting green energy while still leaving room for exceptions.

Article 5 of RED II, another addition, governs the exportation of electricity within the intra-Union market and allows for the support of renewable energy schemes in importing Member States. According to Article 5.1, Member States can decide the extent to which they support electricity from renewable sources produced in another Member State. Member States can provide support for an indicative share of

[133] Roggenkamp et al. (2016), pp. 326–327; Johnston and Block (2013), p. 322.

[134] Directive (EU) 2018/2001 of the European Parliament and of the Council of 11 December 2018 on the promotion of the use of energy from renewable sources.

[135] Article 4.1-3.

[136] Article 4.3-4.

newly-supported capacity, or of the budget associated with it, each year to producers located in other Member States. Participation in these promotion schemes will be facilitated through agreements between Member States, covering principles for the allocation of renewable electricity that is subject to cross-border support.

Another significant amendment in RED II is the "Financial Stability" regulation in Article 6. This article prohibits Member States from revising promotion schemes in a way that negatively affects the rights conferred under TFEU 107 and 108 and the economic viability of projects already receiving support. If they re-regulate promotion schemes, they must adjust the level of support according to objective criteria established in the original design of the scheme. This rule suggests that Member States cannot create new reasons or criteria to re-regulate promotion schemes in a way that endangers the financial stability of operational projects. Article 6 also requires long-term planning for promotion (for 5 years) and assessment of the effectiveness of support schemes for electricity from renewable energy sources and their significant distributive effects on different consumer groups and investments.

Concurrently with the RED, the RED II delineates a framework of regulations on the calculation of renewable energy quotas and statistical transfers among Member States. There is a significant amendment concerning the subject of statistical transfers. Statistical transfers denote non-physical reallocations of renewable energy quotas in the energy matrix, permitting Member States to acquire renewable energy shares from other Member States. Under the RED, statistical transfers were not incorporated into the national objectives; however, this obstacle has been cleared by the RED II. With the RED II, Member States can make statistical transfers in order to attain their national goals. As an illustration, in 2020, Ireland procured a specific portion of renewable energy quotas from Denmark and Estonia, amounting to 50 million euros, to meet its renewable energy target.[137]

A further distinction lies in the establishment of the "Union Renewable Development Platform" (URDP). To expedite the realization of the Union-wide renewable energy quota targets and streamline statistical transfers, the Commission constituted the URDP in 2021. The URDP is a data-matching mechanism (i.e., a database and a set of algorithms) to ensure accurate statistical transfers. On a discretionary basis, Member States submit annual data to the URDP concerning their national contributions to the Union target or any established benchmark for monitoring progress. This data-collection scheme includes the anticipated shortfall or surplus in their contribution, along with an indication of the price at which they would agree to transfer any overproduction of energy from renewable sources from or to another Member State. The Commission is obligated to ensure that the URDP is capable of balancing the demand and supply of the quantities of energy from renewable sources,

[137] The Irish Times (2019) Ireland to pay Denmark, Estonia €50 m for 'statistical' renewable energy transfer. https://www.irishtimes.com/news/ireland/irish-news/ireland-to-pay-denmark-estonia-50m-for-statistical-renewable-energy-transfer-1.4418420.

considered in the computation of a Member State's renewable energy quota, based on prices or other criteria specified by the Member State accepting the transfer.[138]

It is worth noting that Member States are now empowered to facilitate statistical transfers to accomplish their national renewable energy quota targets, thus enhancing the relevance of URDP in the coordination of Union-wide target planning.

A further innovation is that RED 2018 bestows upon the Commission the responsibility of fostering joint projects, a mandate that was absent in RED 2009: "*The Commission shall, upon the request of the Member States involved, facilitate the establishment of joint projects between Member States, particularly through dedicated technical assistance and project development aid*."[139] In alignment with the RED, the RED II governs joint projects with third countries, for instance, Turkey. However, it introduces a new stipulation regarding the international law status of potential partner states. Electricity derived from renewable resources in a third country may be included in calculating the renewable energy shares of the Member States, provided that these partners satisfy certain criteria, such as compliance with international law. Article 13.4 of the RED II envisions that the Commission will disseminate guidelines and best practices and, upon request from the Member States, facilitate the establishment of joint support schemes among the Member States.

Another innovation is that Member States will consult with network operators to consider the impact of energy efficiency and demand response programs, along with specific provisions on renewables self-consumption and renewable energy communities, on the infrastructure development plans of the operators. Article 16 simplifies the process for obtaining renewable energy permits. As per this article, Member States will appoint a single contact point for applicants responsible for the entirety of the permit-granting processes. The permit-granting process should not exceed 2 years for power plants and 1 year for installations under 150 kW capacity, encompassing all relevant procedures of competent authorities. Article 17, akin to the streamlined permit-granting process in Article 16, anticipates a straightforward notification process for grid connections. Additional topics the RED addresses are self-consumers (Article 21), and renewable energy communities (Article 22).

Nevertheless, by 2023, it became evident that a revision to the RED II was necessary, and the time limit for reevaluating the renewable share goal had been reached. By the close of the year, a RED III is anticipated. A provisional consensus was achieved in March 2023 to augment the target to 42.5% by 2030, with an optional 2.5% indicative increase, leading to a total of 45%. The provisional agreement incorporates expedited permitting procedures for renewable energy projects, aiming to expedite the deployment of renewable energies in line with the EU's REPowerEU plan, which seeks independence from Russian gas. Member States will establish Renewable Energy Acceleration Areas, where renewable energy projects will be subject to streamlined and expedited permit approval processes. Moreover, the deployment of renewable energy will be regarded as being in the "overriding

[138] Article 8.2-3.

[139] Article 9.6.

public interest", which will restrict the basis for legal objections to new installations.[140]

4.2.3.5 Temporary Crisis and Transition Framework (TCTF)

In March 2022, the Commission instituted a State Aid Temporary Crisis Framework (TCF), designed to aid Member States in addressing the economic shortfall encountered by the EU economy due to the Russian invasion of Ukraine. This framework was then expanded and refined through the "Temporary Crisis and Transition Framework" (TCTF) in March 2023, effective until December 2025.[141] This extension allowed Member States to facilitate their progress toward a carbon-neutral economy and alleviate the adverse effects of the ongoing energy crisis.[142] The TCTF signifies an additional measure of flexibility within the EU state aid control regime, which, in this instance, is a response more to geopolitical tension than to decarbonization objectives.

Section 2.5 of the TCTF outlines the compatibility criteria for promoting renewable energy and energy storage under the REPowerEU initiative. This part incentivizes investment and operational support for renewable energy sources and storage modalities via state aid exceptions, thereby ensuring a cost-effective reduction in dependence on fossil fuel imports, accelerating the energy transition, and facilitating lower and less volatile prices.

Support pursuant to Sect. 2.5 should be allocated to newly installed or refurbished capacities based on a scheme with a predetermined volume and budget. The provision of this support can persist until December 2025, and projects benefiting from this support must be operational within 36 months following the aid date.

Furthermore, aid may be combined with other forms of promotion for distinct, identifiable eligible costs. Aid can be conferred through direct grants, repayable advances, loans, guarantees, or tax advantages. The amount of aid can invariably be determined through open, clear, transparent, and non-discriminatory competitive bidding procedures. The support level can be set administratively for all technologies except for large solar, wind, and hydropower installations. The aid ceiling is €30 million per enterprise per project, and the installed capacity thresholds set out in

[140] Council of the European Union (2023) Council and Parliament reach provisional deal on renewable energy directive. In: Consilium Europa. https://www.consilium.europa.eu/en/press/press-releases/2023/03/30/council-and-parliament-reach-provisional-deal-on-renewable-energy-directive/.

[141] Communication from the Commission Temporary Crisis and Transition Framework for State Aid measures to support the economy following the aggression against Ukraine by Russia 2023/C 101/03.

[142] European Commission, Guiding template: Investment/operating aid for the reduction and removal of greenhouse gas emissions including through support for renewable energy and energy efficiency, 2023.

point 77(h). The maximum individual aid amount conferred per enterprise must not surpass 10% of the total budget allocated for such a scheme or EUR 200 million.

In relation to operating aid (Sect. 2.5.2), aid can exclusively be conferred in the form of contracts for differences (CfDs) in correlation with the energy output of the installation and with a duration of up to 20 years after the start of operations. The scope and exceptions are identical to the investment aid, excluding sizable solar, wind, and hydro projects, with the addition of projects above an aid ceiling.

Section 2.6 lists the compatibility criteria for schemes designed to encourage investments in the decarbonization of industrial activities. These investments incorporate the electrification and adoption of renewable and electricity-based hydrogen, along with energy efficiency measures in the industry. The aim is to accelerate the decarbonization of the industry, thereby diminishing dependence on Russian gas imports.

Eligibility under Sect. 2.6 of the TCTF necessitates the investment to facilitate a minimum 40% reduction in direct greenhouse gas emissions from the industrial installation presently dependent on fossil fuels or a minimum 20% reduction in energy consumption in industrial installations in relation to the promoted activities. For investments associated with activities encompassed by the EU Emission Trading System (ETS), the aid must reduce the GHG emissions of the installation below the relevant benchmarks for free allocation.

Aid should not be utilized solely to comply with prevailing Union standards or finance an augmentation in the overall production capacity of the beneficiary, although a minor capacity increase may be permitted if deemed necessary for technical reasons. Additionally, the installation or equipment funded under Sect. 2.6 of the TCF must be completed and fully operational within 36 months after the date of granting, with penalties in effect should these deadlines not be met.

Three distinct methodologies have been put forth for the calculation of the aid amount which is (temporarily) exempt from the Commission scrutiny:

1. The first approach determines the eligible costs as the difference between the costs associated with the aided project and the cost savings or additional revenue compared to the scenario devoid of aid throughout the investment's lifespan (i.e., finance gap). The maximum fundamental aid intensity stands at 40% of the eligible costs. This rate may be elevated by 10% for aid extended to medium-sized enterprises and 20% for aid extended to small enterprises. The aid intensity may additionally be increased by 15 percentage points for investments that result in a reduction of direct greenhouse gas emissions by at least 55% or a decrease in energy consumption by at least 25% relative to the situation prior to the investment. A clawback mechanism (i.e., fund recall) is mandated to counteract windfall profits, for instance, in cases of extraordinarily high electricity prices.
2. As per the second approach, the provision of investment aid may be conducted via a competitive bidding process that is open, clear, transparent, and non-discriminatory, based on objective criteria defined in advance.

3. The third approach calculates eligible costs as the investment costs connected to the project for which aid is dispensed (for example, costs related to equipment and construction).[143]

Aid under Sect. 2.6 may be combined with other schemes for varying eligible costs. Aid calculated under the first and second methods can be combined with other aid or support from centrally managed funds for overlapping eligible costs, provided the maximum aid amount under the regulations is respected. Aid calculated under the third method can be merged with other aid or support for overlapping eligible costs, given that the highest aid amount or intensity under any of the applicable rules is respected. The cumulative aid amount should not exceed 100% of the eligible costs.

References

Aidelojie K, Makuch Z (2008) Multilateral organisations, fossil fuels and energy law and policy: the tower of Babel re-visited. Eur Energy Environ Law Rev 17:227–255

Alija N (2016) State Aid for Green Electricity Federal Republic of Germany v European Commission T-47/15 Annotation by Nevin Alija. Eur State Aid Law Q 15:452–457

Asmelash HB (2014) Energy subsidies and WTO dispute settlement: why only renewable energy subsidies are challenged? University of St Gallen Law School - Law and Economics Research Paper Series

Bacon K (2017) European Union law of state aid, 3rd edn. Oxford University Press, Oxford

Bigdeli SZ (2011) Resurrecting the dead - the expired non-actionable subsidies and the lingering question of green space. Manchester J Int Econ Law 8:2

Biondi A, Eeckhout P (2004) State aid and obstacles to trade. In: Biondi A, Eeckhout P, Flynn J (eds) The law of state aid in the European Union. Oxford University Press

Bouchagiar A (2020) When do funds become state resources. Eur State Aid Law Q 19:19–28

Clayton M, Catalan MJS (2015) The notion of state resources: so near and yet so far. Eur State Aid Law Q 14:260–270

Condon BJ (2017) Disciplining clean energy subsidies to speed the transition to a low-carbon world. J World Trade 51

Cosbey A, Mavroidis P (2014) A Turquoise mess: green subsidies, blue industrial policy and renewable energy: the case for redrafting the subsidies agreement of the WTO. J Int Econ Law 17

Craig P, de Búrca G (2020) EU law: text, cases, and materials, 7th edn. Oxford University Press, Oxford

de Sadeleer N (2014) EU environmental law and the internal market. Oxford University Press

den Bossche PV, Zdouc W (2021) The law and policy of the World Trade Organization: text, cases and materials, 5th edn. Cambridge University Press, Cambridge

Espa I, Marín Durán G (2018) Renewable energy subsidies and WTO law: time to rethink the case for reform beyond Canada – renewable energy/fit program. J Int Econ Law 21:621–653

Farah PD, Cima E (2015) World Trade Organization, renewable energy subsidies and the case of feed-in tariffs: time for reform toward sustainable development? Georgetown Int Environ Law Rev (GIELR) 27

Frenz W (2018) Europarecht der erneuerbaren Energien (EEE). In: Frenz W, Müggenborg H-J, Cosack T et al (eds) Erneuerbare-Energien-Gesetz (EEG) Kommentar. Erich Schmidt Verl

[143] Ibid.

Grozea-Knuth C (2016) De Minimis. In: Pesaresi N, van de Castelle K, Flynn L, Siaterli C (eds) EU competition law: state aid, Book One, 2nd edn
Grozea-Knuth C, van de Ven R, Schoser C (2016) Energy and environment. In: Pesaresi N, van de Castelle K, Flynn L, Siaterli C (eds) EU competition law: state aid, Book One, 2nd edn
Heidenhain M (ed) (2010) European state aid law: a handbook. Beck/Hart, München/Portland
Hofmann HCH, Micheau C (eds) (2016) State aid law of the European Union. Oxford University Press, Oxford
Ide A-M (2017) Grenzüberschreitende Förderung erneuerbarer Energien im europäischen Strombinnenmarkt, 1st edn. Nomos, Baden-Baden
Johnston A, Block G (2013) EU Energy Law, 1st edn. Oxford University Press
Kingston S (2011) Greening EU competition law and policy. Cambridge University Press
Klasse M (2013) The impact of Altmark: the European commission case law responses. In: Szyszczak E, van de Gronden JW (eds) Financing services of general economic interest: reform and modernization. Springer
Koenig C, Kühling J (2002) EC control of aid granted through State resources: public undertakings, funds, imputability and the importance of how resources are transferred. Eur State Aid Law Q 1: 12
Könings M (2002) State aid for renewable energy sources: a practical state aid manual for going green. Eur State Aid Law Q 1:14
Krämer R, Krajewski M (2011) State aid (subsidies) in international trade law. In: Szyszczak E (ed) Research handbook on European state aid law. Edward Elgar Publishing
Lester S, Mercurio B, Davies A (2018) World trade law: text, materials and commentary, 3rd edn. Hart Publishing, Oxford
Matsushita M, Schoenbaum TJ, Mavroidis PC, Hahn M (2015) The World Trade Organization: law, practice, and policy, 3rd edn. Oxford University Press, Oxford
Mavroidis PC (2016) The regulation of international trade. MIT Press
Medghoul S (2016) The concept of state aid. In: Pesaresi N, van de Castelle K, Flynn L, Siaterli C (eds) EU competition law: state aid, Book One, 2nd edn
Messenger G (2017) The public–private distinction at the World Trade Organization: fundamental challenges to determining the meaning of "Public Body". Int J Const Law 15:60–83. https://doi.org/10.1093/icon/mox001
Müller W (2017) WTO agreement on subsidies and countervailing measures: a commentary. Cambridge University Press
Plender R (2004) Definition of aid. In: Biondi A, Eeckhout P, Flynn J (eds) The law of state aid in the European Union. Oxford University Press
Roggenkamp M, Redgwell C, Ronne A, del Guayo I (eds) (2016) Energy law in Europe: national, EU and international regulation, 3. Oxford University Press.
Säcker FJ, Montag F (eds) (2016) European state aid law: a commentary. Beck/Hart, München/Oxford
Stoll P-T, Koebele M (2008) WTO - Trade Remedies. Brill Nijhoff
Stoll P-T, Schorkopf F (2006) WTO - world economic order, World Trade Law. Brill Nijhoff
Stoll P-T, Strack L (2009) Article XX lit. b GATT. In: Wolfrum R, Stoll P-T, Hestermeyer H (eds) WTO - trade in goods. Brill Nijhoff
Struckmann K (2017) PreussenElektra – Dead or Alive? In: Buts C, Sierra JLB (eds) Milestones in state aid case law - EStAL's First 15 years in perspective. Lexxicon
Talus K (2015) Renewable energy disputes in the European Union: an overview of current cases. In: Säcker J, Scholz L, Sveen T (eds) Renewable energy law in Europe: challenges and perspectives, 1st edn. Peter Lang
Wolfrum R, Matz-Lück N (2009) Article XX lit. g GATT. In: Wolfrum R, Stoll P-T, Hestermeyer H (eds) WTO - trade in goods. Brill | Nijhoff

Chapter 5
Green Electricity Promotion Schemes

Prior to advancing to an analysis of the green electricity law and policy in Germany and Turkey, it is necessary to delve into the policy, economic, and legal aspects of green electricity promotion schemes. Consequently, this chapter is dedicated to explaining the functioning of green electricity promotion schemes. Each scheme possesses its unique set of merits and disadvantages from policy and economic perspectives and poses particular legal challenges within both international and domestic legal realms. Owing to these reasons, each green electricity promotion scheme will be examined individually and in its own context.

It is worth noting, however, that the promotion schemes discussed herein represent only the most prominent variants. The emergence of novel types of promotion schemes, or the existence of less recognized ones at the local level, is a distinct possibility.

Different classifications can be applied to promotion schemes, ranging from direct promotion—indirect promotion, price support—government revenue foregone—transfer of funds and liabilities or direct transfers—tax concessions—contingent liability assumptions.[1] For the purposes of this work, however, the categorization of "Public Financing and Fiscal Promotion Schemes – Regulatory Promotion Schemes" is opted for, as it more accurately aligns with the theoretical objectives of this study. The primary distinction between promotion schemes resides in their legal nature, which can be scrutinized from a regulatory law perspective.

Some promotion schemes are formulated through direct state actions, either by the transfer of funds or land or by granting tax concessions or guarantees. Conversely, states avoid direct intervention in other categories and regulate the relationships between private market actors and market conditions by adjusting tariffs, establishing quotas, conducting tenders, and limiting carbon emissions. Therefore, the legal nature of the below-mentioned promotion schemes will be examined in the

[1] Morgan (2007), p. 5; Beaton and Moernhout (2011), p. 15; WTO (2006), p. 51.

O. Cagdas Artantas, *Promotion of Green Electricity in Germany and Turkey*, EYIEL Monographs - Studies in European and International Economic Law 33,
https://doi.org/10.1007/978-3-031-44760-0_5

corresponding subchapters. As an additional form of promotion that affects the green electricity sector, "Promotion of Green Electricity Equipment Industry" is examined as a separate category.

In conclusion, it is crucial to note that governments may elect to implement a single promotion scheme for green electricity or amalgamate two or more in a mixed regime.[2] In a majority of countries aiming to promote green electricity, a mix of promotion schemes are in operation.[3] The abundance of parallel promotion makes it challenging to assess the ultimate positive and negative impacts of these schemes, as the market distortions and positive spillovers they engender are likely to intermingle. A comprehensive cause-and-effect analysis of mixed promotion policies should ideally be conducted using specific country examples and detailed sectoral statistics, which is a task beyond the scope of this book.

5.1 Public Financing and Fiscal Promotion

The initial category of promotion schemes to be explored in this study pertains to public financing. Public promotion of green electricity encompasses a diverse array of mechanisms, including grants, public equity finance, soft loans, guarantees, and fiscal measures. While the rationale for incorporating grants in this category is straightforward—they constitute direct financial support from the treasury or other public resources—the inclusion of public equity finance, soft loans, guarantees, and fiscal measures warrants clarification. These measures can be converted into project finance, with public equity finance operating similarly to grants, albeit transferring a degree of control over the project to the public investor. Green electricity projects benefit from eased financial burdens through soft loans, facilitating project finance. Guarantees, likewise, alleviate project finance by mitigating certain risks. Fiscal measures promote green electricity by forgoing tax expenditure that would otherwise be due.

In all these schemes, the public plays a critical role as a stakeholder. Government or other public entities intervene by providing grants, guarantees, interest discounts, or tax rebates. In contrast, the following category, elaborated below, involves the public regulating relationships between private actors while abstaining from direct stakeholder involvement. Finally, land aids will also be examined, representing a specific form of grants and fiscal promotion.

It should be noted that some green economy promotion measures are available at both international (e.g., the "Green Climate Fund" of the UNFCCC) and Union levels (e.g., the "Horizon Europe" or "Recovery and Resilience Facility" of the EU).

[2] Rickerson et al. (2012).

[3] IEA (2020) Macro drivers – World Energy Model – Analysis. https://www.iea.org/reports/world-energy-model/macro-drivers.

Nonetheless, this work will not delve into international and Union level promotion, as its primary focus is on the domestic promotion of green electricity.

5.1.1 Grants

Green electricity grants represent direct financial contributions issued from the treasury or analogous public sources to foster green electricity. Central to these grants are their non-repayable nature and the fact that they do not transfer control of the promoted entity to the promoter. An application process conducted per established legal rules and a guideline with objective criteria characterizes the grant scheme. Subsequently, a "grant decision" ensues, and applicants who are unjustly excluded from the grant can seek judicial review of the decision.

A relevant discussion here involves whether regulation through grant guidelines matches the economic outcomes of regulatory schemes. Although distinguishing between fiscal and regulatory schemes can be difficult, a criterion can be proposed to differentiate these two regimes: regulatory steering typically manifests as a long-term support program, whereas grants are typically one-time payments and do not extend into the long term.

A variety of grants exist for the promotion of green electricity. Grants can be offered to both green electricity producers and consumers.[4] "Capital grants" provide funding for a portion of green electricity investments, aiming to diminish the final cost of the project. While capital grants facilitate green electricity investment, the operation phase can also be supported by grants, which are often conditional upon certain environmental standards.[5] Furthermore, energy exportation may be aided by grants. In theory, the consumption of green electricity can also be fostered via this scheme via one-off grants to green electricity tariff users. However, grant schemes would not be feasible to promote consumption in the long term.

While grant schemes are relatively simple to implement and manage, they do come with certain disadvantages. Primarily, they fail to provide incentives for the beneficiary to develop long term financial sustainability.[6] Some countries, such as Germany, have devised specific scrutiny mechanisms to mitigate this issue, including a grant's potential withdrawal (i.e., clawback provisions) if the criteria outlined in the grant guideline are unmet.[7]

Grant schemes are also susceptible to excess and corruption.[8] Beneficiaries may exploit the grant to temporarily sustain a project, only to abandon it later. To circumvent this, public authorities may opt for an alternative approach similar to

---

[4] Sovacool (2009), pp. 1529–1532.

[5] IPCC, *Renewable Energy Sources and Climate Change Mitigation*, 2011.

[6] Hussain (2013).

[7] VwVfG § 49 Section 3 N. 1-2.

[8] Mendonca et al. (2009), p. 167.

grants yet inherently distinct in its legal nature: equity finance. Like grants, equity finance provides investment funds to beneficiaries, but it also transfers a portion of the project's shares (and control) to the public authority. This arrangement entitles one or more representatives from the public stakeholder to participate in and vote on the executive board of the investing companies, thereby allowing public influence over investments in line with the public good. Equity financing also allows for the potential recovery of funds through unbounded dividend income or the sale of shares, analogous to revolving loan funds.[9] However, equity financing is not without drawbacks, as public sector involvement in project control may result in underperformance and the crowding out of private financing.[10]

As an indirect promotion measure, green electricity research and development (R&D) can be supported by grants. In practice, capital grants for small and medium-sized projects, along with grants for green electricity R&D, are rather prevalent. In contrast, other grant types are relatively scarce. Many grant programs prioritize "green innovation" over the direct promotion of green electricity.[11] Green innovation promotion frequently forms part of industrial policies globally.[12] Indirectly, R&D grants foster green electricity generation through technological advancements and efficiency increases, thereby reducing prices while augmenting output.

At international, supranational, and domestic levels, numerous entities offer many R&D grants for fundamental and applied research. For instance, in 2010, over 150 R&D support programs were available in the USA, offered by 18 federal agencies.[13] At the EU level, one of the pillars of the "Horizon Europe" R&D support program is combatting climate change, which naturally encompasses energy science and innovation. Germany directly supports demonstrative renewable energy projects and energy research through grants. For instance, R&D grants may be considered actionable if specific, given the absence of exceptions for R&D subsidization schemes in the WTO system.[14]

From a legal perspective, grants align perfectly with the category of subsidies under WTO law. According to SCM Agreement 1.1. (a).1, a direct transfer of funds by the government or any public body within the territory of a Member constitutes a subsidy as long as a benefit is conferred, with subparagraph (i) explicitly listing grants. The benefit effect of grants is relatively straightforward to establish. The Appellate Body in Canada – Aircraft underscored that a "benefit is present if 'financial contribution' makes the recipient 'better off than it would otherwise have been, absent that contribution." Given their non-repayable nature, grants inherently make the recipient better off.

[9]BNEF, *Finance guide for policy-makers*, 2016.

[10]Hussain (2013), p. 13.

[11]Bigdeli (2009).

[12]Rodrik (2014), pp. 469–473.

[13]Mendonca et al. (2009), pp. 166–167.

[14]Bundesministerium für Wirtschaft und Energie, *Bundesbericht Energieforschung 2020*, 2020.

Equity funding, conversely, presents a more complex scenario than grants. Though it is enumerated under SCM Agreement 1.1. (a).1. (i) (as equity infusion) as a type of financial contribution, determining whether equity funding confers a benefit requires a market benchmark. If the equity funding is conducted under market conditions and prices, it may be challenging to classify it as a subsidy in the WTO sense. Nevertheless, equity funding schemes targeting renewable energy frequently offer more favorable terms than standard market practices. Consequently, they may assume higher risks for lower compensation. Nevertheless, equity funding schemes should be evaluated against a market benchmark on a case-by-case basis.

Upon being identified as subsidies under WTO law, grants and equity funding schemes will be classified as either actionable or prohibited subsidies by the WTO dispute settlement body. If the grant or equity funding is contingent upon export performance or the use of domestic goods over imported ones, they will be considered prohibited. Otherwise, if deemed specific, the measure will fall under the "actionable subsidies" category.[15]

From the perspective of EU law, grants and equity funding measures may satisfy the four criteria of the state aid definition: they confer an advantage on the recipient; this advantage is granted by a Member State or through state resources; the aid potentially distorts or threatens to distort competition within the EU; and it impacts inter-state trade. Grants for green electricity might fall under the automatic compatibility scope of TFEU 107(2) if the grant has a social character. For instance, a grant program that promotes green electricity consumption in lower-income households may qualify for automatic compatibility.

Grants and equity funding could also fall under the discretionary compatibility scope in European state aid law. Firstly, green electricity promotion might pertain to regional development in the sense of TFEU 107(3)(a) and (c). Alternatively, it might support the execution of an IPCEI as per TFEU 107(3)(b). Other categories falling under discretionary compatibility could be introduced, with the GBER, Energy Tax Directive, CEEAG, and RED II serving as prominent examples.

5.1.2 *Soft Loans*

A soft loan, by definition, is a debt financing form that comes with more favorable conditions compared to typical market terms. In debt repayment schemes, the borrowed amount and any accrued interest are paid back within an agreed-upon timeframe. Debt financing makes up a significant part of renewable energy investment funding and is often the preferred method for energy investors due to certain unique aspects that set it apart from equity funding.[16] Firstly, in debt financing, control over the project does not transfer from the investor to the lender. Secondly,

---

[15] Espa (2015).

[16] IPCC, *Renewable Energy Sources and Climate Change Mitigation*, 2011, p. 893.

lenders supply funds for a fixed return and do not have any claim on the project's profits. However, debt financing does come with its drawbacks. The debt must be repaid regardless of whether the project generates revenue, while equity investors bear the risk of non-repayment. Consequently, debt financing is often considered riskier than equity financing.

Public entities may offer soft loans to mitigate the risks associated with debt finance and promote certain projects. These loans often come with various favorable terms to support the relevant undertaking. The lender may require lower collateral, apply a reduced interest rate, or provide an extended repayment period. Additionally, options such as one-off balloon payments (i.e., bullet repayment) to lessen future interest payments or extended grace periods during which no repayment is needed might be offered.

At present, soft loans are provided by numerous international and domestic bodies. Multilateral development banks, such as the World Bank or the Asian Infrastructure Investment Bank, offer concessional loans for a wide range of projects, from basic infrastructure to energy. At the EU level, the European Structural and Investment Funds provide financing for projects significant for regional development and cohesion of the internal market.[17] Domestically, many countries have public or private soft loan providers. For instance, the KfW (Kreditanstalt für Wiederaufbau), a German state-owned development bank, provides soft loans for renewable energy and energy efficiency projects. The KfW, through its "renewable energy credit" program, covered 100% of the investment costs at lenient interest rates.[18] In Turkey, the "Kalkınma ve Yatırım Bankası", a state-owned development and investment bank, issues soft loans for green electricity projects per agreement. One such investment is a 5.6 MW installation in Antalya.[19]

The provision of soft loans may be predicated on the performance of exports. Globally, export banks endeavor to facilitate the trade of domestically manufactured goods (for instance, the Export-Import Bank of the United States, KfW IPEX in Germany, and Eximbank in Turkey). The dissemination of green electricity equipment may be endorsed through export credits featuring favorable terms. This promotion would fortify the domestic green electricity equipment industry and green electricity generation.

Instead of surfacing as "senior debt", soft loans may materialize as "subordinated debt", also known as "mezzanine finance". In the debt repayment hierarchy, senior

---

[17]The European Commission (2020) European structural and investment funds. In: European Commission - European Commission. https://ec.europa.eu/info/funding-tenders/funding-opportunities/funding-programmes/overview-funding-programmes/european-structural-and-investment-funds_en.

[18]KfW (2020) Erneuerbare Energien – Standard Finanzierung. https://www.kfw.de/inlandsfoerderung/Unternehmen/Energie-Umwelt/Förderprodukte/Erneuerbare-Energien-Standard-(270)/.

[19]Anadolu Ajansı (2020) Türkiye Kalkınma ve Yatırım Bankası'nın desteklediği GES faaliyette. https://www.aa.com.tr/tr/sirkethaberleri/finans/turkiye-kalkinma-ve-yatirim-bankasinin-destekledigi-serra-ges-faaliyete-basladi/659797.

debt is prioritized over subordinated debt. Senior loans enhance the affordability of projects, and investors may augment more capital by securing loans in addition to the primary, senior debt. The subordinated debt status of publicly provided soft loans mitigates the risk for public sources, which could potentially be utilized for novel green electricity projects (such as the "revolving fund scheme"). Although mezzanine finance assumes more risk, it also possesses greater leverage.[20] To encourage renewable energy, public entities might supply mezzanine finance featuring concessional terms, thus minimizing project risk.[21]

Another debt financing method comprises bonds, also referred to as "asset-backed securities". Rather than bank provision, these are interest-bearing instruments issued by corporations to raise capital.[22] The supported project's prospective income secures these bonds.[23] Certain companies propose "green bonds" allocated for environmental ventures, such as green electricity investments. In some instances, governments, municipalities, or development banks also issue green bonds to gather capital for "green" initiatives.[24] For instance, the Danish "Vattenfall Kriegers Flak", an offshore wind project with nearly 1.5 billion USD expenditure, was financed via an asset-based arrangement.[25]

Fiscal measures, such as tax incentives, may be used as the method of choice for governments aiming to promote green bonds. These fiscal measures will be elaborated upon below. Hypothetically, leasing contracts could also serve as a project finance source for green electricity; however, the longevity and more minor scales (relative to conventional forms) of the green electricity projects inhibit this arrangement. Alternatively, governments may issue green bonds, borrow at low-interest rates, and lend to green initiatives.[26]

Financial contributions such as loans are classified under the SCM Agreement 1.1. (a).1. (i). As previously indicated, public banks may proffer soft loans to encourage the export of locally manufactured products. Hence, a soft loan could be contingent on exportation, thereby categorizing the measure under prohibited subsidies. Moreover, the flexible terms of a soft loan agreement or the incentivization of a green bond could also be dependent on the utilization of domestically manufactured goods, and such a scheme would likewise be categorized under prohibited subsidies. Soft loan measures that are not prohibited could

---

[20] Hussain (2013), pp. 14–15.

[21] IPCC, *Renewable Energy Sources and Climate Change Mitigation*, 2011, p. 893.

[22] KfW, *Financing Renewable Energy: Instruments, Strategies, Practice Approaches*, 2005.

[23] Hussain (2013), p. 16.

[24] UN Environment, *Global Trends in Renewable Energy Investment 2019*, 2019, p. 40.

[25] Ibid., p. 40.

[26] Climate Policy Initiative (2020) Solving India's Renewable Energy Financing Challenge: Instruments to Provide Low-cost, Long-term Debt. https://www.climatepolicyinitiative.org/publication/solving-indias-renewable-energy-financing-challenge-instruments-to-provide-low-cost-long-term-debt/.

potentially fall under the actionable subsidies category, provided they constitute specificity.[27]

With regards to EU law, it is essential to reiterate that state aids such as soft loans may be subject to automatic or discretionary compatibility and should be assessed on a case-by-case basis. The case law implies that loans granted on preferential terms are covered by TFEU 107(1).[28] Promoting green electricity through soft loans was identified as financial advantage. Exemption regulation (such as GBER, CEEAG, and RED II) may afford some policy flexibility for policies. Soft loans that fall within the purview of this secondary law could potentially be justified. A soft loan program aimed at promoting green electricity installations could fall under this category and be exempt from the Commission's scrutiny. The KfW's credit service to the renewable energy installations, referenced above, serves as a fitting example.

5.1.3 Guarantees

Guarantees frequently appear in large-scale infrastructure projects due to various reasons: prolonged maturity periods, environmental, economic, and regulatory risks, nascent financial markets in developing nations, and the incapacity of private lenders to factor in externalities.[29] Conventional financial procedures may overlook the negative externalities linked to green electricity generation. As indicated earlier, promoting green electricity may aim to rectify market failures. At this juncture, guarantees facilitate the risk transference of green electricity projects to the public sector. Consequently, the competitive advantages of conventional energy projects are diminished, while the disadvantages of green electricity projects are partially mitigated.

Private banks calibrate the terms of debt financing to align with the risks associated with projects. Despite the absence of "fuel supply risks", which are common in conventional energy projects, green electricity projects present a diverse risk portfolio that encompasses economic, regulatory, political, and environmental risks. The primary risk on the demand side is the possibility of electricity generation exceeding anticipated needs. Potential hazards for these projects include local currency devaluation, high inflation, and steep interest rate hikes. Each green electricity generation technology presents unique risks, such as potential flooding for hydropower plants during wet seasons and frequent pump malfunctions for geothermal projects.[30] Future environmental and economic regulations may alter the project's terms, indicative of regulatory risks. Economic changes (e.g., demand and price volatility) and political instability (e.g., strikes or violent incidents) could

[27] Espa (2015), pp. 6–7.

[28] Podsiadło (2016), p. 72.

[29] Griffith-Jones (1993).

[30] United Nations Environment Programme et al. (2004), p. 18.

compromise the project's viability. Expropriation presents an additional political risk. Ultimately, *force majeure* events may jeopardize the project.[31] Hence, risk management is central to the project finance for green electricity projects. Governments can intervene in this regard, issue guarantees, and decrease the risks for the private lender. Projects can secure higher credit ratings with diminished risks, leading to lower financing costs.

The initial risk management method employed by the state in private debt financing is referred to as "debt guarantees" or "financial guarantees". In the debt guarantee framework, the state shoulders partial or complete responsibility for the debt in the event of borrower default. Multilateral development banks (such as the World Bank and European Investment Bank) and domestic institutions (publicly-owned banks, export credit agencies, or state treasuries) can guarantee debt. Debt guarantees impact debt financing in ways that decrease interest rates or prolong maturities.[32]

The second risk mitigation approach involves "Power Purchase Agreements" (PPAs), which assuage demand-side uncertainties for a segment of the generated electricity. PPAs guarantee a stable revenue stream for green electricity projects. According to the World Bank, PPAs are employed for electricity projects under circumstances of revenue ambiguity, where there is a requirement for assurances on demand volumes and pricing to ensure project feasibility. Additionally, they are used when the consumer seeks supply security. Within the PPA framework, a public electric utility often pledges to purchase a pre-defined share of electricity generation at a fixed price. The price can be subjected to calibrations per specific clauses of the PPA over the agreement term.[33]

The third risk management strategy encompasses private risk mitigation initiatives, such as "risk insurances." These differ fundamentally from public guarantees. Risk insurances mitigate potential hazards, such as business disruption, ancillary expenses, and third-party liability. However, they also entail a financial burden for the investor in the form of a "risk premium" incorporated into the insurance contract.[34] In contrast to guarantees, which establish a relationship among the guarantor, financier, and recipient of finance, insurances create a bilateral relationship between the insurer and insured.[35] International entities, including the Multilateral Investment Guarantee Agency of the World Bank, International Finance Corporation, and International Bank for Reconstruction and Development, extend

---

[31] Bachrach et al. (2003).

[32] Griffith-Jones et al. (2004), pp. 6–7.

[33] The World Bank (2020) Power Purchase Agreements (PPAs) and Energy Purchase Agreements (EPAs) | Public private partnership. https://ppp.worldbank.org/public-private-partnership/sector/energy/energy-power-agreements/power-purchase-agreements.

[34] United Nations Environment Programme et al. (2004), p. 30.

[35] Hussain (2013), p. 17.

insurance against political uncertainties such as expropriation.[36] This insurance may manifest as political risk insurances (PRIs) or partial risk guarantees (PRGs). In the context of PRGs, the guarantee is safeguarded by a corresponding counter-guarantee from the host nation, whereas PRIs do not necessitate such counter-guarantees.[37] In addition to providing counter-guarantees, states might undertake the responsibility of risk premium payments to promote green electricity, a practice akin to grants and subject to comparable legal considerations.

The final risk management method to be detailed in this part is referred to as "grid-related guarantees." Conventionally, energy investors must deal with grid access issues while devising their investment plans. Grid access could be restricted at the juncture where the installation is planned, or future grid connections might be preemptively allocated to other investors. Even when grid access is guaranteed for the project, dispatch priority could be conferred upon other electricity producers at the same dispatch point. Consequently, other producers might be displaced from the grid during peak generation times of the prioritized producers. Restricted grid access or displacement from the grid invariably leads to the same consequence: at least a part of the generated electricity will remain unsold in the market, thereby restricting the project's income stream and jeopardizing its viability.

To mitigate this risk, governments can extend grid-related guarantees to green electricity projects, which can also be classified as regulatory schemes.[38] Primarily, they might assure grid access or confer connection precedence. Logically, a grid access guarantee is economically more beneficial than connection priority since the latter does not necessarily equate to immediate grid access. Additionally, governments may provide dispatch guarantees or priority. Similar to the issue of access guarantee and priority, dispatch guarantee is more advantageous than dispatch priority.[39] Nevertheless, all four kinds of grid-related promotion schemes attempt to diminish risks for the projects, thereby enhancing their credit score and reducing investment costs. Typically, grid-related guarantees are balanced by transferring grid access costs to the plant operator.[40]

5.1.4 Fiscal Concessions

Governments frequently resort to fiscal incentives to promote preferred projects. These incentives often materialize in various forms, including tax credits,

[36] KfW, *Financing Renewable Energy: Instruments, Strategies, Practice Approaches*, 2005, pp. 29–32.

[37] Hussain (2013), p. 18.

[38] Martinot and Beck (2004), p. 368.

[39] Gudas (2015).

[40] Eclareon GmbH (2012) Comparing grid issues. http://www.res-legal.eu/compare-grid-issues/.

deductions, deferrals, exclusions, accelerated depreciation, or preferential tax rates.[41] Fiscal concessions operate akin to a "reverse grant"; they do not constitute a monetary transfer from the state to the investor; rather, they alleviate the investor's economic obligations. Economists acknowledge the economic equivalence of promotional strategies through direct means (such as grants) and indirect fiscal measures (like tax concessions).[42] With a reduced or absolved tax burden, investors find themselves in an improved financial position, enhancing the project's viability and subsequently promoting it. Ultimately, the investor will be "better off" with a tax obligation written off.[43] A school of thought argues that fiscal incentives as superior to other promotion forms, such as grants or regulatory schemes, citing fewer distortions, a lesser strain on public resources, and more valuable benefits to businesses.[44]

The WTO law covers the concept of tax concessions accurately, as described above: According to Article 1.1(a)(1)(ii) of the SCM Agreement, a financial contribution is deemed to exist when *"... government revenue that is otherwise due is foregone or not collected (e.g., fiscal incentives such as tax credits)"*. Any forgone government revenue otherwise due constitutes a tax concession or, in other words, promotion in fiscal form.

Tax concessions can form a vital component of the domestic green electricity promotion system. They can be employed to correct market failures related to energy generation.[45] For instance, the RED II lists "tax exemptions or reductions" and "tax refunds" as support mechanisms that would be green-lit for promoting renewable energy. Governments may selectively promote technologies or offer a technology-neutral tax promotion for green electricity. For example, Sweden exclusively promotes wind energy via taxation, whereas Denmark only supports solar and hydropower. Additionally, governments may stipulate a threshold for tax promotion. For instance, Poland only supports green electricity projects with installed capacities smaller than 5 MW.[46]

Governments may implement tax credit systems for electricity generation. Whereas tax concessions involve an exemption from initial tax liability, tax credits serve as deductions that investors can subtract from their final tax liability.[47] In tax credit systems, the investor is granted tax credits proportional to the quantity of electricity produced. These systems inherently reduce project costs. Some tax credit systems also envisage a "refund mechanism." In such setups, if the value of the tax credit exceeds the owed tax, the taxpayer is entitled to a refund for the excess tax credit value, making these systems a potential income source and further

[41] Espa (2015), p. 4.

[42] Ruiz (2015).

[43] Bigdeli (2009), p. 162.

[44] See: Nicolaides (2015).

[45] Pirlot (2017).

[46] Holzer et al. (2017), p. 362.

[47] Rubini (2012).

incentivizing investment. The USA's renewable energy promotion program, popularly known as the "Federal Solar Tax Credit Program," is an example of this system. Through this program, owners of new residential and commercial solar installations can deduct 22% of the system cost from their taxes.[48] Therefore, tax credit systems bear similarities to grant schemes in their outcomes, as both systems culminate in a net payment to the green electricity investor or operator.

Tax credit systems can also be applied during the investment phase, with certain schemes awarding tax credits for green electricity investment above specified thresholds. For instance, the US introduced a tax credit system for domestic renewable energy installation investments, providing a 30% tax credit for installation costs. However, this tax credit rate is projected to decrease to 10% by 2021 and remain at that level. Accelerated depreciation represents another method of fiscal promotion. In this scheme, investors can depreciate their investments over a shortened duration, such as 5 years, as opposed to the average lifespan of 15–20 years. This mechanism allows the investor to lower their tax base more rapidly.[49] Moreover, certain schemes may offer "bonus depreciation" options for green electricity investments, enabling them to immediately deduct a substantial portion of the purchase price, thus reducing investment costs. India, for instance, has previously allowed a 100% first-year depreciation for wind energy installations.[50]

Fiscal incentives may also be offered at the consumption level. Consumers may receive tax reductions or credits proportional to the amount of electricity used, provided they have opted for green electricity according to their tariff or power purchase agreement with the distributor. This option would encourage the selection of green electricity at the consumer level and supply a more significant revenue stream to the green electricity investor.

Providing fiscal incentives for green electricity while imposing standard taxes on conventional electricity is termed "differentiated taxation".[51] Both generation and consumption-level fiscal promotion schemes necessitate the certification of green electricity to verify its generation or consumption. Despite electricity being a homogenous form of energy, states may apply differentiated tax rates to electricity depending on its source.[52] Italy, Finland, the Netherlands, Poland, and Sweden, all member states of the EU, exemplify countries employing differentiated tax promotion schemes for green electricity.[53]

Under Article 1.1(a)(1)(ii) of the SCM Agreement, as previously referenced, a financial contribution is perceived to exist if *"government revenue that would otherwise be collected is foregone or not collected (e.g. fiscal incentives such as*

[48] EnergySage (2020) The Solar Tax Credit Explained. https://www.energysage.com/solar/cost-benefit/solar-investment-tax-credit/.

[49] Sherlock (2018).

[50] Kitson (2015).

[51] Espa and Holzer (2015).

[52] Holzer et al. (2017), p. 8.

[53] Cottier et al. (2014).

tax credits)". Given that the remaining two criteria for identifying a subsidy as stipulated by the SCM Agreement (being granted by a government or a public body and conferring benefit) are met, the Dispute Settlement Body will conclude that a subsidy exists and proceed to assess its specificity (also determining whether it is prohibited or actionable). Differential tax schemes may potentially initiate disputes under WTO law based on the violation of the non-discrimination principle if conventional electricity constitutes a significant portion of electricity imports while domestically produced electricity is predominantly green.[54] Such measures will be deemed prohibited or actionable, given that green electricity and electricity generated from conventional sources are viewed as "like products" according to the Dispute Settlement Body interpretation.

In the context of the EU law, fiscal concessions are not explicitly specified; however, they may be encapsulated under the state aid category. As stated in Article 107(1) TFEU, fiscal incentives may be covered within the scope of state aid and must be subjected to legal scrutiny to determine whether they are conferred by a Member State or via state resources, and whether they distort or threaten to distort competition and affect trade between Member States. Nonetheless, tax aids might qualify for the exemptions outlined in Articles 107(2) and 107(3) TFEU.[55] As previously mentioned, the Energy Tax Directive is a key legal source regarding fiscal incentive issues. According to Article 15(1)(b) of the Directive, "*... Member States may apply under fiscal control total or partial exemptions or reductions in the level of taxation to...*" green electricity. Member States are also permitted to refund the producer some or all of the tax paid by the consumer on green electricity.[56] They may further apply tax reductions on the consumption of energy products in favor of energy-intensive businesses.[57]

In summary, the Energy Tax Directive provides extensive policy room for the fiscal promotion of green electricity within the EU. However, it is worth noting that the "energy-intensive businesses" exemption potentially discourages investment in energy efficiency and decarbonization. In July 2021, the Commission proposed a revision to the Energy Taxation Directive. The intention of this proposal was to harmonize the taxation of energy products with EU energy and climate policies, to endorse clean technologies, and to eliminate outdated exemptions and reduced rates that currently incentivize the use of fossil fuels. As of 2023, the amendment to the Directive has not yet been implemented.

---

[54] Holzer et al. (2017), p. 367.

[55] Micheau (2014), p. 80.

[56] Article 15(2)

[57] Article 17(1)

5.1.5 Land Aid

Land aid, a form of support often overlooked in scholarly literature, constitutes a significant component of any physical investment, such as green electricity projects. Procuring property, an essential yet costly aspect of these investments, involves acquiring project sites that offer conducive conditions for electricity generation, including energy capacity (e.g., strength of solar radiation or wind) and grid access. National legislation often establishes land and energy laws governing land procurement for electricity projects. Where present, green electricity legislation may introduce additional advantageous or onerous provisions to the existing legal framework on land procurement.

However, it is essential to distinguish between land planning regulations and the laws concerning land acquisition. Making the former more accommodating for new renewable energy installations would be considered regulatory promotion, not an aspect of public financing. In this section, the focus will be on the promotion of green electricity through land control provided to investors.

Land aid can be conceived as a form of a grant, often referred to as "land grants". However, due to their significance, they will be treated as a separate category in this book. The importance of land aid becomes evident in cases such as Turkey, where the treasury owns vast plots of land suitable for green electricity projects. Additionally, it is important to elucidate that land aids operate as a form of fiscal promotion. They involve the transfer of ownership or possession rights of a plot of land, potentially including the transfer of property to the investor or the granting of usage rights for a specified period (e.g., 49 years).

Various models of land aid may be implemented. Firstly, states may offer public properties for new investments. If a government charges a green electricity investor less than the due amount for the land or does not levy any charges at all, we can confirm that a promotion is in effect. The expropriation of private land and the transfer of its rights, or "third-party beneficiary expropriation", may serve as the second model.

For instance, under Turkish law, investors may be granted the right to use state-owned land for small unlicensed green electricity generation projects.[58] Third-party beneficiary expropriation is also frequently employed in Turkey, occasionally taking the form of "emergency expropriation", favoring green electricity projects or the grid investments required by them. In the emergency expropriation model, land plots are expropriated via an expedited process for the benefit of green electricity projects, such as geothermal or hydroelectricity units.[59]

WTO law does not unambiguously categorize land aid as a financial contribution. Nonetheless, the two aforementioned models can potentially be classified under two

[58] Başbakanlık Mevzuatı Geliştirme ve Yayın Genel Müdürlüğü (2014) Milli Emlak Genel Tebliği No: 362. https://www.resmigazete.gov.tr/eskiler/2014/02/20140207-16.htm.

[59] Anadolu Ajansı (2020) Enerjide acele kamulaştırma kararları. https://www.aa.com.tr/tr/ekonomi/enerjide-acele-kamulastirma-kararlari/2062544.

categories stipulated in Article 1.1(a)(1) SCM. The first model, involving the transfer of property or usage rights of public lands without appropriate compensation, could fall under subparagraph (ii), which states that *"... government revenue that is otherwise due is foregone or not collected (e.g., fiscal incentives such as tax credits)."* This subparagraph specifically lists examples of fiscal promotion schemes. However, the general provision of the subparagraph could extend beyond these cases. If any government revenue that would otherwise be collected is forgone, a financial contribution might be deemed to exist. Correspondingly, the first model envisages the foregoing of due government revenue. The government either does not charge the investor the full amount for the land or refrains from charging any amount at all. Consequently, this subparagraph may be invoked in the context of this land aid scheme.

As for the second model, which involves state intervention in procuring land from public individuals, subparagraph (i) may be relevant: *"...a government practice involves a direct transfer of funds (e.g., grants, loans, and equity infusion), potential direct transfers of funds or liabilities (e.g., loan guarantees)."* This subparagraph also does not enumerate the second land aid method mentioned above, but its scope may be interpreted to include this model. The state intervention would involve the payment of a certain sum to the landowner, sometimes in addition to the sum paid by the buyer. This additional sum could be construed as a grant under subparagraph (i). If the state provides this payment as a soft loan with favorable terms to the investor, this subparagraph may also be applicable.

In the EU law, the regulation of land and property aid is primarily guided by a non-binding text, "Commission Communication on State Aid Elements in Sales of Land and Buildings by Public Authorities".[60] This Communication provided guidance on procedures for public land and building sales in compliance with EU state aid law, delegated responsibility to Member States to inform the Commission about specific sales, and outlined the Commission's stance on third-party claims concerning these sales.

The Communication clarified a sale that does not constitute state aid as follows: *"A sale of land and buildings following a sufficiently well-publicized, open, and unconditional bidding procedure, comparable to an auction, accepting the best or only bid is by definition at market value and consequently does not contain State aid".*[61] Utilizing an *a contrario* argument, one can accurately depict a land sale as state aid. If the sale of public land was not executed at market value, it could be deduced that the sale contained state aid. The deviation from market value may occur due to various reasons, as outlined in the Communication. An auction may not have been conducted, wherein the sale is granted to the best or only bid. Member States may replace the auction process with an independent expert evaluation: *"... an independent evaluation should be carried out by one or more independent asset valuers prior to the sale negotiations in order to establish the market value on the*

[60] 97/C 209/03 of 10.7.1997.

[61] Para 2(b).

basis of generally accepted market indicators and valuation standards".[62] A deviation from the market price determined by one or more independent experts would also be regarded as state aid. The Communication relaxed this criterion with a 5% margin, applicable if a reasonable effort to sell the land at the real value fails.[63] Member States were obliged to notify the Commission if the sale was executed without a valid auction or below the value determined by the experts.

In 2016, the "Commission Notice on the Notion of State Aid as referred to in Article 107(1) of the Treaty on the Functioning of the European Union" replaced the aforementioned Communication.[64] Although the Notice retained the fundamental elements of the Communication regarding land sale, it incorporated additional details. According to the Notice, tenders must now be "transparent" and designed to attract bidders from Europe and worldwide. A tender must be sufficiently well-publicized, ensuring that all potential bidders have an opportunity to consider it.[65] Buyers cannot be burdened with special obligations beyond those stemming from general domestic law or a decision made by planning authorities.[66] Member States should aim for measures of central tendency, such as the average or the median, within a set of comparable transactions (i.e., pari-passu transactions) when benchmarking for market value.[67] It is worth noting that while the Communication solely applied to land and building sales, the Notice extends to all types of transactions.

The European Court of Justice (ECJ) prioritizes market value as the primary criterion concerning land sale matters. In the case of *BVVG Bodenverwertungs-und-verwaltungs GmbH*, the Court concurred that Member States could disregard any bid in auctions that substantially deviates from the market price.[68]

5.2 Regulatory Promotion

The second type of promotional scheme explored in this work pertains to regulatory promotion, encompassing various types to be individually addressed. Contrary to public financing and fiscal promotion, regulatory promotion involves public regulation of the relationship between private entities, with the public authority refraining from directly participating. This part discusses the seven most prominent methods of regulatory promotion within the green electricity sector. Initially, the focus will be

[62] Para. 2(a).

[63] Para. 2(b).

[64] 2016/C 262/01 of 19.7.2016.

[65] Paras. 84(ii), 91.

[66] Para. 95.

[67] Para. 100.

[68] Case C-39/14, BVVG Bodenverwertungs-und-verwaltungs GmbH [2015] ECLI-470. See: Giraud and Petit (2016).

on the most common ones, Feed-in Tariffs (FITs) and Feed-in Premiums (FIPs). This will be followed by an exploration of quota setting for green electricity and the trading of certificates for these quotas. Subsequently, the discussion will move to the tendering process for green electricity and net metering. Then, carbon-related schemes will be covered, encompassing carbon taxes, carbon pricing, and emissions trading. The final subject will be regulatory easing as a promotional method.

It is important to reiterate that the regulatory schemes delineated in this chapter do not constitute an exhaustive list. Alternative regulatory schemes may be formulated to support green electricity. However, the "regulatory easing" subchapter will include some open-ended content to address a portion of the potential possibilities.

5.2.1 Feed-in Tariffs and Feed-in Premia

This subchapter will examine Feed-in Tariffs and Feed-in Premiums concurrently, given their similarities and the benefits inherent in a comparative analysis. Primarily, the FITs (also referred to as "Renewable Energy Payments" or "Advanced Renewable Tariffs") will be defined. Essentially, a FIT is a mechanism that establishes a fixed rate for the purchase of electricity, usually delineated per kilowatt-hour (kWh). These are typically long-term agreements spanning several decades. Additional components, such as grid guarantees and technology-specific provisions, may be incorporated within FITs.[69]

FITs were first introduced in the United States in 1978 as a component of "The Public Utility Regulatory Policies Act", formulated in response to oil crises.[70] Throughout the 1980s and 1990s, the first FITs emerged in Europe. Given the slow growth in installed renewable energy capacity, these were seen as a promotional method for the swift deployment of renewable energy sources. Until recent years, FITs have proliferated globally. In 2019, FITs were implemented in 111 countries at regional or national levels, with Turkey and Germany being two such examples.[71] FITs have also become the most prevalent method of promoting green electricity within the EU.[72]

There are notable advantages to FITs. Firstly, they are simple to adopt and implement. FITs may be the least complex green electricity generation scheme with a straightforward base: A fixed rate for electricity generated. Moreover, with the design options discussed later, FITs can also be fine-tuned to address specific policy objectives. Secondly, FITs provide investors with complete protection from

[69] See: Mendonca et al. (2009); Couture et al. (2010); Jacobs (2012); Wilke (2011); Kettner and Kletzan-Slamanig (2016); Martinot and Beck (2004).

[70] Mendonca et al. (2009), p. 77; Couture et al. (2010), p. 9.

[71] REN21, *Renewables 2019 Global Status Report*, 2019.

[72] The EU Parliament, *Promotion of renewable energy sources in the EU: EU policies and Member State approaches*, 2016.

demand-side risks. A fixed-rate, even if set low, offers the investor total predictability. The reasonable expectations emerging from the tariff are generally safeguarded by local public law regimes, in addition to foreign direct investment law. Thirdly, as a generation-focused promotion method, FITs aid in rapidly developing targeted types of green electricity. In practice, FITs have performed exceptionally well in fostering wind energy development in Northern Europe and solar power in Southern Europe, even sparking debate on whether these investments have been overcompensated.

A primary consideration of FITs concerns financing the gap between the market price and the fixed FIT rate for green electricity. The FIT support can be shouldered by the grid operator, distributors, or consumers. However, the financing burden of the promotion will be passed along each step, eventually reaching the consumer. For example, if the grid operator is liable for the "green electricity fee" under the FIT design, this cost will be transferred to the distributors, who, in turn, will pass it on to the consumers. Consequently, with FITs, consumers will invariably bear the FIT costs.[73] The cost of green electricity promotion often appears on bills as a "system fee" (also known as "System Benefit Charge"). A specific example of the FIT system fee is the "EEG-Umlage" in the German promotion system, whereby the costs of green electricity promotion are transferred to German electricity consumers. A similar fee is present in the Turkish system ("YEKDEM Birim Maliyeti").

Hence, FITs introduce political-economic risks. The electric bill increases can unsettle voters, forcing governments to choose between maintaining the FIT, using fiscal and public expenditure methods, passing the costs onto all taxpayers rather than just electricity consumers, or foregoing green electricity support altogether. However, many governments often do not want to abandon green electricity promotion due to political and legal reasons. Moreover, financing the energy transition through levying electricity bills is generally considered more reasonable than passing the cost onto taxpayers. Those who consume more electricity will pay more under the FIT scheme, which is deemed a more equitable system.

Indeed, FITs pose certain challenges. One of them is that they do not encourage investors to respond to market price signals since they are completely shielded from them. As a result, FITs do not create incentives to adjust supply in line with demand or peak generation with peak demand in their basic formulation.[74] While existing solar photovoltaic or wind installations may not be able to align with demand due to their intermittent nature, feed-in tariff schemes can influence the investment decisions of investors, potentially leading them to add new units to their facilities when it may not be necessary or beneficial for the overall grid balance.

Another concern with FITs is the potential for overcompensation. Setting the rates at an appropriate level can be challenging due to the inherent "information asymmetry" between the investor and the regulator. Regulatory capture, wherein the regulated entity has an undue influence over the regulatory authority, can also be an

[73] Mendonca et al. (2009), p. 29.

[74] Couture et al. (2010), p. 61.

issue while setting the rates. This can result in higher remuneration than is necessary to adequately promote green electricity. This perceived overcompensation could lead to a significant legal issue: the government backtracking on the FIT. If a government re-regulates or cancels a FIT, it could trigger investment disputes, a complex legal area beyond the scope of this discussion.

As delineated above, the fundamental elements of the Feed-in Tariff (FIT) scheme encompass a fixed tariff rate for generated electricity. Nonetheless, FIT designs may embody additional variants rich with integral components. The following are such potential design options:

1. A pivotal design option is the distinction between technology specificity and technology neutrality. FITs may stipulate differing rates for varying renewable electricity technologies, such as a higher rate for more costly solar and a lower rate for less expensive wind. Alternatively, FITs may support technology neutrality, applying a uniform rate to all technologies. Even within a single energy type, technology specificity can be executed. For instance, more recent solar panel technologies may qualify for elevated rates over new designs suchlike perovskite cells. Differential rates for technologies are typically established following scientific analysis of parameters such as efficiency, demand, energy capacity, and costs.[75]
2. The installed capacity of projects could lead to differences in FIT rates, an outcome hinged on the FIT design decision. This FIT type typically prioritizes micro and small-scale projects by reflecting higher operational costs and fostering citizen-level investments.[76]
3. The density of the energy source might be a factor for differentiation in FIT. Greater generation per installed capacity, reduced intermittency, or construction in locations determined by governmental scientific evaluations could result in higher remuneration rates for investors.[77]
4. Geographic location can also result in varied FIT rates. For instance, building-integrated solar installations could be granted a higher rate than free-standing installations; likewise, installations on public buildings may be incentivized more than residential buildings. Alternatively, low-income regions may be prioritized.
5. Adherence to generation forecasts provided by investors could be incentivized in FIT systems. Day-ahead and intra-day forecasts are often mandatory submissions in many energy grid systems. These forecasts assist grid operators in reconciling energy demand with supply. Forecasting becomes more challenging as renewable electricity technologies typically exhibit greater intermittency compared to conventional electricity generation methods in the absence of

[75] Jacobs (2012), pp. 44–50.
[76] Mendonca et al. (2009), pp. 17–19.
[77] Couture et al. (2010), pp. 29–33.

robust storage options. Therefore, FIT systems might incentivize compliance with forecasts.

6. The tariff structure may demonstrate a downward trajectory. A higher rate might be set during the initial investment years, during which the investor's financial condition is most fragile. Subsequent years may witness annual reductions, as stipulated by the government.
7. Conversely, the tariff may exhibit an upward trajectory. A higher rate may be established for the years following the investment commencement, potentially as a result of inflation. Alternatively, the agreement could incorporate an "inflation adjustment clause", or hard currency based "update clauses".[78]
8. A "revaluation interval" may be proposed, during which authorities will assess tariff rates at regular intervals, employing scientific and market data.
9. Investors may be granted the choice between a longer term of lower remuneration or a shorter term of higher remuneration. Shorter terms could span approximately 5–10 years, while longer terms could extend to around 20 years, corresponding to the average lifespan of many renewable electricity projects.[79]
10. PPAs may constitute components of FITs. These agreements ensure the purchase of all generated electricity or electricity generated up to a certain threshold.
11. "Priority Grid Access" is frequently an element of FITs. It ensures grid connection priority over traditional electricity plants.
12. FIT frameworks may incorporate local content requirements (LCRs). LCRs compel the investor to utilize a specified proportion of locally produced equipment in the project.

In a Feed-in Tariff (FIT) scheme, governments, generators, grid operators, distributors, and consumers are assigned distinct roles. Governments bear the responsibility of establishing the legal framework and setting the tariffs, though they typically abstain from meddling with the financial flow. Generators adhere to technical standards, procure licenses, and submit generation forecasts and disruption reports (e.g., due to technical failures). Grid operators ensure grid connection, balance demand with supply, collect payment from distributors, and compensate the green electricity tariff to the generator. Distributors handle billing and gather the green electricity fee from consumers. Consumers, in the end, pay these bills.[80]

The Feed-in Premium (FIP, also known as Premium FITs or "Market-Dependent Tariff") is another regulatory incentive system exhibiting similarities to feed-in tariffs. Under a FIP scheme, generated green electricity is sold on the market at market price. An additional "premium" is subsequently rewarded to the investor atop

[78] Ibid., pp. 37–40.

[79] Mendonca et al. (2009), pp. 27–28.

[80] European Renewable Energy Council, *Future investment: a sustainable investment plant for the power sector to save the climate*, 2007.

the market price of the electricity.[81] Several policy design options exist for FIPs, analogous to the case with FITs:

1. FIPs can opt between "fixed premium" and "sliding premium" schemes. In fixed premium frameworks, the premium remains constant based on criteria other than the volume of generated electricity. Increased electricity generation results in higher premiums for investors. However, this system may pose a risk of overcompensation, as there is no established maximum price limit or cap. Consequently, some FIP schemes may adopt the "sliding premium" system. Under the sliding FIP system (also known as "Contract for Difference", CfD), a reference electricity price is established, and the premium is calculated based on the difference between this cap and the market electricity price. Hence, sliding FIPs bear a resemblance to FITs by capping maximum remuneration.
2. A minimum limit, or "floor," for the price of electricity might be imposed to shield the investor from the risk of exceedingly low market prices. Premiums are then calculated and paid on top of this floor price.
3. Most design options applicable for FITs may also be plausible for FIPs (e.g., Technology specificity, size specificity, downward or upward tendency).

FIP systems have pros and cons concerning the promotion of green electricity. The principal advantage of the FIP lies in its capacity to incentivize market participation and competition. The FIP system allows market signals to reach the investor in a damped form. By lowering the risk for the investor, the premium encourages participation in the electricity market, fostering competition among participants. As market signals reach the investors, grid management becomes more straightforward, as investors can adjust supply and demand and respond to peak-hour demands.

The FIP system's primary disadvantage is that the electricity payments per kilowatt-hour (kWh) frequently exceed those associated with FITs. Additionally, FIP schemes may not guarantee purchases, thereby escalating risks for investors. Lastly, despite being more market oriented, FIP systems significantly dampen market signals, potentially leading to delayed investor responses to demand fluctuations.

Having discussed the key aspects of FITs and FIPs, it is pertinent to transition to the legal issues revolving around these systems. Given the substantial similarities between these two systems and the higher prevalence of FITs, the focus will be on the legal framework governing FITs.

The most notable case in ECJ jurisprudence pertaining to FITs is *PreussenElektra*. Under the German FIT regulated by the StromEinspG of 1990, local energy distributors were obligated to purchase green electricity generated within their supply area. This requirement imposed additional costs on the companies. The distributor Schleswag A.G., in response, sought compensation from the grid operator and supplier company, PreussenElektra A.G. Initially, PreussenElektra

[81] Mendonca et al. (2009), p. 40; Couture et al. (2010), p. 22; Beaton and Moernhout (2011), pp. 16–17; Muñoz et al. (2007).

A.G. made the payment with reservations and directed the matter to the local court. The local court opted to suspend proceedings and refer the matter to the ECJ for a preliminary ruling under Article 267 TFEU.

The ECJ confirmed the conferred advantage of the FIT to the companies, as it enabled them to reap substantial profits without incurring risks.[82] However, as delineated above, in *PreussenElektra*, the ECJ ruled that the payments made to electricity generators via the FIT scheme did not constitute a transfer sanctioned by a Member State or facilitated through State resources. Hence, the specific FIT design was deemed compatible with the internal market. In *PreussenElektra*, resources were provided directly by private electricity supplier companies and transferred to local companies. The ECJ would have reached a different conclusion if the surcharge used to fund local green electricity generators were instituted as a public levy by the State or a public body.[83] As discussed above, this approach was affirmed in subsequent *EEG 2012* and *EEG 2014* decisions.

Cases concerning green electricity promotion via FITs that reach the WTO dispute arm necessitate a comprehensive examination. Several complaints about FITs have been brought to the WTO dispute resolution arm, but only one such dispute has been adjudicated by the Appellate Body. This case, *Canada – RE*, was lodged against Canada by the EU and Japan. The measures of Canada under scrutiny in these decisions were identical: Ontario's FIT scheme, introduced in 2009. Ontario FIT possessed typical elements of a FIT scheme, such as a long-term power-purchase agreement at a rate exceeding average market prices.[84] However, Ontario FIT also introduced stipulations that could be interpreted as LCRs. The scheme demanded the usage of a certain percentage of locally produced equipment and local labor.[85] The EU and Japan contended that these measures indeed constituted LCRs and were thus prohibited under Article 3 of the SCM Agreement. In this section, *Canada – RE* will be addressed solely concerning the legal aspects of the FIT scheme.

Certain challenges exist in evaluating FITs within the WTO law context. Firstly, it is difficult to categorize FITs under the "*by a government or any public body*" criteria. Secondly, it is equally challenging to categorize FITs under any of the four types of financial contribution specified in Article 1.1(a)(1), or the price support in Article 1.1(a)(2). It could be asserted that the fundamental design of FITs delegates the responsibility to electricity market actors to collect a specific levy from consumers and distribute it to green electricity investors. Moreover, it could be argued that this payment is akin to grants, differing minimally from traditional governmental practices. This line of reasoning may categorize FITs under Article 1.1(a)(1)(iv) of the SCM Agreement, thus qualifying them as subsidies.

[82] Para. 54.

[83] Säcker and Montag (2016), p. 1242.

[84] See: Carmona (2016); Kent and Jha (2014); Hildreth (2014).

[85] Lai (2016), p. 304; Wilke (2011), p. 3.

However, both the Panel and Appellate Body in *Canada – RE* abstained from a detailed analysis and comparison of these alternatives and instead proceeded according to Canada's argument. Two central issues arose in the Panel's decision in the case: determining financial contribution or income or price support and the issue of benefit. As discussed previously, an assessment of benefit requires a "market investor analysis". Canada contended that FITs represented "government purchases of goods" and that there was no "market" in the electricity sector, as prices were established by the government in some way to maintain a balanced supply-demand relationship.[86]

The Panel commenced with the benefit issue. The complainants proposed the use of out-of-province benchmarks derived from the prices in the electricity markets of comparable Canadian provinces and US states. The Panel did not adhere to this reasoning, instead arguing that Canada's FIT measures did not confer a benefit to investors. Subsequently, the Panel concurred with Canada's assertion that FITs are "government purchases of goods" under SCM Article 1.1(a)(1)(iii) and designated the relevant market as the wholesale competitive electricity market, irrespective of the generation technology employed.

The Appellate Body upheld the Panel's conclusion on the benefit issue. According to the Appellate Body, the existence of a subsidy does not necessitate a positive determination of benefit. For them, a determination of a benefit requires a comparison between actual remuneration and a market-based benchmark or proxy. This comparison between amounts is needed to establish the existence of a benefit.[87]

The Appellate Body continued their review of the Panel's benefit analysis with an examination of the relevant market. The Panel had concluded that the relevant market for benefit analysis, in this case, was all electricity produced. However, the Appellate Body criticized the Panel's position for two reasons. Firstly, they claimed that the Panel should have begun its analysis with the determination of the relevant market, not ended with it. Secondly, the Appellate Body noted that there were demand and supply-side distinctions specific to green electricity.

They stated that the disparities in cost structures and operational characteristics of wind and solar electricity compared to other technologies made it improbable that the former could impose any price constraint on the latter. In contrast, conventional generators produced an identical commodity, useful for both base-load and peak-load electricity. They benefited from larger economies of scale and exerted price constraints on wind and solar PV generators.[88]

However, the Appellate Body concluded that due to the unique situation of green electricity at that time, the government could not be considered as conferring a benefit. This conclusion was based on the absence of a market in this case and the fact that the existence of green electricity in the electricity mix resulted primarily from government intervention. The government's choice of supply-mix of electricity

[86] See: Bigdeli and Delimatsis (2016), pp. 123–128.

[87] Paras. 5.165, 5.166.

[88] Para. 5.174.

generation technologies created markets for wind and electricity. A government might choose the supply-mix by setting fixed prices for technologies that would otherwise be unable to recover their costs on the spot market. The government's definition of a specific supply-mix could not, in and of itself, be considered conferring a benefit within the meaning of Article 1.1(b) of the SCM Agreement.[89]

Finally, the Appellate Body noted that green electricity's supply and demand-side characteristics should be considered when determining the relevant market. The unique situation of green electricity suggests that their relevant markets should be the competitive markets for each of the green electricity generation technologies. In cases where the government has defined an energy supply-mix that includes green electricity generation, a benchmark comparison for purposes of a benefit analysis for wind and solar PV electricity generation should be made with the terms and conditions available under market-based conditions for each of these technologies, taking the supply-mix as a given.[90] Ultimately, the Appellate Body was unable to conclude the legal analysis due to a lack of substantial factual evidence and undisputed facts in the Panel report.[91]

The *Canada – RE* case played a crucial role in clarifying the WTO law on FITs. However, ambiguity surrounds the proper categorization of FITs under Article 1.1 (a). There is still uncertainty about whether FITs are considered one of the financial contribution types listed in 1.1(a)(1) or as income or price support under 1.1(a)(2). A "two-tiered approach" should be employed to address this question. The first tier involves looking at the financial contribution types listed in Article 1.1(a)(1), with a focus on 1.1(a)(1)(iv). A FIT mechanism might be seen as a funding system given a role typically carried out by the government. For instance, comparing the European *Vent de Colere* and *PreussenElektra* cases, the French government grants contributions in the former, while the German government assigns this task to transmission system operators in the latter. Within the WTO context, *Vent de Colere* would come under Article 1.1(a)(1)(i), while *PreussenElektra* would be analyzed under 1.1(a)(1) (iv).

The second tier comes into play if a financial contribution under Article 1.1(a) (1) cannot be identified. We then need to look at 1.1(a)(2), which includes "*any form of income or price support.*" Article 1.1. (a)(2) widens the application of the SCM Agreement. Generally, income or price support relates to government actions in agriculture.[92]

In conclusion, it is suggested that if a FIT mechanism does not fit into 1.1(a)(1) (i) or 1.1(a)(iv), it could be classified under 1.1(a)(2). However, building a case based on income or price support can be challenging due to the possible lack of comparable energy product exports.[93]

[89] Para. 5.175.

[90] Para. 5.190.

[91] Para. 5.224.

[92] Müller (2017), p. 124.

[93] Espa (2015), p. 6.

Canada – RE has provided a technology-based approach to green electricity. It factors in the higher investment costs and externalities of green electricity while determining the relevant market.[94] However, the Appellate Body refrained from providing a method for benefit tests in FIT-related cases. Nevertheless, a hypothetical benefit test could be considered. If market prices for green electricity were to be compared with the tariff rates, the difference could potentially represent the total benefit. This could be a simplistic application of the "Private Investor Test" from *Canada – Aircraft*. It is crucial to remember that conventional markets for green electricity are heavily regulated, and green electricity projects are often promoted in various ways. As such, a "market" in the conventional sense may be non-existent for green electricity.[95]

The question of how to discern the benefit in green electricity promotion schemes is one that remains unresolved by *Canada – RE*. An independent economic test that accounts for external factors such as emissions and pollution reduction, as well as localization and decentralization, should be employed. This test could identify an "appropriate price" for green electricity, which can then be compared to the FIT rate. If a positive difference exists between these two values, it could be inferred that the benefit lies in the magnitude of this positive difference.

In conclusion, *Canada – RE* might be interpreted as suggesting that FITs without LCRs were consistent with WTO law at that time. However, technological advancements may have transformed the present economics of green electricity. With the decline in investment costs for solar PV and wind electricity units, coupled with the impetus of storage and cross-border electricity trade growth, there is now a potential for FITs to be effectively contested in the WTO system.

5.2.2 Local Content Requirements

Local Content Requirement (LCR) provisions represent integral elements within numerous green electricity promotional systems, such as FIT/FIPs. An LCR is a provision obligating investors and businesses to adhere to a minimum criterion for procuring goods and services from local sources.[96] Typically, LCRs establish a percentage quota on the utilization of domestically manufactured components or necessitate the incorporation of specific locally produced elements. A case in point is the Chinese LCR in the wind power sector, which mandates a 70% target for domestic production. Conversely, the Brazilian LCR obliged the use of certain locally made components, e.g., blades.[97]

[94] Shadikhodjaev (2013); Shadikhodjaev (2015); Lee (2016).

[95] See: Kent and Jha (2014).

[96] UNCTAD, *Local Content Requirements and the Green Economy*, 2014; Kuntze and Moerenhout (2012); Farah and Cima (2015), p. 519.

[97] Hansen et al. (2020).

From an economic perspective, LCRs serve as textbook examples of "demand-pull" incentives, engendering demand for domestically manufactured goods and consequently augmenting median profitability.[98] Enhanced profitability facilitates increased investment capacity in production and R&D within the green electricity equipment industry of the promoting nation, contributing to its prosperity. The ramifications include the development of a more resilient and globally competitive green electricity industry.

However, the effects of a government's LCR on other countries may manifest inversely. The demand for green electricity equipment production could diminish, negatively impacting their profitability and global competitiveness.[99]

As discussed above, the prohibition of LCRs under WTO law is expressly stated. Initially, the "National Treatment Principle" outlined in GATT Article III(4) poses a substantial barrier to such provisions. As articulated in SCM Agreement Article 3(1)(b), "subsidies contingent, whether solely or as one of several other conditions, upon the use of domestic over imported goods" are deemed prohibited and considered inherently specific. Furthermore, TRIMs Article 2(1) and (2) preclude measures akin to LCRs. These clauses collectively highlight the WTO's perspective that LCRs potentially distort global trade and, thus, must be eliminated.[100]

Notwithstanding this, a potential leeway for LCRs may be found within GATT Article XX.[101] States may declare that their LCRs are indispensable for fostering their "green economies" in order to mitigate climate change and local environmental degradation. However, the possibility of LCRs being deemed compliant with WTO law through a GATT Article XX exception, as previously discussed, remains remote. Additional policy space for LCRs could exist in GATT Article III(8)(a), which shields government procurement measures from WTO law intervention. Nevertheless, this option is equally remote for justifying nationwide policies.

The specific prohibition delineated by the WTO has not deterred many states from incorporating LCRs into their promotion schemes. Notable examples include China, India, Brazil, South Africa, and Turkey. LCRs may constitute components of larger industrial policies and yield considerable benefits for energy transition, particularly in developing nations. Most of these nations grapple with chronic trade and currency deficits, making them susceptible to currency shocks. By safeguarding their domestic green electricity equipment industry, these developing nations can gain access to a consistent supply of affordable green electricity technology. This equipment flow, in turn, would facilitate a smoother process of global energy transition.

While calling for reform in the SCM Agreement may extend beyond the scope of this discussion, it is certain that green electricity LCRs offer benefits beyond the

[98] OECD, *Domestic Incentive Measures for Renewable Energy With Possible Trade Implications*, 2013/1, 2013, p. 76.

[99] Ibid., p. 84.

[100] Farah and Cima (2015), p. 522.

[101] Kuntze and Moerenhout (2012), p. 38.

traditional "infant industry protection", such as employment creation and local industry growth. Therefore, LCRs used in promoting green electricity may possess unique advantages crucial for the much-needed energy transition.[102]

LCRs have been subjected to criticism from various perspectives. The predominant view is that LCRs are inefficient, diverting resources from pursuits that might otherwise enhance overall welfare. Further, it is maintained that they are ineffective in cultivating local firms' ability to compete globally, as they excessively prioritize manufacturing at the expense of other areas, such as services and research. Thirdly, LCRs are deemed detrimental to global trade due to their inherently protectionist nature. According to this line of argument, protectionism diminishes global welfare by reallocating resources to less efficient local manufacturers rather than globally competitive entities with higher efficiency. A potential drawback of LCRs could be their contribution to increasing electricity prices, as they could potentially shift the equilibrium towards a higher price-quantity point.[103] The Doha Ministerial Declaration advocated for *"the reduction or, as appropriate, elimination of tariff and non-tariff barriers to environmental goods and services"*.[104] This aspiration to eliminate protectionist measures for environmental goods may have originated from similar criticisms.

Implementing an LCR represents a complex policy decision, entailing legal risks within the WTO domain. One could argue that developing nations might require these non-tariff barriers to foster their developing green industries. Contrarily, the view that local content requirements diminish global welfare also carries considerable significance within the current economic discourse.

However, it is crucial to note that LCRs are not mere protectionist measures. They also embody the aspirations of developing nations to safeguard and foster their green industries. Given the pressing climate crisis, it is essential to differentiate between measures that protect local green industries and those inherently prohibited or actionable under WTO law. LCRs might be interpreted as the manifestation of a new "Right to Green Industry" for developing nations, aimed at promoting their technologically lagging green electricity equipment industries. Such local green electricity equipment industries could prove instrumental in combating climate change by bolstering local supply chains and financial infrastructures.

Nonetheless, several cases have emphasized the WTO's stringent stance on LCRs within green electricity promotional schemes. The case of *Canada – RE* stands out in this context. The Ontario FIT system incorporated a "Minimum Domestic Content Level" prerequisite for eligibility for tariff payments.[105] The complainants contended that these stipulations were proscribed under WTO law and should be either removed or counterbalanced. Canada maintained that the Ontario LCR was essentially a "government procurement" measure, thereby justified under GATT

---

[102] Lester (2011); Johnson (2013); Meyer (2015); Cottier (2014).

[103] Johnson (2013), pp. 11–12; Kuntze and Moerenhout (2012), p. 7.

[104] Para. 31.

[105] Hestermeyer and Nielsen (2014).

Article III(8)(a). The Panel, however, disagreed with Canada, ruling that the Ontario FIT LCR constituted a commercial measure not covered by GATT Article III(8)(a). Consequently, the Panel found the Ontario LCR to be inconsistent with WTO law, specifically TRIMs Article 2. Canada appealed the decision, and the Appellate Body upheld the Panel's ruling, affirming that Canada's LCR measure was incongruous with WTO law.[106]

Several subsequent rulings echoed this approach. The *China – Wind* case served as a prominent example.[107] China provided grants to companies that produced specific wind power equipment domestically, rather than relying on imports. The United States challenged this promotional system in the WTO, leading China to abolish the scheme before the case advanced further.

The *EU – RE* was a following case.[108] The issue at hand involved LCRs tied to FITs in Greece and Italy, both EU member states. The complainant, China, lodged consultations against the EU due to the application of RED. It was inferred from the consultation request that the LCRs in question applied to goods produced within the EU or European Economic Area. China invoked a series of regulations against the aforementioned measures, including, *inter alia,* GATT Article III and SCM Article 3.1(b).

Another significant case was *India – Solar Cells.*[109] As part of the "Jawaharlal Nehru National Solar Mission", the Indian government purchased electricity from solar power producers via power purchase agreements at favorable prices. The government then resold this electricity to distribution companies. This scheme incorporated content requirements for domestically produced solar cells and modules, implemented in a gradual fashion. The United States challenged this system in the WTO, concerned that it might impact their solar equipment exports to India. The Panel determined that the LCR in question was in conflict with GATT Article III (4) and TRIMs Article 2(1), namely the National Treatment Principle. Furthermore, it dismissed India's assertions under GATT Article III(8)(a), referred to as the "Government Procurement Derogation", and Article XX(j), the "Short Supply of a Certain Good Exception", as well as Article XX(d), the "Necessary Compliance with Laws and Regulations Exception". In the appeal phase, the Appellate Body endorsed the Panel's stance on all three of India's claims.[110]

The final case to be assessed under this chapter is the recent US – RE. India reported detecting 11 instances of LCRs in the US about its solar exports to the

---

[106] Lai (2016); Leal-Arcas and Filis (2014), p. 408.

[107] Request for Consultations, WT/DS419/1 of 6 January 2011, China – Measures Concerning Wind Power Equipment.

[108] Request for Consultations, WT/DS452/1 of 07 November 2012, European Union and certain Member States—Certain Measures Affecting the Renewable Energy Generation Sector.

[109] Request for Consultations, WT/DS456/1 of 11 February 2013, India – Certain Measures Relating to Solar Cells and Solar Modules.

[110] See: Karttunen and Moore (2018); Deshpande and Bansal (2017).

country.[111] These 11 measures were implemented in various states across the US. For instance, the measure in Washington comprised a system akin to FITs for local renewable electricity producers. Utilization of equipment produced in Washington State resulted in more lenient payment factors and thus increased income.

Following the establishment of the Panel and prior to the Panel's decision being formed, some of the measures under scrutiny were repealed, while others were amended. Consequently, the Panel centered its focus on three measures. The first was the "Washington State Additional Incentive", which proposed lenient payments for the use of renewable energy equipment produced in Washington. The second measure was the "California Manufacture Adder". An addendum to the "California Self-Generation Incentive Program", this measure provided additional promotion for renewable electricity generation for the needs of a facility (either partially or entirely) when equipment produced by "California Manufacturers" was used. The benchmark was 50% of the capital equipment value, and the "California Manufacturers" were to be determined by the State.[112] The third measure (initially eighth in the list before repeals) was the "Michigan Equipment Multiplier". In this system, projects utilizing locally produced equipment were awarded higher energy credits, which could subsequently be used as origin guarantees in the State-wide green electricity quotas. This effectively meant higher payments to reward the use of locally produced equipment.[113]

The Panel also reached a decision on the repealed measures since they were in place at the establishment of the Panel. The Panel ruled that the measures in question influenced "*the internal sale, offering for sale, purchase, transportation, distribution or use*" of products and "*accorded less favourable treatment*" within the context of GATT Article III:4.

The aforementioned cases collectively illustrate the stance of the WTO Dispute Resolution Arm and its application of the relevant legal framework. As per GATT Article III:4, TRIMs Article 2 and, more critically, SCM Agreement Article 3.1 (b) and 3.2, LCRs are explicitly forbidden. The "Government procurement derogation" or the exemptions under GATT Article XX have proven to be of limited utility for governments who granted benefits under LCR schemes. The future policy scope for green LCRs remains uncertain at present. Conceivably, a developing country with a smaller industry than India might push the boundaries of the WTO and invoke GATT Article XX exemptions.

[111] The Panel Report, WT/DS510/R of 27 June 2019, United States - Certain Measures Relating to the Renewable Energy Sector.

[112] Paras. 2.14–2.19.

[113] Paras. 2.40–2.50.

5.2.3 Green Quotas and Certificate Trading

Renewable energy quotas represent a regulatory mechanism designed to promote the use of renewable resources. These quotas are often referred to as "Renewable Energy Quota Obligations" or "Renewable Energy Portfolio Standards" in academic discourse. For consistency in this context, these will be characterized as "green quotas".

Green quotas typically establish minimum thresholds for the inclusion of green electricity within the energy mixes provided by suppliers.[114] In some instances, the consumption patterns of major electricity consumers may also be subject to these green quota stipulations. Frequently, electricity firms meet their quota obligations by procuring power from green electricity producers in their respective regions. However, this may not always be viable.

In scenarios characterized by a dearth of green electricity or a shortage of green electricity producers within a particular region, electricity suppliers may have to purchase "tradable green certificates" (TGCs) from green electricity producers in other countries or regions to meet their obligations. TGCs enhance the scheme's flexibility and provide an additional revenue stream for green electricity producers, even when suppliers in their regions exceed their green quota obligations.[115] Suppliers who fail to meet their quota obligations face penalties.

Green quota systems can either be technology-specific or technology-neutral. In technology-specific instances, the green quotas may encompass a "portfolio" comprising varying shares of different technologies. Portfolio obligations prevent electric suppliers from fulfilling their quota exclusively with the "most cost-effective" form of green electricity, such as wind energy. Demand for all forms of green electricity can be cultivated by determining different ratios for technology-specific quotas.

Quota systems offer certain benefits. Inherently, green quota systems align more closely with market principles when compared to FIT or FIP systems. A distinct market materializes alongside the conventional electricity market: the TGC market. This secondary market determines the prices per unit of produced green electricity, which tend to be higher than those of traditional electricity. In this way, green electricity promotion employs a method that reflects market signals.[116] Another advantage of this scheme is that the promotional funds are not sourced from the state treasury or an entrusted intermediary, thus shielding the system against state aid claims.

However, fluctuations in the price level for TGCs can also present challenges for green electricity. If TGC prices decrease excessively, a funding issue for green electricity producers may arise. Conversely, a significant increase in TGC prices

[114] EPA, *Energy and Environment Guide to Action: State Policies and Best Practices for Advancing Energy Efficiency, Renewable Energy, and Combined Heat and Power*, 2015; Resch et al. (2007); Ide (2017), p. 58; Buchmüller (2013), p. 90; Parker (2016), p. 26.

[115] Mitchell et al. (2011), p. 896.

[116] Ide (2017), p. 59; Jacobs (2009).

could result in overcompensation for green electricity, pressuring the government to dismantle the quota system. Furthermore, some tradable green certificate systems have been criticized as lacking ambition in promoting robust growth of renewables.[117]

Certification represents a pivotal aspect of green quotas. Without it, quota systems would not function, thus necessitating an accurate certification system for green quota schemes.[118] Certification can be entrusted to either private or public bodies. However, typically the "Transmission System Operators" issue the certificates.[119] TGCs can be traded and banked without the physical presence of the commodity, electricity, and can also serve as a guarantee in long-term financing.

An example of such a scheme is the public procurement of green electricity. Given that public authorities are substantial electricity consumers (accounting for an estimated 6–7% of the total European consumption), electricity could be procured from renewable sources through "Green Public Procurement". Such procurement decisions would generate a smaller "secondary market" characterized by an elevated market price for the electricity purchased by the public authority, consequently promoting green electricity generation through this higher price.

The public procurement of green electricity resembles quota systems due to the requirement for a "guarantee of origin" for the green electricity procured. The fundamental distinction between the two schemes lies in the purchasing entity: in public procurement, the public authority directly purchases the electricity, whereas, in the quota system, private market actors make the purchase. However, the "secondary market effect" is common in both regimes.

PPAs can be orchestrated between private entities, contingent on regulatory provisions permitting such arrangements. These kinds of contracts, referred to as "Corporate PPAs", can be executed "on-site" between a green electricity facility and a consumer in the range of private electric lines or microgrids. Conversely, they could be implemented "off-site," utilizing the national grid, involving parties that do not engage in the physical exchange of electricity. Regardless, even in off-site scenarios, the PPA provides essential stability in pricing and demand over the long term, promoting the initial financing of the investment.

Within the EU, numerous Member States are experimenting with green quotas, with more potentially following suit. The Belgian and Swedish mechanisms serve as key examples of green quota implementations. Initiated in 2002 and 2003, respectively, Belgium and Sweden mandate that electricity suppliers purchase a certain quantity of green electricity certificates. Both systems impose penalties for non-compliance with this obligation.[120]

[117] Ide (2017), p. 60.

[118] Mendonca et al. (2009), p. 153; Martinot and Beck (2004), p. 372.

[119] Johnston and Block (2013), p. 336.

[120] Pavaloaia et al. (2015); Energypedia.info (2021) Renewable Energy Quota and Certificate Schemes. https://energypedia.info/wiki/Renewable_Energy_Quota_and_Certificate_Schemes.

Article 19 RED II provides an elaborate system of TGCs, referred to as "Guarantees of Origin" (GOs) in the EU system, to validate the renewable quality of energy sources. It mandates Member States to ensure that the origin of energy can be confirmed following objective, transparent, and non-discriminatory criteria. A standard GO must correspond to 1 MWh of energy; for each unit of energy produced, no more than one GO should be issued. This regulation helps prevent double promotion by stipulating that the same unit of renewable energy is accounted for only once.

Furthermore, each GO must explicitly detail at least the following attributes: the energy source from which the energy was generated; the commencement and completion dates of production; the identity, location, type, and capacity of the facility where the energy was produced; whether the installation received investment support; whether the unit of energy benefitted in any other manner from a national promotion scheme, including the nature of that scheme; the operational start date of the installation; and the date and country of issuance, coupled with a unique identification number.

Member States or their designated competent authorities are required to implement appropriate mechanisms to ensure that GOs are issued, transferred, and canceled electronically and that GOs remain accurate, reliable, and resistant to fraudulent practices. Each Member State must recognize GOs issued by other Member States. However, a Member State may refuse recognition of a GO if it maintains justified doubts concerning its accuracy, reliability, or authenticity. Such a refusal, along with its rationale, must be reported to the Commission. Lastly, Member States are permitted to incorporate objective, transparent, and non-discriminatory criteria for the usage of GOs within their national legislation, as long as these criteria comply with the EU law.

A Europe-wide certificate trading system is not currently in place. The only suggestion for a quota and certificate system covering the European Union (EU) was rejected in 2008.[121] Nonetheless, 18 of 28 EU Member States, joined by Norway and Switzerland, actively participate in the "Association of Issuing Bodies". This body sets a standard for green certificates, also known as the European Energy Certificate System.[122]

A key challenge linked to the quota and TGC (or GO) systems is the promotion of electricity generated in other countries. This situation becomes more probable as interconnections are built, enabling electricity trade.[123] The main points of concern are whether TGCs are issued in these foreign countries and, if so, whether they are recognized. The principle of free movement of goods is also relevant within the EU.

Alands Vindkraft was a notable judgment in this context.[124] In 2009, Finland's "Oskar" wind plant sought recognition in the Swedish TGC system. Approval would

---

[121] Ide (2017), p. 61.

[122] Association of Issuing Bodies (2021) AIB. https://www.aib-net.org/.

[123] Buchmüller (2013), p. 101.

[124] European Court of Justice Judgement, C-573/12 Ålands Vindkraft AB v Energimyndigheten,. [2014] ECLI:EU:C:2014:2037.

have allowed the Oskar plant to benefit from the Swedish quota system, as it was linked to the Swedish grid. Denying Swedish TGCs to the Oskar plant would have resulted in a significant disadvantage against Swedish green electricity producers, which were benefiting from the quota system. The Swedish regulator denied the application, and the Swedish Administrative Court took the issue to the ECJ. The company, Alands Vindkraft, alleged a breach of TFEU Article 34 (ex. Article 28 TEC), which restricts quantity-based import limitations.[125] The ECJ found the Swedish regulator's denial to be a violation of Article 34 and that the refusal itself created a barrier to trade within the single market. However, the ECJ deemed the refusal "proportionate" for three reasons. First, it was difficult to identify the source of electricity once it entered the grid. Second, the Court emphasized the territorial focus of the national renewable energy targets under RED (of 2009).[126]

In the end, the Court affirmed the Swedish regulator's decision to deny the inclusion of green electricity promotion to producers from other Member States.[127] The key aspect of the decision was Article 3(3) RED. This Article stated that Member States have the right to decide the extent of their support for renewable energy produced in another Member State.[128] As previously outlined, RED II introduced cooperation mechanisms between Member States, which now allows for mutual recognition of GOs. However, they can decide how to apply these GOs in their national promotion schemes. This implies that the principle of territoriality in EU green electricity promotion is still in effect. Under RED II, Member States are required to work together on joint support mechanisms rather than extending the reach of national support schemes to installations in other Member States. This situation illustrates the gap between the requirements of the European energy system and the level of harmonization of green energy promotion.[129]

5.2.4 Tendering

Simply put, green electricity tenders, or auctions, represent strategies where investors compete for authorization to construct a green electricity installation or to secure promotional concessions.[130] The terms "auctioning" and "tendering" are frequently

[125] *"Quantitative restrictions on imports and all measures having equivalent effect shall be prohibited between Member States."*

[126] Paras. 95–103.

[127] Ankersmit L (2014) 'Facilitating' infringements of article 34 TFEU and the territorial nature of green electricity support schemes: Case C-573/12 Ålands Vindkraft AB v Energimyndigheten. In: European Law Blog. https://europeanlawblog.eu/2014/07/07/facilitating-infringements-of-article-34-tfeu-and-the-territorial-nature-of-green-electricity-support-schemes-case-c-57312-alands-vindkraft-ab-v-energimyndigheten/; Fouquet and Guarrata (2014).

[128] Fouquet and Guarrata (2014).

[129] See: Gerig and Helbig (2014).

[130] Beaton and Moernhout (2011), p. 18; Jacobs (2012), p. 26.

used interchangeably and are considered synonymous in this context. An auction or tender can be described as *"an allocation procedure based on a precise evaluation criterion specified by the auctioneer, and a pre-defined publicly available set of rules designed to allocate or award objects or products (e.g. contracts) on the basis of a financial bid"*.[131] Renewable energy tenders are market-based, competitive bidding processes aimed at identifying the most suitable renewable projects to be built within a specific timeframe and geographical location, as well as distributing appropriate support payments to these projects.[132]

Investors participate in the bidding process and, if necessary, demonstrate their compliance with additional criteria. These may encompass preconditions about materials, technology, size, experience qualification thresholds, or financial prerequisites. Tenders may be "single criterion", i.e., based on price, or "multi-criteria", where awards are determined by a range of factors, including price. The winner will secure the right to construct the green electricity installation with a defined installed capacity.[133] Conversely, if the installation pre-exists, the winning party may become eligible for FIT/FIP payments, certificate rights, grid guarantees, tax incentives, and other forms of promotional support for their green electricity production.

Green electricity tenders can be technology-specific or technology-neutral, while they are typically technology-specific.[134] In certain instances, green electricity generation sites were directly auctioned with a technology-specificity stipulation, such as in Turkish tenders. The global trend in green electricity tendering is also inclining towards technology-specific tenders. In particular, solar photovoltaic and offshore wind tenders were the most prevalent types during the 2017–2018 period.[135]

Green electricity tenders offer several notable benefits. When well-structured, these tenders serve as effective price discovery mechanisms and are less susceptible to corruption compared to their alternatives. The alternatives to tendering, such as direct negotiations or "beauty contest" designs (where applicants highlight the strengths of their projects, and a winner is chosen by the public authority in a non-transparent manner), often risk straying from economically viable outcomes for new green electricity capacity or access to promotion.

Nevertheless, green electricity tenders are not without drawbacks. Tenders involve bureaucratic procedures and high transaction costs.[136] These costs ultimately impact the final financial support. However, when accurately reflected,

---

[131] Maurer and Barroso (2011), p. 4.

[132] AURES (2017) Auctions for renewable energy support - Taming the beast of competitive bidding. In: AURES. https://auresproject.eu/publications/auctions-renewable-energy-support-taming-the-beast-of-competitive-bidding.

[133] Council of European Energy Regulators, *Sustainable Development Work Stream: Tendering Procedures for RES in Europe: State of Play and First Lessons Learnt*, 2018.

[134] Jerrentrup et al. (2019); Gephart et al. (2017).

[135] IRENA, *Renewable Energy Auctions: Status and Trends Beyond Price*, 2019.

[136] IRENA, *Renewable Energy Auctions: A Guide to Design*, 2015.

these bureaucratic costs are economically deducted from the final support level and do not create a disadvantage. Moreover, tenders make it simpler to regulate the volume of green electricity generation, thus offsetting a share of the transaction costs. In contrast, FITs may lead to over-generation as they typically do not impose a production cap. That being said, the bureaucracy associated with tenders could potentially deter smaller actors, thereby reducing competitiveness.[137]

Secondly, tenders heavily rely on the quality of bidders and the value of bids. Over-compensation in situations of low competition or under-compensation in cases of high competition (a phenomenon known as the winner's curse) are possible outcomes. Mitigating these issues requires well-defined criteria and well-publicized tender processes.[138] Otherwise, projects may either burden consumers or taxpayers, or they might not come to fruition at all.

As such, smaller installations and nascent technologies may be exempted from tendering and instead subjected to FIT/FIP mechanisms. Establishing a ceiling price for the tender is another strategy to mitigate excessive or insufficient bids.[139]

Constructing a tender may be achieved through a diverse array of policy options. Notably, the energy sector predominantly employs the "sealed bid" and "descending clock" tender varieties. Sealed-bid tenders, which necessitate all participants to simultaneously offer concealed bids to ensure anonymity, comprise a single round of bidding, thereby preventing the modification of bids in response to competition. This category can be further subdivided into two distinct types: "First Price Sealed Bid" and "Pay-as-bid". The former requires each participant to submit a single bid for one item, whereas the latter involves multiple units of the same item, thus giving rise to an array of prices. The Pay-as-bid method is frequently employed in energy tenders, particularly for new green electricity capacity, as it generally involves the allocation of multiple units of capacity, most commonly measured in megawatts.[140]

In contrast, the descending clock tender model is a dynamic, multi-round system. This model begins with the auctioneer proposing a high price and requesting the participants to declare the quantities they are willing to sell at that price. Should the offered quantity exceed the target, the price is subsequently decreased in the next round. The rounds continue until the total quantity offered aligns with the target.

Each of these policy options bears its own merits and drawbacks. The sealed-bid model, for example, is straightforward to implement but potentially inhibits price discovery and bidder competition. Dynamic designs such as the descending clock model can enhance price discovery and competition, yet they are notably complex and challenging to operate.[141]

---

[137] del Río and Linares (2014); Bento et al. (2020).

[138] del Río and Linares (2014), p. 43.

[139] AURES (2017) Auctions for renewable energy support - Taming the beast of competitive bidding. In: AURES. https://auresproject.eu/publications/auctions-renewable-energy-support-taming-the-beast-of-competitive-bidding, p. 4.

[140] Maurer and Barroso (2011), p. 8.

[141] Ibid., pp. 9–11.

The sealed-bid model has emerged as the predominant tendering method for green electricity promotion allocation in the EU Member states. On the other hand, Brazil tends to employ a hybrid approach that merges sealed-bid and dynamic tendering for new green electricity capacity.[142]

There is a discernible global shift from FIT/FIPs and quota/TGC mechanisms to tenders. In 2019, the cumulative total of tendering policies in the electricity sector nearly equaled that of FIT policies worldwide.[143] This trend can be attributed to multiple factors. Primarily, in contrast to FIT/FIPs, tenders often yield cost-effective and competitive winning bids.[144] The European Commission asserts that a well-crafted auction can create considerable competition between bids, thereby exposing the actual costs of individual projects, promoters, and technologies. Consequently, this leads to cost-efficient support levels and minimizes necessary support.[145] Moreover, in contrast to quota schemes, the extent of the support in tendering is fully disclosed at the outset, thereby fostering investor confidence and security. This transparency tends to produce more competitive bids. Finally, tenders are praised for their "price discovery" characteristics, in stark contrast to the administrative price setting prevalent in FIT/FIPs.[146]

Tendering is not a promotional strategy in and of itself but rather a method to identify eligible parties to endorse green electricity or establish new capacities. As such, any legal implications concerning the form of promotion become relevant when offered via the medium of tendering. Per WTO law, there are no limitations to conducting tenders for promotional schemes, provided that the promotion scheme complies with the WTO law.

The RED II envisages various rules regarding green electricity tenders. As stated in Article 4(4)-1 RED II, *"Member States shall ensure that support for electricity from renewable sources is granted in an open, transparent, competitive, non-discriminatory, and cost-effective manner."* Despite this, per Article 4(4)-2, Member States reserve the right to exempt small-scale installations and demonstration projects from tendering procedures. Furthermore, per Article 4(5), they may restrict tendering procedures to particular technologies where the inclusion of all producers of electricity from renewable sources could potentially result in suboptimal outcomes, given: (a) the long-term potential of a specific technology, (b) the need to foster diversification, (c) the grid integration costs, (d) network constraints and grid stability, and (e) for biomass, the requirement to evade distortions of raw materials markets.

[142] Gephart et al. (2017).

[143] REN21, *Renewables 2020 Global Status Report*, 2020.

[144] Bento et al. (2020).

[145] European Commission, "European Commission Guidance for the design of Renewables Support Schemes: Delivering the Internal Market in Electricity and Making the Most of Public Intervention", Communication, SWD(2013):439 Final, 2013, p. 6.

[146] IRENA, *Renewable Energy Auctions: Analysing 2016*, 2017.

The RED II may give rise to a multitude of legal consequences for the Member States. Primarily, tendering has now been mandated under RED II, with very restricted exceptions. Consequently, RED II provides minimal policy space to Member States for the non-competitive allocation of green electricity promotion. Secondly, tenders discriminating among technologies are no longer permissible, excluding those cases explicitly stipulated in Article 4(5) RED II. This further curtails the policy space available to Member States for conducting technology-specific tenders. However, it is noteworthy that technology-specific tendering, especially for solar photovoltaics and offshore wind, is prevalent, as demonstrated by Germany's practices. In fact, technology-specific tenders are common in the EU.[147] This situation raises questions concerning the compatibility with RED II.

Solar PV and offshore wind technologies may currently be deemed "mature technologies" with economies of scale, considering the substantial reduction in their cost per kilowatt over the past decade. Consequently, the justification provided in the first subparagraph of Article 4(5), on "the long-term potential of a particular technology" may no longer apply to these technologies. Only the "diversification" and "grid stability" subparagraphs may retain economic relevance.[148] The Commission, when justifying exemptions from the tendering requirement, commonly cites these two reasons.[149] These two subparagraphs might be interpreted as a singular justification for technology-specific tenders, given that regional energy source diversification typically aims at grid stability. Therefore, the placement of solar photovoltaic installations in a region abundant in wind power, or vice versa, could be justified under Article 4(5). This implies that RED II restricts the policy scope of the Member States not only through the tendering requirement but also by demanding technology-neutral tendering.

Nevertheless, Member States might attempt to circumvent the technology-neutral tendering requirement by invoking Article 4(5). For instance, a decision to situate a solar photovoltaic installation in an area rich in solar energy could be grounded on Article 4(5)-a, the "long-term potential of a particular technology" subparagraph. To prevent such circumstances, the Commission may have to issue a new policy guideline that addresses the maturity of certain technologies, such as solar PV and offshore wind.

Tendering holds significance not merely for domestic green electricity promotional schemes but also for the EU-wide renewable energy financing mechanism, which is similarly grounded on promotional allocation through tendering.[150] This mechanism pursues two objectives: filling the gaps in the Union's trajectory of renewable energy capacity deployment, which serves the gap-filling function, and providing support for renewable energy irrespective of the Union's trajectory, thus

---

[147] Jerrentrup et al. (2019).

[148] Article 4(5)-b and d.

[149] Jerrentrup et al. (2019).

[150] Commission Implementing Regulation (EU) 2020/1294 of 15 September 2020 on the Union Renewable Energy Financing Mechanism.

fulfilling the enabling function. According to Article 4 of the Financing Mechanism Regulation, the funds necessary to finance the Union-wide renewable energy support tenders must be collected from Member States, Union funds, or private sector contributions. Upon the submission of an application by a contributing state, a call for proposals will be disseminated.[151] Technology-neutral, multi-technology, or technology-specific tenders are all viable candidates for support.[152] The commodity and volume granted in the tender may be quantified in terms of kilowatts (kW) or kilowatt-hours (kWh). Alternatively, the volume may be expressed in terms of budget.[153] This system essentially suggests that the EU-wide renewable energy financing mechanism accommodates all kinds of tenders for the allocation of renewable energy support.

The distinguishing feature of this mechanism is its scope of application: Contrary to domestic tenders, this mechanism envisages Union-level tenders. Consequently, this mechanism manifests the EU's distinct preference in terms of the allocation of green electricity promotion: The EU prefers tenders over the non-competitive allocation of green electricity promotion.

5.2.5 Net Metering

Net metering, commonly abbreviated as NEM, is a promotion scheme designed to facilitate the sale of surplus green electricity generated by small-to-medium scale producers.[154] Typically, these net-metering operators engage in both the consumption of electricity from the grid and the production of green electricity via relatively small installations, such as a few solar panels or wind turbines.

According to the US National Renewable Energy Laboratory (NREL), net metering is defined as *"a metering and billing arrangement intended to reimburse owners of distributed energy generation (DG) systems for any energy production that is exported to the utility grid"*.[155] This model allows customers utilizing on-site DG to balance out the electricity they procure from the grid during the billing cycle (for instance, on a monthly basis). The utility customer is then charged for the net energy drawn from the utility grid.

Implemented predominantly through a utility meter, net metering quantifies the net commercial relationship between the electricity supply company and the producer/consumer, or "Prosumer". The system is subject to FIT analogous rates, often perceived as unfavorable by the producers. However, it is noteworthy that a

[151] Article 15.

[152] Article 16.

[153] Article 22.

[154] Martinot and Beck (2004), p. 380; Andra (2016).

[155] NREL (2020) Basics of Net Metering. https://www.nrel.gov/state-local-tribal/basics-net-metering.html.

fluctuating tariff for net metering has been introduced in certain scenarios.[156] Grid costs are typically invoiced separately and subtracted from the producer's payments.

Despite these challenges, the net metering scheme has been instrumental in facilitating sooner return on investment for smaller green electricity installations, as the surplus energy generated can be monetized. For instance, rooftop solar installations may produce an electricity surplus during summer, resulting in what can be described as "negative electricity bills" for a brief period. Electricity supply companies may offer energy credits in exchange for these negative bills or alternatively provide monetary compensation. Conversely, during the winter months, the electricity bill would be positive; however, it is typically reduced due to moments of peak generation. In essence, while its impact may be relatively minor on an industrial scale, net metering serves as an effective strategy to incentivize the production of green electricity at the domestic level.

One notable disadvantage of the net metering scheme is its potential to instigate grid congestion, particularly in countries characterized by outdated electrical grids. Furthermore, given the unpredictability of installation investments made by smaller operators, surplus electricity generation could emerge as a frequent occurrence in several regions.[157] This, in turn, necessitates that electricity suppliers reduce their procurement of electricity from large-scale generation installations, thereby leading to significant revenue losses for substantial investors. Without adequate advancements in electricity storage technology that can keep pace with the expansion of grid-connected small operators, net metering might not be a sustainable promotion method at larger scales.

The regulatory complexity associated with net metering is also evident. It mandates a robust regulatory framework for efficient operation. The relationship between electricity suppliers and prosumers requires comprehensive regulation. Moreover, technical nuances, such as those about two-sided meters or dual-meter systems, need to be explicitly addressed within the regulatory framework.

In sum, net metering presents a regulatory challenge yet exhibits a degree of efficacy in promoting green electricity. It has been adopted in both developed nations, such as Denmark, and developing countries, suchlike Turkey, and it is expected to remain in use for the foreseeable future. This method shows promise in the wake of "smart grid" plans for more sizable prosumer installations.

5.2.6 *Carbon Pricing*

Another significant method for promoting green electricity lies within carbon emission limitation strategies, specifically through carbon pricing. Though not directly tied to the promotion of green electricity, these measures indirectly foster its growth.

[156] Mendonca et al. (2009), p. 166.

[157] Andra (2016).

Despite the term "carbon pricing," these initiatives apply to all GHG emissions. The United Nations Framework Convention on Climate Change (UNFCCC) describes the principles of carbon pricing as follows: *"Carbon pricing mitigates greenhouse gas emissions by imposing a charge on emission or by providing incentives for reduced emissions. The price signal thus created influences consumption and investment patterns, harmonizing economic development with climate protection".*[158]

Carbon pricing schemes are often deemed cost-efficient due to their technology-neutral and market-based nature.[159] They are even considered optimal policies for emission reduction. However, empirical evidence supporting these properties remains limited.[160]

Carbon pricing takes two forms: Carbon taxation and Emission Trading Systems (ETS). Carbon taxation directly sets a price on carbon by defining a tax rate on greenhouse gas emissions or the carbon content of fossil fuels. Conversely, an ETS establishes a cap on the total level of greenhouse gas emissions and permits industries with low emissions to sell their extra allowances to bigger emitters.[161]

Carbon taxes, discussed in the first chapter, are examples of Pigouvian measures. They are imposed to correct negative climate externalities and to divert resources away from emission-intensive economic activities. Carbon taxes embody the negative externalities associated with these activities when applied to emission-intensive forms of electricity generation.[162] In response, investors will likely increase their investment in the green electricity sector. As such, the green electricity sector stands to gain from a carbon tax.

Prominent instances of this approach are the Swedish and Danish carbon tax schemes. Established in the 1990s, these systems now cover 40% of domestic emissions in Sweden and Denmark, with tax rates ranging from 20 to 100 Euros per ton of CO2. By comparison, the median in Europe is 35 Euros per ton of CO2, covering 30% of domestic emissions.[163]

Nonetheless, carbon taxes have certain drawbacks. The experience with carbon taxes, particularly their full effects on emission-intensive energy generation sectors, remains substantially uncharted. Additionally, energy taxes introduce a level of unpredictability into carbon pricing, potentially generating unforeseen revenues and imposing unanticipated burdens on the energy sector. This unpredictability makes them politically challenging to implement.[164]

---

158 UNFCCC (2020) About Carbon Pricing. https://unfccc.int/about-us/regional-collaboration-centres/the-ci-aca-initiative/about-carbon-pricing#eq-1.

159 Abrell et al. (2019).

160 Groba and Breitschopf (2013).

161 The World Bank (2020) Pricing Carbon. https://www.worldbank.org/en/programs/pricing-carbon.

162 Weisbach and Metcalf (2009).

163 Asen (2020).

164 Ansuategi and Galarraga (2012).

While energy taxes are relatively straightforward mechanisms, ETS systems are more complex in regulatory terms. ETS limits the total level of greenhouse gas emissions and enables industries with lower emissions to sell their excess allowances to larger emitters. The benefits of ETS are multifaceted. Firstly, ETS provides certainty regarding the quantity of emissions avoided. Secondly, it is a cost-effective, market-based system that generates revenue for environmental objectives through auctions. Thirdly, unlike certain other promotional measures, ETS does not strain the government's budget.[165]

Despite its cost-effectiveness, a major disadvantage of ETS is the potential for non-auctioned (i.e., unsold) ETS permits to accumulate, leading to a significant decrease in their costs. This could hinder the system's ability to achieve its emission reduction goals.[166]

The WTO law implications of ETS schemes deserve examination. In implementing an ETS, governments need to distribute permits to private firms. The methodology of distributing these permits could potentially be viewed as a subsidy under WTO law. Therefore, governments must exercise caution to avoid subjecting their trading industries to claims under the WTO with ETS permits. The free allocation of permits (e.g., due to grandfathering rights) may provoke WTO disputes.[167]

A notable example of emission trading mechanisms is the EU ETS, established by the ETS Directive.[168] The EU ETS caps the emission of one-ton equivalent of carbon and gradually reduces the cap to meet the EU's emission reduction goals. Installations can trade permits or obtain them in public auctions. Designed to operate in phases, the system will enter its fourth phase in 2021. With each phase, the scope of the system extends to new countries and sectors. Nonetheless, electricity installations with a capacity exceeding 20 MW have been included in the system since its initial phase.[169]

A crucial aspect of the EU ETS pertinent to this discussion is the free allocation of permits. From 2013 (the third phase), the system ceased free permit allocations for the electricity generation sector. However, the ETS Directive not only establishes an emission trading mechanism but also permits some temporary state aid measures for electricity generation.[170] The ETS Guidelines, designed by the European Commission, further clarify the Commission's approach to electricity generation aid concerning the ETS. The Commission suggests that exemptions from the ETS

---

[165] The European Commission (2016) EU Emissions Trading System (EU ETS). In: Climate Action - European Commission. https://ec.europa.eu/clima/policies/ets_en.

[166] Leal-Arcas and Filis (2014).

[167] Leal-Arcas et al. (2015), p. 479; Jegou and Rubini (2011), ID 1914997; Deane (2015), p. 133.

[168] Directive 2003/87/EC of the European Parliament and of the Council of 13 October 2003 Establishing a Scheme for Greenhouse Gas Emission Allowance Trading within the Community and Amending Council Directive 96/61/EC.

[169] Jacobs (2016), p. 34; Kreuter-Kirchhof (2017)., Seres (2016).

[170] Bacon (2017), p. 386.

could be introduced to renew conventional electricity plants and build highly efficient plants with carbon capture technology. However, these exemptions do not directly relate to green energy. The only significant aspect is that some of the auction revenues will be allocated to fund the development of renewable energy technologies.[171] From a policy perspective, the EU ETS's state aid exemptions seem to prioritize the modernization of conventional electricity generation over the swift development of green electricity. Consequently, these aid exemptions could be viewed as detrimental to the green electricity sector.

The European ETS is not without issues. One significant problem concerning the European ETS, relevant to electricity generation, is the so-called "Waterbed Effect". This phenomenon arises in three scenarios. Firstly, when member states to phase out CO2-emitting lignite and coal-fueled plants, they achieve considerable emission reductions, thereby reducing the demand for emission allowances. Imported electricity from lignite and coal-fueled plants in other member states could fill the electricity demand gap, known as the "waterbed effect via direct displacement of activities". Secondly, when emission allowances are traded inexpensively to other member states and used for high-CO2 impact investments, this is referred to as the "waterbed effect via CO2 price channel". Lastly, the "waterbed effect via banking channel" refers to situations where cheap allowances are "banked" for future use in high-CO2 impact investments.[172] The waterbed effect becomes particularly relevant in instances of coal phase-outs, such as in Germany. The German coal phase-out plan will inevitably lead to a surplus of allowances and a reduction in allowance prices.

Nevertheless, the Commission has initiated new mechanisms to mitigate the waterbed effect. In Phase 3, the "Backloading mechanism" was launched, whereby tenders for 900 million allowances were postponed until 2019–2020 as a short-term solution. In Phase 4, the "Market Stability Reserve" was initiated as a long-term solution. Firstly, the 900 million allowances backloaded in Phase 3 were not auctioned but transferred into the reserve.[173] Unallocated allowances in Phase 4 will also be transferred to the reserve. From 2023 onwards, allowances held in reserve above the previous year's auction volume will cease to be valid. In other words, from 2023 onwards, the reserve will commence the cancellation of "banked" emission allowances.[174] Some posit that the Phase 4 mechanism will temporarily

---

[171] The European Commission, *EU ETS Handbook*, 2015, pp. 35–38.

[172] Clean Energy Wire (2019) National climate measures and European emission trading: Assessing the 'waterbed effect'. https://www.cleanenergywire.org/factsheets/national-climate-measures-and-european-emission-trading-assessing-waterbed-effect.

[173] Kreuter-Kirchhof (2017).

[174] The European Commission (2016) Market Stability Reserve. In: Climate Action - European Commission. https://ec.europa.eu/clima/policies/ets/reform_en.

"puncture" the waterbed.[175] Others argue that the reserve mechanism is intrinsically flawed since it operates as a banking mechanism.[176]

Both the Phase 3 and Phase 4 mechanisms, aimed at tackling the waterbed effect, are inadequate, if not counterproductive. Ultimately, back-loading and "banking" in reserve will create a specific form of the waterbed effect, as mentioned above, "the waterbed effect via banking channel". These allowances may be used in the future for high-CO2 impact projects. Cancellation of the allowances, set to occur after 2023, will be limited and likely will not eliminate the aforementioned three forms of waterbed effect. The European ETS requires a significant reduction of the system's emission cap. Alongside this, an earlier cancellation of allowances in the market stability reserve could contribute to the effort to mitigate emissions.

Another issue with the European ETS is the so-called "Carbon Leakage". This term refers to instances where investments are transferred to countries with lenient environmental regulations and subsequently export their products back to their original country. The carbon leakage problem is particularly prevalent in energy-intensive sectors. However, relocating electricity investments is not straightforward, given that electricity trade with neighboring regions remains minimal. Nonetheless, we could conceive of a hypothetical scenario where German coal energy companies relocate their investments to a third country with more relaxed (or non-existent) emission control regulations, only to export their production back to the EU via ENTSO-E connections. This scenario could resemble carbon leakage. To address this problem, the "Carbon Border Adjustment Mechanism" has been devised as a component of the EU Green Deal. With a carbon border tax measure, the emission externality of an imported product is reflected more accurately. In practical terms, this signifies an additional tariff on imports with a higher carbon footprint.

Indeed, the compatibility of ETS schemes with green electricity promotion measures is a topic of debate within the literature. The first perspective argues that these two instruments can be coupled to achieve deeper decarbonization and more significant emission reductions.[177] Conversely, the second perspective opposes this, arguing that utilizing multiple instruments to pursue the same policy goal can lead to inefficiencies and additional transaction costs.[178]

However, these two schemes serve two related but distinct policy objectives: emission reduction and the rapid deployment of green electricity installations. Neither of these two policy objectives is inherently superior to the other. While promoting green electricity does contribute to emission reduction, it also serves other objectives, as explained in the first chapter. Secondly, emission trading schemes and the promotion of green electricity are not mutually exclusive. In fact, they can mutually reinforce each other.

---

[175] Perino (2018).

[176] Rosendahl (2019).

[177] Geroe (2019), Lehmann and Gawel (2013).

[178] Riechmann et al. (2013); Frondel and Schmidt (2006).

As mentioned earlier, emission trading can be viewed as an "indirect promotion scheme" that favors green electricity. By pairing emission trading with direct forms of green electricity promotion, the goal of rapid deployment of green electricity installations can be more successfully achieved. Moreover, reaching the electricity mix share target will be much more feasible with policy coupling between these two measures.

While it is true that merging these two systems might increase transaction costs, these costs could be viewed as the price of faster green electricity deployment. The ultimate aim is to create a sustainable, green energy sector, and combining these two measures could accelerate the achievement of this goal.

5.2.7 Regulatory Easing

Indeed, the notion of reducing regulatory requirements, commonly phrased as "cutting red tape", could potentially act as a stimulus for encouraging investments in the green electricity sector. It is not rare when potential investors express their concerns about the bureaucratic difficulties involved in investing in green electricity. These procedures are often perceived as overly complex, lengthy, and burdensome, creating a discouraging environment for initiating new projects in this field.

Moreover, the regulatory landscape becomes more demanding for projects of larger scale, as well as for those deploying cutting-edge technologies in the green electricity domain. The underlying reason is that such projects can pose more significant potential risks, given their size or the unproven nature of the technologies involved. This regulatory severity often results in investors opting for smaller-scale projects or more conventional green electricity investments. Consequently, this can suppress the impetus of the energy transition towards more sustainable options, thereby prolonging the dependence on non-renewable electricity sources. In this context, easing regulatory requirements for not just the initiation of new investments but also during the projects' operational phase could promote the green electricity sector.

The Turkish "Unlicensed Generation" model is an example of the regulatory easing approach. This model was designed for green electricity projects that do not exceed certain predetermined thresholds. While these investments are not entirely exempted from regulatory processes, the bureaucratic procedures, and legal requirements they must comply with have been substantially relaxed. This streamlined process simplifies the steps for investors to execute green energy projects, creating a promotion effect.

However, it is crucial to recognize that easing regulations should not undermine safety, environmental protection, or other vital concerns. The need to ensure safety standards, preserve ecological integrity, and maintain due diligence should not be compromised in the quest for regulatory simplicity. Striking the right balance between regulatory easing and the need for adequate safeguards and standards becomes a critical factor.

References

Abrell J, Rausch S, Streitberger C (2019) The economics of renewable energy support. J Public Econ 176:94–117

Andra J (2016) What is net metering and why does it matter? Renewable Energy World. https://www.renewableenergyworld.com/2016/11/15/what-is-net-metering-and-why-does-it-matter/

Ansuategi A, Galarraga I (2012) Carbon pricing as an effective instrument of climate policy: searching for an optimal policy instrument. In: Castellucci L, Markandya A (eds) Environmental taxes and fiscal reform. Palgrave Macmillan UK, London, pp 145–167

Asen E (2020) Carbon Taxes in Europe. Tax Foundation. https://taxfoundation.org/carbon-taxes-in-europe-2020/

Bachrach D et al (2003) Comparing the Risk Profiles of Renewable and Natural Gas Electricity Contracts: A Summary of the California Department of Water Resources Contracts

Bacon K (2017) European Union law of state aid, 3rd edn. Oxford University Press, Oxford

Beaton C, Moernhout T (2011) A literature review on subsidies to electricity from renewable energy sources, pp 16–17

Bento N, Borello M, Gianfrate G (2020) Market-pull policies to promote renewable energy: a quantitative assessment of tendering implementation. J Clean Prod 248

Bigdeli SZ (2009) Incentive schemes to promote renewables and the WTO law of subsidies. In: Nartova O, Bigdeli SZ, Cottier T (eds) International trade regulation and the mitigation of climate change: World Trade Forum. Cambridge University Press, Cambridge, pp 155–192

Bigdeli SZ, Delimatsis P (2016) Feed-in-tariffs and the WTO regulation of subsidies—a moment of progressive adjudication in Canada–Renewable Energy. In: Research handbook on climate change and trade law. Edward Elgar Publishing

Buchmüller C (2013) Strom aus erneuerbaren Energien im WTO-Recht, 1st edn. Nomos, Baden-Baden

Carmona FR (2016) The feed-in tariffs entanglement: a comparative study of the analytical approaches followed by the EU and WTO judiciary bodies regarding renewable energy subsidies. Legal Iss Econ Integr 43

Cottier T (2014) Renewable energy and WTO law: more policy space or enhanced disciplines? Renew Energy Law Policy Rev 5:40–51

Cottier T et al (2014) Differential Taxation of Electricity: Assessing the Compatibility with WTO Law, EU Law and the Swiss-EEC Free Trade Agreement

Couture T et al (2010) A policymaker's guide to feed-in tariff policy design, 6 October 2010

Deane F (2015) Emissions trading and WTO law: a global analysis. Edward Elgar Pub, Cheltenham; Northampton

del Río P, Linares P (2014) Back to the future? Rethinking auctions for renewable electricity support. Renew Sustain Energy Rev 35:42–56. https://doi.org/10.1016/j.rser.2014.03.039

Deshpande C, Bansal V (2017) The India – solar cells dispute: renewable energy subsidies under World Trade law and the need for environmental exceptions. NUJS Law Rev 10

Espa I (2015) Subsidies, clean energy and climate change

Espa I, Holzer K (2015) Greening electricity through taxing: an analysis of GATT constraints

Farah PD, Cima E (2015) World Trade Organization, renewable energy subsidies and the case of feed-in tariffs: time for reform toward sustainable development? Georgetown Int Environ Law Rev (GIELR) 27

Fouquet D, Guarrata A (2014) Judgment of 1st July 2014 in Ålands Vindkraft AB v Energimyndigheten: Comments on Case C-573/12. Renew Energy Law Policy Rev 5:52–59.

Frondel M, Schmidt C (2006) Emissionshandel und Erneuerbare-Energien-Gesetz: Eine notwendige Koexistenz?, 1 January 2006

Gephart M, Klessmann C, Wigand F (2017) Renewable energy auctions – When are they (cost-) effective? Energy Environ 28:145–165. https://doi.org/10.1177/0958305X16688811

Gerig M, Helbig E (2014) Rechtliche Instrumente zur Vollendung des europäischen Energiebinnenmarktes. Wirtschaftsdienst 2014:887–891

Geroe S (2019) Addressing climate change through a low-cost, high-impact carbon tax. J Environ Dev 28:3–27. https://doi.org/10.1177/1070496518821152

Giraud A, Petit S (2016) BVVG Bodenverwertungs-und –verwaltungs GmbH · Case C-39/14. Eur State Aid Law Q 15:142–144

Griffith-Jones S (1993) Loan guarantees for large infrastructure projects: The issues and possible lessons for a European facility. Report prepared for the commission of the European communities. European Communities, Luxembourg

Griffith-Jones S et al. (2004) Alternative Loan Guarantee Mechanisms and Project Finance for Infrastructure in Developing Countries, pp 6–7

Groba F, Breitschopf B (2013) Impact of renewable energy policy and use on innovation: a literature review, 1 January 2013

Gudas K (2015) Promotion of Renewable Energy in the EU

Hansen UE, Nygaard I, Morris M, Robbins G (2020) The effects of local content requirements in auction schemes for renewable energy in developing countries: a literature review. Renew Sustain Energy Rev 127:109843. https://doi.org/10.1016/j.rser.2020.109843

Hestermeyer HP, Nielsen L (2014) The legality of local content measures under WTO law. J World Trade 48

Hildreth V (2014) Renewable energy subsidies and the GATT. Chicago J Int Law 14

Holzer K, Espa I, Payosova T (2017) Promoting green electricity through differentiated electricity tax schemes. In: Espa I, Cottier T (eds) International trade in sustainable electricity: regulatory challenges in international economic law. Cambridge University Press, Cambridge, pp 356–389

Hussain M (2013) Financing renewable energy options for developing financing instruments using public funds.

Ide A-M (2017) Grenzüberschreitende Förderung erneuerbarer Energien im europäischen Strombinnenmarkt, 1st edn. Nomos, Baden-Baden

Jacobs D (2009) Quotas and tender schemes

Jacobs D (2012) Renewable energy policy convergence in the EU: the evolution of feed-in tariffs in Germany, Spain and France, 1st edn. Routledge

Jacobs M (2016) Europäischer Emissionshandel, Erneuerbare-Energien-Gesetz und das Recht der Umweltbeihilfen: Plädoyer für einen "more environmental approach" im EU-Wettbewerbsrecht. Nomos

Jegou I, Rubini L (2011) The allocation of emission allowances free of charge: legal and economic considerations, ID 1914997, 23 August

Jerrentrup L, Lotz B, Tiedemann S, Hirth L (2019) Technology-neutral auctions for renewable energy: EU Law vs. member state reality: an assessment of the EU environmental and energy state aid guidelines 2014–2020 and their application. J Eur Environ Plan Law 16:386–406

Johnson O (2013) Exploring the effectiveness of local content requirements in promoting solar PV manufacturing in India

Johnston A, Block G (2013) EU energy law, 1st edn. Oxford University Press

Karttunen M, Moore MO (2018) India–solar cells: trade rules, climate policy, and sustainable development goals. World Trade Rev 17:215–237

Kent A, Jha V (2014) Keeping Up with the changing climate: the WTO's evolutive approach in response to the trade and climate conundrum: a comment on Canada – certain measures affecting the renewable energy sector. J World Invest Trade 15:245–271

Kettner C, Kletzan-Slamanig D (2016) Renewable electricity support in the EU – what lessons can be learnt? In: Stoianoff NP, Kreiser L, Butcher B et al (eds) Green fiscal reform for sustainable future: reform, innovation and renewable energy. Edward Elgar Publishing, pp 155–168

Kitson L (2015) India's accelerated depreciation policy for wind energy

Kreuter-Kirchhof C (2017) Klimaschutz durch Emissionshandel? Die jüngste Reform des europäischen Emissionshandelssystems. EuZW 412–418

Kuntze J-C, Moerenhout T (2012) Local content requirements and the renewable energy industry - a good match? SSRN Electronic Journal. https://doi.org/10.2139/ssrn.2188607

Lai H (2016) The climate-trade conundrum: a critical analysis of the WTO's Jurisprudence on subsidies to renewable energy. In: Matsushita M, Schoenbaum TJ (eds) Emerging issues in sustainable development: international trade law and policy relating to natural resources, energy, and the environment. Springer, pp 297–319

Leal-Arcas R, Filis A (2014) Legal aspects of the promotion of renewable energy within the EU and in relation to the EU's obligations in the WTO. Renew Energy Law Policy Rev 1

Leal-Arcas R, Filis A, Gosh ESA (2015) International energy governance: selected legal issues. Edward Elgar Pub, Cheltenham

Lee J (2016) SCM agreement revisited: climate change, renewable energy, and the SCM agreement. World Trade Rev 15:613–644

Lehmann P, Gawel E (2013) Why should support schemes for renewable electricity complement the EU emissions trading scheme? Energy Policy 52:597–607. https://doi.org/10.1016/j.enpol.2012.10.018

Lester S (2011) GATT Article XX and Domestic Production of Environmental Goods. International Economic Law and Policy Blog. https://ielp.worldtradelaw.net/2011/04/article-xx-domestic-production-of-environmental-goods.html

Martinot E, Beck F (2004) Renewable energy policies and barriers. In: Cleveland CJ (ed) Encyclopedia of energy, 1st edn. Elsevier Science, Amsterdam

Maurer LTA, Barroso L (2011) Electricity auctions: an overview of efficient practices, p 4

Mendonca M, Jacobs D, Sovacool BK (2009) Powering the Green economy: the feed-in tariff handbook, 1st edn. Routledge, London, Sterling

Meyer T (2015) How local discrimination can promote global public goods. Boston Univ Law Rev 95

Micheau C (2014) State aid, subsidy and tax incentives under EU and WTO law. Wolters Kluwer

Mitchell C, Sawin J, Pokharel GR, et al (2011) Policy, financing and implementation

Morgan T (2007) Energy subsidies: their magnitude, how they affect energy investment and greenhouse gas emissions, and prospects for reform. UNFCCC Secretariat

Müller W (2017) WTO agreement on subsidies and countervailing measures: a commentary. Cambridge University Press

Muñoz M, Oschmann V, David Tàbara J (2007) Harmonization of renewable electricity feed-in laws in the European Union. Energy Policy 35:3104–3114. https://doi.org/10.1016/j.enpol.2006.11.006

Nicolaides P (2015) Grants versus fiscal aid: in search of economic rationality. Eur State Aid Law Q 14:410–416

Parker L (2016) International law and the renewable energy sector. In: Gray KR, Tarasofsky R, Carlarne C (eds) The Oxford handbook of international climate change law

Pavaloaia L, Georgescu I, Georgescu M (2015) The system of green certificates - promoter of energy from renewable resources. Proc Soc Behav Sci 188:206–213. https://doi.org/10.1016/j.sbspro.2015.03.374

Perino G (2018) New EU ETS Phase 4 rules temporarily puncture waterbed. Nat Clim Change 8: 262–264. https://doi.org/10.1038/s41558-018-0120-2

Pirlot A (2017) The inadequacy of EU state aid law and WTO law on subsidies to regulate energy tax reliefs. Eur State Aid Law Q 16:25

Podsiadło P (2016) The interference of law and economics: the case of guarantees for bank debt and their impact on the competitiveness of the EU member states. Eur State Aid Law Q 15:72–90

Resch G, Ragwitz M, Held A et al (2007) Feed-in tariffs and quotas for renewable energy in Europe. CESifo DICE Report 5:26–32

Rickerson W, Laurent C, Jacobs D et al (2012) Feed-in tariffs as a policy instrument for promoting renewable energies and green economies in developing countries. UNEP

Riechmann C, Müsgens F, Peichert P et al (2013) Emissionshandel oder Förderung Erneuerbarer Energien in Europa: Wer sollte langfristig das Steuer übernehmen? Energiewirtschaftliche Tagesfragen 63:8–12

Rodrik D (2014) Green industrial policy. Oxford Rev Econ Policy 30:469–491. https://doi.org/10.1093/oxrep/gru025

Rosendahl KE (2019) EU ETS and the waterbed effect. Nat Clim Change 9:734–735. https://doi.org/10.1038/s41558-019-0579-5

Rubini L (2012) Ain't Wastin' time no more: subsidies for renewable energy, the SCM agreement, policy space, and law reform. J Int Econ Law 15:525–579. https://doi.org/10.1093/jiel/jgs020

Ruiz MAG (2015) Tax expenditures to promote environmentally responsible investment. In: Kreiser L, Andersen MS, Olsen BE et al (eds) Environmental pricing. Edward Elgar Publishing, pp 100–114

Säcker FJ, Montag F (eds) (2016) European state aid law: a commentary. Beck/Hart, München/Oxford

Seres EL (2016) The question of compliance with the polluter-pays principle and State aid rules within the European Emission Trading Scheme. J Agric Environ Law 21:63–95

Shadikhodjaev S (2013) First WTO judicial review of climate change subsidy issues. Am J Int Law 107:864–878

Shadikhodjaev S (2015) Renewable energy and government support: time to 'Green' the SCM agreement? World Trade Rev 14:479–506

Sherlock MF (2018) The energy credit: an investment tax credit for renewable energy

Sovacool BK (2009) The importance of comprehensiveness in renewable electricity and energy-efficiency policy. Energy Policy 37:1529–1541. https://doi.org/10.1016/j.enpol.2008.12.016

United Nations Environment Programme, Division of Technology I and Economics, UNEP Sustainable Energy Finance Initiative (2004) Financial risk management instruments for renewable energy projects: summary document. United Nations Environment Programme, Division of Technology, Industry and Economics, Paris

Weisbach D, Metcalf G (2009) The design of a Carbon Tax. Harv Environ Law Rev 33. https://doi.org/10.2139/ssrn.1327260

Wilke M (2011) Feed-in tariffs for renewable energy and WTO subsidy rules: an initial legal review, p 3

WTO (2006) World Trade Report 2006: Exploring the Links Between Subsidies, Trade and WTO. WTO Publishing

Chapter 6
Green Electricity Promotion in Germany

Renowned for its commitment to green electricity promotion, Germany has been a pioneer in this field. This was inaugurated with the inception of the Stromeinspeisungsgesetz (The Feed-In Tariff Act, StromEinspG) in 1990 when Germany began the utilization of its FIT to promote the growth of green electricity.[1] Furthermore, Germany has been adept at energy regulation since the introduction of the Energiewirtschaftsgesetz (EnWG, Energy Industry Act) in 1935. Consequently, Germany boasts an extensive collection of acts and secondary regulation at the federal level, further supplemented by the pertinent EU legislation and state-level norms.

This discussion will initially cover the foundations of Germany's contemporary energy policy, given that the policy backdrop considerably enhances the understanding of the legal dimensions. Thereafter, an outline of Germany's energy regulation framework will be presented. The comparison of the policy and law evolution concerning green electricity promotion in Germany will illustrate the core subject of this book. In conclusion, Germany's green electricity promotion strategies will be examined, with primary emphasis on the EEG 2023. The evolution of the EEG will be explored further in this chapter.

6.1 Policy Background

The primary focus of this chapter is the legal aspects of green electricity promotion in Germany. However, any assessment of the promotion strategies would be unproductive without a thorough understanding of the political and legal context. Thus, this part intends to furnish the political background in Germany. As previously

[1] Fouquet (2018).

O. Cagdas Artantas, *Promotion of Green Electricity in Germany and Turkey*, EYIEL Monographs - Studies in European and International Economic Law 33,
https://doi.org/10.1007/978-3-031-44760-0_6

noted, Germany is a pioneer in green electricity promotion, a status that did not materialize in a vacuum. Preceding its green electricity promotion schemes, Germany had a rich history of environmental movements. A brief investigation into the history of modern environmentalist movements in Germany is thus required, a history that extends into very recent. Lastly, the influence of this environmental legacy on the German model of green electricity promotion deserves a thorough analysis.

Since the 1970s, Germany has been a nexus of influential environmental movements. The inception of a popular anti-nuclear initiative as early as 1972, originating with protests against a proposed nuclear power plant in Wyhl, marked the beginning of a significant shift in German public sentiment. This movement found resonance among various sections of society, encompassing farmers, academia, clergy, and daily commuters. Consequently, there was an increased awareness regarding the risks associated with nuclear energy, paving the way for a broader spectrum of environmentalism. This encompassed advocacy groups campaigning for organic farming practices, recycling initiatives, increased use of public transportation, and climate protection.[2]

Although differentiated by political context, environmentalism found traction in both West and East Germany. Post-reunification, environmentalist groups from both the West and East merged to form mainstream political movements. Overall, it is apparent that elements of environmentalism are evident in all mainstream parties, profoundly impacting the contemporary political landscape.

Energy has invariably remained at the core of Germany's environmentalist agenda. The movement initially gained momentum as an anti-nuclear initiative, but the demands concerning the energy mix evolved over time. Phasing out nuclear energy was a significant step but necessitated the development of replacement energy sources. Energy efficiency measures could only reduce this requirement to a certain extent. Consequently, alternative solutions needed to be developed. Even in the 1970s, renewable energy was considered a promising alternative, a perception further galvanized by the Oil Crises of 1973 and 1979. However, renewable energy technology was still in its infancy during this period. Although wind turbines were based on ancient technology, their utilization for electricity generation was in the developing stage. Solar energy remained primarily theoretical, and only hydroelectricity was accessible in significant amounts. Unfortunately, Germany's hydroelectric potential was limited. Hence, nuclear power and coal plants continued to sustain Germany's substantial industrial and domestic energy needs.[3]

By the 1990s, it became increasingly noticeable that renewable energy options could potentially replace at least a portion of conventional energy sources. As early as 1990, a national FIT was established to bolster renewable energy generation via the StromEinspG. Eventually, this act evolved into the Erneuerbare-Energien-Gesetz

---

[2]Morris and Jungjohann (2016), p. 15.

[3]Praetorius (2020), p. 80.

(The Renewable Energies Act, EEG). The evolution of these two acts will be examined in detail below.

The 1990s marked a pivotal shift in global climate consciousness, with the growing discourse around "global warming" and later "climate change". An increasing concern regarding the rate of Earth's warming and the potential for more frequent natural disasters provoked new policy formulation. Particularly from the late 2010s, governments began to experience mounting pressure from younger demographics to implement policy changes to mitigate climate-altering emissions. A significant strategy to curtail these emissions involved the development of a "green economy", central to which was electricity generation. Consequently, the demand for transitioning to green electricity escalated.[4] While this transition, or "decarbonization", was widely supported in Germany, there were critical voices concerning the methodology of this shift and the siting of new infrastructure. Nevertheless, the decarbonization process signified the first substantial objective of German Energiewende. Germany has set ever-increasing national energy mix targets for the future under the RED II framework. These targets involved a gradual phasing out of carbon-sourced electricity generation, heating, and transportation by 2050, with a complete coal power plant phase-out by 2038.[5]

Prior to the adoption of the Climate Act in 2019, Germany sought to reduce its greenhouse gas (GHG) emissions by 80–95% by 2050. The enactment of the German Climate Act (Klimaschutzgesetz, KSG) in 2019 stipulated a 55% carbon emission reduction by 2030 and a complete GHG emission phase-out by 2050. However, critics asserted that the KSG 2019 was not ambitious enough. The Act postponed 45% of decarbonization until after 2030, with the 2050 target deemed "too far away" by critics. This issue was adjudicated by the Federal Constitutional Court (Bundesverfassungsgericht, BVerfG), which ruled in March 2021 that the KSG 2019 was partially unconstitutional.[6] The case hinged on the state's environmental protection obligation under Article 20a GG. The BVerfG ultimately concluded that the KSG 2019's dynamics violated the freedoms of the youthful complainants by deferring a substantial part of decarbonization until after 2030. For the targets of the Paris Agreement to be achieved, "the reductions still necessary after 2030 were to be achieved with ever greater speed and urgency".

In response to this ruling, the German Parliament enacted a new Climate Act, the KSG 2021. This updated legislation aims for a 65% CO2 emissions reduction by 2030 (a 10% increase from previous targets), an 88% reduction by 2040, and total CO2 neutrality by 2045, 5 years ahead of the previous target. These revised targets will necessitate an even more rapid deployment of renewables, particularly green electricity installations. Thus, it could be asserted that Germany's green electricity promotion policy will need to continue into the 2040s to ensure complete climate neutrality.

[4] Ohlhorst (2019), p. 102; von Hirschhausen (2018), p. 30.

[5] Oei (2018).

[6] Order of 24 March 2021, 1 BvR 2656/18, 1 BvR 288/20, 1 BvR 96/20, 1 BvR 78/20.

The Fukushima Daiichi disaster in 2011 prompted a worldwide review of nuclear energy programs. While some nations opted to reinforce nuclear technology regulations without significantly altering their energy mix plans, Germany took a resolute stance by choosing to completely phase out nuclear energy by 2022. This move, termed "Denuclearization", constituted Germany's second significant energy policy objective.[7] While many nations shifted to a more positive stance on nuclear energy after 2022, Germany kept the phase-out deadline intact and shut down its last reactors in April 2023.

Energy security serves as the third critical aspect of German energy policy. As explained above, energy security is a complex concept encompassing various elements. One such element is energy reliability, which correlates with the uninterrupted provision of energy. A second constituent of energy security is the supply security, aimed at eliminating dependence on imported energy. Such dependency can give rise to considerable geopolitical challenges. For instance, Germany's reliance on imported gas meant that global political tension could significantly impact energy generation. As was demonstrated in the winter of 2022–2023, unforeseen price surges or supply shocks could potentially jeopardize a vital fraction of the energy mix, the industrial sector, and ultimately the broader economy.[8]

The fourth objective of European and German energy policy is stimulating economic growth and fostering job creation. The intention is to maintain the competitiveness of German industry, drive economic growth, and generate new jobs through a "Green New Deal." Drawing on the historical precedent of the American New Deal implemented during the Great Depression, contemporary Green New Deals across the globe aim to spur economic growth and public prosperity through green investments. The EU, similarly, pursues its own "European Green Deal" to bolster the green economy within its Member States. These green economic policy objectives are further discussed above.

The term "Energiewende" was introduced by Germany in the 2010s to encapsulate a range of issues, from decarbonization to green economic goals. This term, translatable as "Energy Transition", refers to the shift across all energy sectors towards more sustainable, secure, and affordable modes of generation.[9] Energiewende has rapidly become an international term representing a comprehensive energy transition in the twenty-first century: from conventional to green, efficient, climate-friendly, secure, and affordable sources. Between 2011 and 2012, the Energiewende evolved into a substantial legislative program with amendments to the EnWG and EEG.[10] Subsequently, the term "Energiewende" became an essential component of governmental reports on the energy sector in Germany. Other acts, such as the Kraft-Wärme-Kopplungsgesetz (KWKG, Combined Heat and Power Act) came into force in 2002, the Erneuerbare-Energien-Wärmegesetz (EEWärmeG,

---

[7] Sattich (2018), p. 169.; Maubach (2014), p. 9.; Beveridge and Kern (2013).

[8] Praetorius (2020), p. 46; Jurca (2014); Gentzsch (2018), p. 86; Schafhausen (2018), p. 31.

[9] von Hirschhausen (2018), p. 34.

[10] Müller (2013).

Renewable Energies Heat Act) in 2008, and the Windenergie-auf-See-Gesetz (WindSeeG, Offshore Wind Energy Act) in 2017.

The concept of Energiewende encompasses several integral components. The most pivotal among these is the metamorphosis from conventional, largely pollutant-rich energy production methods to environmentally friendly, sustainable energy generation. This transformation encapsulates the shift towards green electricity, heating, and mobility. Various renewable energy sources, such as solar, wind, hydro, and biomass, inter alia, are intended to be harnessed to diversify the energy mix, concurrently diminishing the reliance on nuclear and coal power generation. As a contingency plan to tackle the intermittency of renewables, natural gas serves as a supplementary energy source until substantial energy storage capacities can be established.

A second crucial aspect of the Energiewende is its focus on energy efficiency. This is deemed a critical part of the initiative as it is poised to facilitate the transition to green energy by reducing energy demand.[11] The implementation of energy efficiency largely relies on the advent of new technologies and construction methodologies, encompassing reductions in electricity usage by industry and households, the adoption of passive heating and cooling techniques, and the improvement of mobility efficiency. The country seeks to effectuate an "uncoupling" of economic growth from the escalation in energy demand. The gains of heating efficiency, particularly through the *Wärmewende* (Warming Transition), is deemed essential in order to achieve the outlined energy efficiency objectives.

The third distinct characteristic of Energiewende is the process of "Democratization" of energy. The concept of energy democracy aligns with the idea of decentralized, citizen-centric energy generation, primarily for personal use or use within a community collective. As previously stated, net metering provisions allow self-generating consumers to sell excess energy back to the primary grid. The democratization of energy is pursued with the intention of stimulating a competitive energy market that caters to the public welfare.

The fourth and final defining aspect of the Energiewende is the promotion of innovative energy technologies.[12] Energiewende functions as a catalyst for the development of emergent technologies by offering technology-specific incentives and bolstering R&D support. These include advanced chemical batteries, Power-to-X technologies (such as hydrogen and methane), electric and hydrogen mobility solutions, Smart Grids, and blockchain-based digital decentralization. The proliferation of these emerging technologies is expected to not only enhance the German

---

[11] World Energy Council, Issues Monitor 2020: Decoding New Signals of Change, 2020, p. 87; Cassel (2018), p. 25.; Eichhammer (2015), p. 29.

[12] See: Bundesministerium für Wirtschaft und Energie, Zweiter Fortschrittsbericht 'Energie der Zukunft', 2018, p. 220; DENA, Die Energiewende – Das neue System gestalten. Das deutsche Energiesystem im Jahr 2050: klimafreundlich, sicher und wirtschaftlich. Die Deutsche Energie-Agentur GmbH (dena) skizziert den Weg, 2019, p. 34; Müller (2010), p. 65; Schiffer (2018), p. 522; Säcker (2016).

industrial sector but boost export capabilities as well, thereby driving economic growth and employment.

The following issues represent key debates that surround the concept of Energiewende in Germany:

The first discussion regarding Energiewende concerns its efficiency. "Efficiency" refers to the program's success in achieving its stated objectives. The fundamental goal of Energiewende is to establish an environmentally friendly energy infrastructure. Some views assert that Energiewende's methods do not sufficiently fulfill the efficiency criterion, especially when compared with alternative strategies. The primary point of contention is that the rapid expansion of renewables was less efficient than potential carbon pricing schemes.[13] However, this opinion does not adequately acknowledge the significance of Energiewende's renewable energy expansion. Given that the energy sector is the primary source of GHG emissions, the shift towards renewables is strategically sound. Complementary strategies, such as carbon pricing schemes, should not be considered as alternatives to promoting green electricity but rather as supplementary mechanisms.

One methodological critique of Energiewende is that the promotion of green energy should be market-oriented and competitive. This approach, according to a majority of economists, would facilitate promotion at lower costs and higher efficiency.[14] Tendering and carbon pricing are viewed as effective mechanisms to achieve this aim. As discussed later, Germany successfully transitioned from FITs to a tendering system, at least for medium to large-sized projects.

The second issue is whether Energiewende creates geopolitical risks through the decommissioning of the country's fossil-fuel and nuclear energy capacities. To a certain extent, natural gas (via direct imports or in LNG form) is envisioned as a backup power source, considered a practical substitute for coal and nuclear energy. Undeniably, natural gas plants do not emit as much GHG emissions as their coal counterparts. They are simpler to construct and operate, typically encountering limited public resistance. When compared to nuclear energy plants, gas plants hold the upper hand as they pose no risk of nuclear meltdown and do not present substantial waste management issues.

However, the drawback of Germany's natural gas power plants is that they rely on imported fuel, engendering energy security risks. As mentioned earlier, by 2038, Germany intends to phase out nuclear and coal energy sources. This could lead to two potential outcomes. In a "business-as-usual" scenario, it could exacerbate Germany's dependency on imported gas, subsequently invoking geopolitical risks. Alternatively, in a technologically optimistic scenario, significant advancements in energy storage technologies, coupled with the expansion of renewables, could see Germany dismantle its nuclear and coal industries and reduce dependency on foreign gas. The future technological and geopolitical implications of Energiewende remain to be seen.

---

[13] Morey and Kirsch (2014).

[14] Heinrich Böll-Stiftung, Zukunft der Energiewende, 2017, p. 8.

The third issue surrounding Energiewende concerns its coherence. It is worth restating that the cornerstone of the Energiewende is the establishment of an environmentally friendly energy infrastructure. It is evident that nuclear and carbon industries have inherent environmental risks; thus, a detailed enumeration is unnecessary here. In brief, nuclear energy is a cause for concern due to its potential for meltdowns and waste management issues. The coal industry, conversely, results in extensive land use and significant GHG emissions. The questions posed are: Which risk is more tolerable, and which is more compatible with the objectives of Energiewende? The coal industry is entirely inconsistent with the goals of Energiewende due to its substantial GHG emissions. The persistence of the coal industry could signify Germany's retreat from its environmental targets, especially within the context of climate change. Alternatively, nuclear energy could potentially serve as a "bridge technology", providing a buffer against the intermittency of renewables until energy storage technologies mature. At this juncture, the plan to phase out nuclear energy by 2022 while allowing a gradual phase-out of the coal industry by 2038 was not entirely consistent.

However, it is crucial to recognize Germany's internal dynamics, such as employment within the coal industry, and the fact that dismantling a historical aspect of the economy requires time.[15] These dynamics have recently impeded the transition in the energy mix from conventional sources to renewables. The deployment of "Carbon Capture and Storage" (CCS) technology could serve as a mitigation strategy to offset the delayed phase-out from the carbon industry.[16] While the premature nuclear phase-out increased the cost of emission mitigation, the absence of long-term CCS capacity could amplify it.

Fourth, the affordability of the Energiewende constitutes an area of concern. According to EnWG § 1, the German energy industry is mandated to ensure the provision of affordable energy. Within the Energiewende context, affordability should be construed as the accessibility of green energy for lower-income groups. Over the past decade, Germany's energy costs have seen a rise, eliciting criticism against the Energiewende.[17] Even the Federal Audit Office (*Bundesrechnungshof*) has expressed concerns about the dwindling affordability of the Energiewende. In its 2021 report, the Federal Audit Office exhorted the Ministry about the affordability issues associated with the Energiewende, indicating eroding public support for the program.[18] Collectively, the affordability issue is Energiewende's "Achilles' heel." Public support is crucial for Energiewende's continuation since the program hinges on it.

---

[15] Braaksma and Fleming (2020), p. 277.

[16] Held (2021).

[17] Schmidt (2018), p. 87; The European Commission, Mission-oriented R&I policies: In-depth case studies - Case Study Report - Energiewende, 2018, p. 47.

[18] Bundesrechnungshof (2021) Bund steuert Energiewende weiterhin unzureichend. https://www.bundesrechnungshof.de/de/veroeffentlichungen/produkte/sonderberichte/2021/bund-steuert-energiewende-weiterhin-unzureichend.

According to the Federal Audit Office report, approximately 75% of an average household's energy bill is composed of taxes, green energy surcharges, and network charges. Measures to reduce the green electricity surcharge could be envisaged.[19] One method could involve higher compensation from the treasury, thereby increasing taxpayer burden, which finally took place in 2022 as will be mentioned below. Alternatively, a "social waiver" for low-income households could be proposed.

Fifth, Energiewende introduces the issue of geographical energy capacity mismatch. Northern Germany, particularly offshore, is endowed with wind resources, while Southern Germany, more abundant in solar energy, generates a significant proportion of its energy from nuclear and coal sources. The phasing out of coal and nuclear energy, along with the swift expansion of wind energy in the north and solar energy in the south, creates this mismatch. The mismatch would be less problematic if Germany had a more robust electricity transmission infrastructure between regions and neighboring countries.[20]

However, Germany's national electricity grid capacity is currently constrained. In some instances, this results in negative electricity prices in some seasons as surplus electricity cannot be transferred to southern distributors. Germany's strategy to mitigate this issue involves constructing a new, smarter, more resilient grid with higher transmission capacity.[21]

Naturally, this undertaking is fraught with challenges. Under Germany's federal structure, national-level projects may face obstruction due to local legislation. The German "Planning Law" poses many limitations for such initiatives. Additionally, local communities often resist the installation of transmission lines across their land (i.e., the "not in my backyard" phenomenon). Politically, it also proves challenging to persuade local policymakers and citizens.[22] Whether Germany will succeed in its new grid venture remains to be seen. However, constructing a new smart grid with underground lines instead of overhead lines entails significant costs. These costs will be passed on to the end consumer through network charges, risking public support for the Energiewende.

Sixth, the longevity of the promotion schemes and what follows after their termination are questioned. Investors generally seek legal security and a level playing field. The question in Germany revolves around the sustainability of these

[19] Bundesministerium für Wirtschaft und Energie (2021) Prüfung der Energiewende durch den Bundesrechnungshof: Fakten und Informationen. https://www.bmwi.de/Redaktion/DE/Downloads/P-R/pruefung-der-energiewende-durch-brh.html.

[20] Sopher (2015); German Development Institute, Germany's Green Industrial Policy Stable Policies – Turbulent Markets: The Costs and Benefits of Promoting Solar PV and Wind Energy, 2014.

[21] DENA, Die Energiewende – Das neue System gestalten. Das deutsche Energiesystem im Jahr 2050: klimafreundlich, sicher und wirtschaftlich. Die Deutsche Energie-Agentur GmbH (dena) skizziert den Weg, 2019; Bundesministerium für Wirtschaft und Energie, Fünfter Monitoring-Bericht zur Energiewende: Die Energie der Zukunft, 2015.

[22] Koch (2020).

promotion schemes. Solar energy promotion schemes were withdrawn in some EU Member States, such as Spain and Czechia, leading to numerous investment arbitration claims. While there is no indication that Germany plans to retroactively withdraw its promotion schemes, they experience amendments every few years (e.g., EEG 2014, 2017, 2021, 2023), which apply to future investors. At the very least, this suggests that the future environment for green investment in Germany may not be as stable as some would hope, even though the guarantees are retroactively protected.

Seventh, another potential issue with the Energiewende is the possibility of carbon and nuclear leakage to other EU Member States. There are times when Germany imports electricity from France, a nation reliant on nuclear energy, and Poland, where coal still makes up half of the electricity mix. Furthermore, Poland is considering developing its nuclear energy capacity by 2033. Consequently, the rapid advancement of renewables in Germany with a slower rate of storage deployment leads to a partial dependence on coal and nuclear energy from its neighbors on days with low solar or wind power. This situation contradicts Germany's environmental and climate objectives. To address this issue, harmonization of energy policies across Europe is critical. However, developing storage technologies is the most effective solution to eliminating the need for imported conventional energy. Increased storage capacity would serve as a counterbalancing factor that should be considered alongside the rapid expansion of renewable energy.

Finally, discussions persist around the democratic nature of Energiewende. One argument suggests that Energiewende was an agenda conceived and implemented by bureaucrats and technocrats, with only symbolic public participation. The discourse around the initiative often intensifies when energy prices escalate.

Assessing the success of the Energiewende brings mixed opinions and could be considered subjective to a degree. One perspective views the Energiewende as falling short, mainly when assessed from the angle of catalyzing an efficient shift towards a green economy.[23] However, this viewpoint typically originated before the EEG 2012. After the enactment of EEG 2012, market-oriented mechanisms gained prominence in the German energy promotion system, subsequently boosting efficiency.

Another perspective suggests that the Energiewende impairs the global competitiveness of the German industry. However, within the span of 20 years since the inception of the EEG, renewables have evolved to become a primary electricity source in Germany.[24] This achievement would not have been conceivable without promotion schemes and the guiding principles of the Energiewende to motivate policymakers. Moreover, Energiewende has stimulated significant employment shifts, creating new job opportunities and transitioning traditional roles into new, green, high-tech positions. Significant strides have been made towards energy

[23] Frondel et al. (2010); Frondel et al. (2014).

[24] Egerer et al. (2018).

efficiency and GHG emission reduction targets.[25] Therefore, one could reasonably regard the Energiewende as a program of modest success with ongoing challenges. Its economic downsides, particularly the high utility prices, may be resolved over time, given the decreasing trend in renewable energy investment costs and installations exiting FIT guarantees to compete in the market to sell their output.

In essence, the Energiewende represents a long-term investment.[26] It is crucial not to overlook the ecological benefits of the Energiewende, such as the elimination of hidden negative externalities from the German industry. The true effects of the Energiewende will appear over time. However, the challenges associated with it must be addressed without delay to expand public support and make the program more resilient for at least two decades to come.

6.2 Legal Background

Prior to delving into the details of Germany's promotion of green electricity initiatives, it is imperative to establish an understanding of the legal foundation underlying German energy law. The aim of this part is to offer insights into German energy law, specifically focusing on significant milestones and regulatory provisions such as the EEG and other relevant Energiewende acts. However, the developmental trajectory of these enactments will be subjected to a comprehensive examination in the subsequent subchapter. Considering the evolution of EU energy law is equally critical, given its impact on Germany's energy policies.

The German Basic Law (*Grundgesetz*, GG) of 1949 does not explicitly include a clause about the energy sector; however, certain clauses can be interpreted as applicable to this field.[27] The GG Article 2(2) stipulates that "Every person shall have the right to life and physical integrity." The right to access energy can potentially be extrapolated from this clause under the auspices of the right to physical integrity.

GG Article 20(1) classifies Germany as a social state, which may lay the foundation for affordable and accessible energy provisions. Furthermore, GG Article 20a obligates the state to safeguard the environment, stipulating that the state, bearing in mind its responsibility towards future generations, shall protect the natural foundations of life and animals. This mandate could potentially be extended to policymaking in the energy sector, positioning the state as a promulgator of environmental and climate-friendly energy policies.

Moreover, GG Article 28(2) upholds the principle of local self-government, which is of critical importance for numerous facets of the promotion of green electricity, including energy communities. Furthermore, GG Article 74(1)

---

[25] Oschmann (2010).

[26] Kemfert et al. (2018), p. 377.

[27] Altenschmidt (2015).

(11) stipulates that concurrent legislative power shall encompass "the law relating to economic matters (mining, industry, energy, crafts, trades, commerce, banking, stock exchanges, and private insurance)", shared between the federal government and states. GG Article 72(1) posits that the states retain the power to legislate until and unless the Federation enacts a law by exercising its legislative power. Conversely, GG Article 72(2) affirms the Federation's right to legislate on energy matters if and when the establishment of equivalent living conditions throughout the federal territory or the maintenance of legal or economic unity necessitates federal regulation in the national interest. Therefore, GG Articles 72 and 74 must be comprehensively understood in conjunction to determine the boundaries of Federal legislative power regarding energy matters. Factors such as the affordability and accessibility of energy, as well as energy security, may serve as the impetus for federal energy legislation.

The Federal Constitutional Court of Germany (*Bundesverfassungsgericht*, BVerfG) has previously underlined the preservation of energy supply as a "public interest of paramount significance", analogously associating the need for energy with the universal demand for daily sustenance.[28] In one particular decision, energy supply was characterized as an essential public service that is "indispensable for ensuring a dignified existence".[29] Nevertheless, BVerfG does not categorize the energy sector as an "administrative monopoly" similar to railroads or post, thus permitting its unbundling.[30]

As one of the first industrialized nations, Germany has been actively engaged in large-scale energy production and consumption. In the late nineteenth century, the inception of the first electricity companies, such as the "AG Städtische Betriebswerke" in Berlin, marked the initiation of the energy sector. These enterprises operated under minimal regulatory oversight, collaborating locally with states (*Länder*) and city municipalities. Their operations spanned divided geographical markets, delineated by concession and demarcation contracts with local administrations and other companies.

The first significant federal legislation, the Energy Industry Act of 1935 (*Energiewirtschaftsgesetz*, EnWG), emerged to regulate the energy sector. This act reinforced the concession system, imposing expanded responsibilities on the supply companies. Given the segmented and vertically integrated nature of the supply areas, competition between energy companies was non-existent. In terms of responsibilities, energy companies were obliged to connect energy producers and consumers to the grid within their respective supply areas. Additionally, the EnWG 1935 introduced public supervision over electricity and gas prices.[31] This straightforward and effective act, appropriate for its era, remained in force with minor amendments until 1998.

---

[28] Pielow et al. (2019).

[29] Dümke (2015), p. 48.

[30] Pielow et al. (2019).

[31] See: Pritzsche and Vacha (2017), p. 15; Dümke (2015), p. 47; Schneider et al. (2013), p. 4.

Throughout the 1990s, the initial European directives for the internal energy market were instituted.[32] These directives mandated Germany to establish regulations fostering competitive, transparent energy markets. Among the four energy directives introduced during that decade, the Internal Market in Electricity Directive was particularly impactful.[33] This directive compelled European states to (1) unbundle energy production, transmission, and distribution; (2) foster competition at the producer level; (3) regulate third parties' access rights to the grid; and (4) open the market to facilitate the creation of a unified European electricity market.

These directives required Germany to revise the EnWG 1935 and competition law, and to incorporate the new stipulations into national law. The EnWG 1998 introduced comprehensive changes. Most notably, the central principles of German energy law were overhauled, and the energy industry underwent a "liberalization" process.[34] The prohibitions on demarcation agreements, which had previously segmented the geographical markets, were lifted. Energy cartels were outlawed to facilitate competition in energy markets. The companies vertically integrated in generation, transmission, and distribution were unbundled. The scope of concession agreements was limited to matters regarding the use of public roads and the installation of energy cables.

Further comprehensive amendments to the EnWG were made in 2005. The EnWG 2005 established an array of rules to regulate the energy sector. Significantly, the Federal Network Agency (*Bundesnetzagentur*, BnetzA) was instituted to oversee and regulate "network industries" at the federal level, including energy, telecommunications, water, and railroads.

In 2009, the European Union adopted the "Third Energy Package," encompassing the Electricity Regulation, Electricity Directive, and the "Agency for the Cooperation of Energy Regulators" (ACER) Regulation.[35] The first two stipulations necessitated further unbundling. Unbundling, within the context of the Third Energy Package, can be conceptualized in terms of three distinct methods:

[32] 90/547/EEC of 29 October 1990, Council Directive on the transit of electricity through transmission grids. 92/13/EEC of 25 February 1992, Council Directive coordinating the laws, regulations and administrative provisions relating to the application of Community rules on the procurement procedures of entities operating in the water, energy, transport and telecommunications sectors. 98/30/EC of 22 June 1998, Directive of the European Parliament and concerning common rules for the internal market in natural gas.

[33] 96/92/EC of 19 December 1996, Directive concerning common rules for the internal market in electricity.

[34] von Danwitz (2006), p. 423.

[35] Regulation (EC) No 714/2009 of 13 July 2009 on conditions for access to the network for cross-border exchanges in electricity and repealing Regulation (EC) No 1228/2003.; Directive 2009/72/ of 13 July 2009 concerning common rules for the internal market in electricity and repealing Directive 2003/54/EC.; Regulation (EC) No 713/2009 of 13 July 2009 establishing an Agency for the Cooperation of Energy Regulators.

1. The ownership unbundling method, which entailed the split of vertically integrated energy companies by compelling them to divest (i.e., exit) their subsidiary companies.
2. The "independent system operator" method, in which the energy supplier also owns the transmission network but separates it as an independent entity.
3. The independent transmission system operator method, wherein the parent company retains ownership of a subsidiary transmission company, yet all pivotal decisions are independently made by the subsidiary.

In 2011, the German government announced a new "Energy Package." Subsequent to this announcement, significant amendments were incorporated into the EnWG and related energy legislation. A commitment to phase out nuclear energy was an integral component of this package, complemented by plans to augment the share of renewable energy in the energy mix and construct a new energy grid network.[36]

The EnWG 2011 is, effectively, Germany's "energy constitution." Although it pertains to the generation, transmission, and distribution of electricity and gas, its primary focus is electricity.[37] Section 1(1) EnWG outlines the objectives of German energy law, asserting that the Act aims to ensure the most secure, affordable, consumer-friendly, efficient, and environmentally friendly grid-based supply of electricity and gas to the public, which should progressively rely on renewable energies. Moreover, Section 1(2) of the EnWG elucidates the objectives of German energy grid regulation, stating that the regulation of electricity and gas supply grids serves to ensure effective, undistorted competition in the supply of electricity and gas and the long-term efficient and reliable operation of energy supply networks.

It is evident that German energy law is a synthesis of the national law and EU law. In recognition of this, Section 1(3) EnWG highlights the role of the EU law in German electricity regulation, emphasizing that another purpose of the Act is the implementation and application of the EU law in the field of grid-based energy supply.

Section 1(4) EnWG describes the strategies to accomplish the objectives laid out in Section 1(1). According to this subsection, German energy authorities should attempt to facilitate the market-oriented formation of prices and balance supply against demand. The authorities should operate in the most environmentally sound, grid-compatible, efficient, and flexible manner possible, to the extent necessary to ensure the security and reliability of the electricity supply system and make strategic investments in neighboring countries. Section 1(a)(1) EnWG governs the principles of the electricity market, reaffirming that prices should be determined via market-oriented, competitive, transparent methods and that supply should be balanced against demand.

Having elucidated the general characteristics of the EnWG, attention can now be turned to the federal authorities that oversee energy matters in Germany. The

[36] Pritzsche and Vacha (2017), p. 21; Petersen and Thomas (2014), p. 52.

[37] Theobald and Danner (2019).

primary authority responsible for shaping the energy sector resides at the ministerial level. The duties and competencies related to the energy sector are consolidated within one ministry: the Federal Ministry for Economic Affairs and Climate Action (*Bundesministerium für Wirtschaft und Klimaschutz,* BMWK). Following the BMWK, the BnetzA is arguably the second most crucial entity concerning energy matters. Since 2005, the BnetzA, under the administrative jurisdiction of the BMWK, has been responsible for monitoring and regulating the electricity industry. Its responsibilities include, inter alia: (1) certification of transmission system operators, (2) approval of grid fees, (3) ensuring unrestricted network access for all suppliers and consumers, (4) improving the grid, and (5) organizing auctions for new capacity under the EEG.

State Regulatory Authorities (*Landesregulierungsbehörden*) operate at the state level, overseeing energy companies that serve no more than 100,000 customers or projects that do not extend to other states. Above these thresholds, the BnetzA assumes responsibility. In some states, such as Berlin and Hamburg, which chose not to establish a State Regulatory Authority, the BnetzA also regulates energy issues falling under the aforementioned de minimis threshold.[38]

Market formation in Germany, as previously mentioned, has been liberalized. The three pillars of the electricity industry—generation, transmission, and distribution—are unbundled. A diverse array of entities, from large and small companies to municipalities, communities, collectives, and individual citizens, generate and sell electricity through various mechanisms such as market exchanges, FITs, PPAs, and net metering. Nevertheless, five major electricity production companies dominate the landscape: RWE, E.ON, Vattenfall, LEAG, and EnBW (i.e., the "Big Five"), accounting for almost 70% of total generation. The number of distribution system operators (DSOs) is significant, with 865 DSOs active in Germany. Conversely, transmission system operators (TSOs) are limited, with only four companies - TenneT, 50Hertz, Amprion, and TransnetBW - functioning as TSOs.[39]

The liberalization of the energy market has led to the development of energy exchange mechanisms in Germany. The European Energy Exchange (EEX) dictates the price of electricity and trades in specific energy types, emission certificates, and physical commodities like coal and oil. The regulation of electricity trade in Germany falls under the remit of the EnWG and the Electricity Market Law (*Gesetz zur Weiterentwicklung des Strommarktes*, Strommarktgesetz) of 2016.[40] Due to the market's liberalization on the demand side, end-consumers in Germany are able to choose energy from various sources. For instance, a customer of an energy company can opt for a plan that guarantees a 100% renewable energy supply.

The energy law - climate law nexus is another facet of the German energy economy. A key legislative source for German emission control is the Federal Emission Control Act (*Bundes-Immissionsschutzgesetz*, BImSchG) enacted in

[38] Pielow et al. (2019).

[39] Bader (2019).

[40] Kühling (2019).

1974. This act fundamentally safeguards air quality whilst concurrently placing restrictions on noise, heat, and light pollution.[41] According to §4 BImSchG, hazardous installations contributing to these emissions are conventionally prohibited; nevertheless, exemptions permitting the construction and operation of such facilities may be granted to investors.

When examining green electricity, a range of energy sources could be deemed "hazardous installations" as stipulated by the supporting regulation of the BImSchG, specifically, the 4th Regulation on the Application of Federal Emission Control Act (*Vierte Verordnung zur Durchführung des Bundes-Immissionsschutzgesetzes*, BImSchV), implemented in 2017. Instances include wind energy towers, which under certain conditions, must secure permits for construction and operation.[42] Permits are also mandatory for biogas, biomass, and waste gas plants.

An additional significant element of German energy law involves planning for new transmission capacity.[43] As previously noted, Germany is dealing with the ramifications of the coal and nuclear phase-outs, as electricity generation faces inconsistency due to the intermittent nature of renewable sources. As early as 2009, it was evident that new transmission capacity was a pressing requirement. Consequently, the Energy Line Expansion Act (*Energieleitungsausbaugesetz*, EnLAG) was enacted in the same year. The EnLAG aimed to expedite the evolution of transmission and proposed 22 renovation and construction projects for high-voltage electricity transmission lines. A cursory examination of the geographic alignment of these projects reveals a distinct north-south orientation, reflecting Germany's strategy to harmonize the wind-rich north with the solar-rich south. A secondary objective was to attain a degree of interoperability for the pan-European electricity grid, known as the ENTSO-E. §1(2) EnLAG furnishes the necessary legal foundation for these projects, designating them as both "urgent and necessary".

Subsequent legislative progression towards grid expansion was marked by the introduction of the Grid Expansion Acceleration Act (*Netzausbaubeschleunigungsgesetz Übertragungsnetz*, NABEG) in 2011. Under § 18 and subsequent sections of the NABEG, the competence to approve grid expansion projects is vested in the BnetzA. In this context, §§ 4 – 17 NABEG set forth a uniform, federal planning procedure. A 2019 amendment to the NABEG further elaborated on the roles and responsibilities of the BnetzA in matters relating to transmission grid expansion and introduced novel rules for the protection of environmental standards during these processes.[44]

The third legislative act promoting grid expansion in Germany was the Federal Requirements Plan Act (*Bundesbedarfsplangesetz*, BBPlG), enacted in 2013. In essence, the BBPlG can be regarded as an extension of the EnLAG, encompassing a list of active projects eligible for fast approval at the federal level. Once again,

---

[41] Fischer (2018), p. 856.

[42] Franke (2018).

[43] Kloepfer (2011), p. 328.

[44] See: Kelly and Schmidt (2019).

these projects predominantly adhere to a North-South orientation, advancing the integration of green electricity sources. Some projects outlined in the BBPlG aim to bolster a pan-European electricity grid. For instance, one project facilitates a connection between the German high-voltage grid and its Danish counterpart, while another establishes a similar linkage with Austria.

However, the EnLAG, NABEG, and BBPlG are exceptions rather than the rule. The primary legal framework for network expansion is delineated in EnWG, referencing the Administrative Procedure Act (*Verwaltungsverfahrensgesetz*, VwVfG) of 1976. According to this "conventional process", transmission network operators are obligated to annually present a joint national network development plan. This plan must enumerate all effective measures necessary for requirement-based optimization, reinforcement, and network expansion, ensuring safe and reliable operation for the ensuing decade, as mandated by § 12b EnWG. The BnetzA scrutinizes this network development plan and submits it as a proposal for a federal requirement plan to the federal government. Subsequently, at a minimum of every 3 years, the federal government presents this draft to the federal parliament (§ 12e EnWG). For cross-border or high-voltage lines as designated in the BBPlG, federal technical planning is conducted to ascertain the route corridors (§§ 4 ff. NABEG). Upon provisional approval from the *Bundesrat*, plan approval is executed by the BnetzA (§§ 18 ff. NABEG). For transmission lines at the state level, the authority of the states remains intact as per § 43 EnWG. In accordance with §§ 72 ff. VwVfG, a "plan approval committee" is convened to evaluate the grid expansion plan.[45]

Lastly, as outlined in §§ 4 ff. BImSchG, onshore wind power towers with a height exceeding 50 meters, as well as biogas and biomass plants, are subjected to a federal approval process. State approval is required for wind power towers standing between 10–50 meters tall. Micro wind towers measuring less than 10 meters in height are typically exempt from approval mandates.[46] As for offshore wind power facilities, approval competence is vested in the Federal Maritime and Hydrographic Agency (*Bundesamt für Seeschifffahrt und Hydrographie*, BSH).

In sum, German planning law plays a substantial role in Energiewende. Planning stipulations act as a stumbling block, causing delays in the energy transition due to the expensive and time-consuming nature of grid expansion procedures. Another facet of planning law is the empowerment of German federal bodies, a stark contrast to the situation at the generation level. Although heavily regulated, the German energy industry does not exhibit the traits of a "Planned Economy" (*Planwirtschaft*).[47] It is true that at the generation level, competition is still lacking. However, free-market competition at the grid level is untenable due to the inherent monopoly character of these activities. Instead, German federal bodies aim to establish "regulatory competition," e.g., tendering processes. Even in the absence

[45]Hirschfeld and Heidrich (2013).

[46]Stecher (2015).

[47]Fehling (2014).

of a genuine competitive market, regulatory frameworks can be designed to simulate competition, thereby enhancing efficiency, mitigating costs, and fostering innovation.

6.3 Promotion Schemes and Debates

This subchapter delves into the evolution of green electricity promotion in Germany, taking into account pivotal legislative landmarks in the realm of green electricity. The notable acts in this respect include the StromEinspG, EEG, KWKG, and WindSeeG. Naturally, the emphasis of this subchapter will be on the EEG 2023, given its significance as the most recent and substantial legislation concerning green electricity promotion.

Germany's expertise is not confined to energy regulation but also extends to the promotion of green electricity. The promotion of green electricity in Germany commenced in 1990 with the introduction of the StromEinspG. This legislation mandated electricity suppliers to procure electricity from green electricity producers in exchange for a proportion of the electricity market price. The StromEinspG underwent considerable amendments in 1998. Post the unbundling accomplished by the EnWG amendment, the obligation to purchase green electricity shifted from electricity supply companies to grid operators. Grid operators were then obligated to purchase merely 5% of the electricity they sold from renewable sources. This was the so-called "hardship clause" encapsulated in the StromEinspG.[48]

Unfortunately, the StromEinspG failed to effectively stimulate the promotion of green electricity, attributable primarily to two reasons. Firstly, the act's remuneration system, which entailed paying a certain percentage of the market price of electricity, generated insufficient incentives. Secondly, the "5% limit" on green electricity posed significant challenges to expanding green electricity in certain regions.

Considering the structural inefficiencies of the StromEinspG in promoting green electricity, it was supplanted by the Erneuerbare-Energien-Gesetz (EEG) in 2000. The EEG leaned on a typical FIT system as opposed to the market price-fixed remuneration employed by the StromEinspG. Four dynamics underpinned the EEG 2000. First, it stipulated a fixed tariff for green electricity, providing degressive remuneration over a span of 20 years. Second, it granted unconditional priority to green electricity. Third, it transferred the remuneration obligation from grid operators to TSOs and, in turn, to energy supply companies. The fourth and final dynamic was the introduction of the "direct marketing option", allowing electricity supply companies to purchase at least half their electricity mix from renewable sources, thereby exempting them from FIT obligations.[49]

---

[48] Hazrat (2017), p. 127.

[49] Pielow et al. (2019); Pritzsche and Vacha (2017), p. 58; Hazrat (2017), p. 127.

The EEG was subjected to two amendments in 2003. The first amendment instituted the so-called "special compensation scheme" for energy-intensive enterprises, aiming to reduce their EEG costs. The second amendment bolstered the tariff rate for solar energy installations.[50]

The EEG 2000 was superseded in 2004, with a new EEG coming into effect. While the core tenets of the EEG 2000 remained intact, the EEG 2004 introduced some minor modifications. The remuneration rates for all types of renewable energy, save for wind energy, saw an uptick with the enactment of the EEG 2004. This act also set national renewable energy targets (12.5% by 2010 and 20% by 2020). The "energy-intensive enterprises" exception introduced by the EEG 2000 was extended to the railroad industry. The EEG 2004 underwent an amendment in 2006, which further broadened the energy-intensive enterprise exception and further diminished their costs. This, in turn, escalated the EEG costs for end consumers who were ineligible for this exception.

The EEG of 2009 superseded the 2004 version and was incorporated into the "Climate and Energy Package." Its primary objective was to amplify renewable electricity production to at least 30% by 2020. This aim necessitated a more efficient and effective remuneration of green electricity producers and an increased market integration of renewable energy sources. Despite retaining the overall structure of its 2004 counterpart, the EEG 2009 elaborated on remuneration rules to bolster legal certainty. This new legislation conferred additional investment security by extending the FIT system to certain levels of green electricity generation, particularly from wind energy, which had previously been governed by agreements. This signaled the final expansion of the FIT system in Germany before its subsequent retraction. Additionally, the market sale of green electricity was subject to new regulations to curtail the "cherry-picking" of favorable prices and conditions. The EEG 2009 also permitted remuneration for the self-utilization of solar energy.

Concurrently in 2009, the Compensation Mechanism Ordinance (*Ausgleichsmechanismusverordnung*, AusglMechV) was enacted. Before this compensation system, energy suppliers were required to purchase green electricity from TSOs and pay the price (including remuneration) directly. Per the AusglMechV, the TSOs sell electricity directly on the electricity exchange and the energy suppliers settle the difference between the sale price and the EEG benefit.

The EEG 2009 was amended in 2010 with the "Photovoltaic Amendment," designed to adapt the EEG 2009 to the rapidly evolving photovoltaic equipment market. The escalating efficiency and competition within the market had precipitated a sharp decline in costs and prices for solar energy equipment, rendering the remuneration for solar energy excessive. Thus, the amendment resulted in a reduction in remuneration for solar energy.

The EEG 2012 replaced the EEG 2009, with the aim of making energy transition more market-oriented, cost-effective, and transparent while simultaneously maintaining the brisk pace of transition. The act introduced new green electricity

[50] Hazrat (2017), pp. 130–131.

share targets: 35% by 2020, 50% by 2030, 65% by 2040, and 80% by 2050. While preserving the tariff system of the EEG 2009, the tariffs were streamlined, adjusted, and broadly reduced. The degression rates were primarily amplified, except in the case of geothermal energy, where they were postponed.[51] Nevertheless, the EEG 2012 did herald a significant novelty: the Feed-in Premium system. The act offered enhanced incentives to green electricity producers to sell their electricity directly in the market. The FIPs were designed to compensate for the difference between the market price and the tariff remuneration. In simpler terms, the "moving" premium mirrored the gap between the technology-specific feed-in tariff remuneration and the typically lower market price.

The EEG 2012 expanded the exemption for energy-intensive enterprises from the EEG surcharge, making it accessible for small and medium-sized enterprises. The threshold of 10 GWh was reduced to 1 GWh, and the limit for the electricity cost share was lowered from 15% to 14%. In the same year, the EEG 2012 underwent an amendment, which came into effect on 1 April 2012 and lowered the remuneration levels for solar installations.[52] An overall expansion target of 52,000 MW was set for solar installations, after which the remuneration for new plants would decrease to zero.

The EEG 2014 replaced the EEG 2012, driven by a grand coalition that aligned on objectives of cost dynamics, an efficient expansion management scheme through corridors, and the promotion of market integration. The primary aim of the EEG 2014 was to enhance the affordability of energy alongside the expansion of renewables. The law established annual expansion corridors for onshore and offshore wind installations, increasing planning security for investors and network operators. Technology-differentiated expansion targets were introduced to regulate the expansion and emphasize the focus on wind energy, which was expected to hold a high potential for cost reduction. However, the most noteworthy novelty in the EEG 2014 was the introduction of a tendering scheme and the compulsory direct marketing of green electricity. The FIT system was limited in the EEG 2014, making the FIP the primary system. Tendering was mandatory only for a pilot amount of solar energy, approximately 400 MW. Another new development was the abolition of the "green electricity privilege" system, as the FIP system was deemed more effective in promoting market integration. Lastly, the threshold for eligibility for the energy-intensive enterprise exception was raised in an effort to harmonize the EEG 2014 with the EU law.

The EEG 2017 introduced significant changes to the previous legislation, primarily characterized by the introduction of "tendering for new capacity" and "tendering for market premia" schemes.[53] Under the new capacity scheme, as per § 22 of EEG 2017, new capacity rights for wind and photovoltaic installations with a capacity of 750 kW or more, and biomass installations with a capacity of 150 kW

---

[51] Ibid., p. 139.

[52] Pielow et al. (2019).

[53] Bahmer and Loers (2017).

or more, were allocated through a competitive tendering process. For smaller installations, the FIP system from EEG 2014 applied, except for the FIT for "micro" installations and grandfathering rights for existing FIT recipients. The tendering process under the EEG 2017 was technology-specific and was facilitated by the BNetzA, with sufficient notice given. Notably, a portion of the tenders between 2018–2020 was technology-neutral, opening up possibilities for both solar and onshore wind entries. The transition to a tendering scheme was designed to control the rapid expansion of renewable energy sources in a way that was compatible with the existing grid. In particular, the expansion of wind installations in northern Germany was heavily regulated and planned ahead with the tendering system.

The EEG 2017 also established development corridors for specific technologies. For instance, one of the objectives was to achieve an annual gross build of new solar installations with an installed capacity of 2500 megawatts as per § 4(3). In line with § 22, the BNetzA conducted the tendering for premia (i.e., "competition-based determination of the market premium") in Germany. Furthermore, the EEG 2017 introduced a "tendering for new capacity" scheme, with expansion corridors for new capacity set each year (as per § 28).

The EEG 2021, which came into effect on 1 January 2021, aimed for a continuous, cost-efficient, and grid-compatible expansion of green electricity, aligning with long-term climate goals. The new act set forth two targets: achieving a 65% green electricity share in gross electricity consumption by 2030 and ensuring 100% greenhouse gas emission-free electricity generation by 2050. The EEG 2021 laid down four principles:

(1) The integration of green electricity into the grid,
(2) The direct marketing of green electricity,
(3) Setting remuneration for green electricity via tenders targeting a diversity of investors,
(4) Keeping the price of green electricity as low as possible while considering macroeconomic factors.

One of the most significant elements of the EEG 2021 was the expansion paths (or development corridors) for specific renewable energy sources, set through tendering volumes. Similar to the EEG 2017, the primary promotion scheme involved tendering for a sliding premium on the market price. The EEG 2021 increased the threshold for solar photovoltaic installation tenders significantly, along with on-land wind project tenders. The expansion goals for 2030 were: 71 Gigawatts for on-land wind, 100 Gigawatts for solar photovoltaics, and 8.4 Gigawatts for biomass. This indicated a substantial growth compared to the EEG 2017. The EEG 2021 also included biomethane plants in the tendering scheme. While it reduced the maximum tender volumes for first-segment solar and onshore wind installations by 15–20%, it allowed the Federal Government to increase these values if necessary for achieving climate targets.

The EEG 2021, in § 39k, introduced a quota for southern wind and biomass projects, allocating 15–20% of the tenders to these projects, often referred to as the

"Southern Quota" (*Südquote*). This initiative represents a direct intervention to balance renewable energy generation across Germany, aiming to alleviate potential risks of grid congestion and instability.

The act also introduced two distinct segments for solar tenders. The first segment included ground-mounted installations or those mounted on structures other than buildings and noise barriers (§§ 37-38b). This segment carried over almost all of the tendering capacity from previous years.

The second segment comprised installations on buildings or noise barriers (§§ 38c-38i). Historically, this segment struggled to compete against the first segment. Therefore, the division of solar installations into two categories in the EEG 2021 promoted solar photovoltaic installations on buildings and noise barriers.

Additionally, the EEG 2021 allowed for the construction of first-segment solar power plants in proximity to motorways and railroads, increasing the range from 110 meters (as per EEG 2017) to 200 meters (§ 37(2)(c) EEG 2021). This change encouraged solar energy investments on idle land surrounding such transportation lines.

The EEG 2021 continued the process of tendering for renewable energy sources established in the EEG 2017. For distinct types of renewable energy sources, distinct regulations were outlined. Broadly, the procedure involved bidders registering with the BNetzA, securing necessary permits as per the BImSchG or zoning requirements, and providing a financial guarantee per kilowatt for their bid size.

This financial guarantee could take the form of a bank guarantee letter or a direct payment to the BNetzA suspense account. Penalties incurred in subsequent steps were deducted from this guarantee. In the tendering process, the award price equaled the bid price (a pay-as-bid system), and a static sealed, multiple-item process was carried out. The bidding also had a ceiling price. Once bids were accepted, the awardees had 30 months to implement the project, with penalties applicable after 24 months. These projects were awarded installed capacity in megawatts (MW).

The German government selected the "tendering for market premia" model for its "price discovery" potential, hoping to drive down prices for renewable energy. However, this model had its limitations. While it might be efficient for large installations, smaller and medium-sized projects often found the tendering process costly and bureaucratic, limiting its effectiveness for price discovery.

Another challenge was the continued use of technology-specific tenders. While the RED II encouraged technology-neutral allocation schemes, the German system largely maintained technology-specific tendering. While this specificity could aid the deployment of certain types of installations, it could potentially hinder price competition. For instance, newer or experimental technologies could struggle to compete with low-cost solar installations in Southern Germany or wind installations in Northern Germany. Therefore, these novel technologies would be promoted only through technology-specific tendering.

The EEG 2021 introduces some important provisions regarding the use and production of hydrogen. Under § 69b, hydrogen producers are granted a partial exemption from the EEG surcharge when procuring electricity. This initiative is particularly important for promoting the use of "green" hydrogen, which is hydrogen produced from water via an electrochemical process powered by renewable energy sources. As this production process is highly energy-intensive, the exemption from the EEG surcharge could be a significant incentive for further adoption of green hydrogen production.

However, the EEG 2021 also allowed for partial EEG surcharge exemptions for "blue" and "grey" hydrogen production in energy-intensive industries, reducing the surcharge to 15% of the total. Blue hydrogen is produced from water via an electrochemical process but powered by conventional energy sources such as nuclear power, whereas grey hydrogen is produced from fossil fuels. This suggests that Germany was interested in promoting hydrogen production from these alternative sources at the time of the amendment's inception.

Interestingly, Germany did not provide a direct promotion scheme for hydrogen production because it could lead to double promotion, which would contradict the RED II. The question then arises whether a surcharge waiver for hydrogen production is sufficient to support the European and German goals of increased hydrogen technology adoption. It might not be sufficient, and a relevant amendment in the RED III could be necessary, allowing member states to promote hydrogen production directly.

Regarding the post-promotion period for green electricity installations, the EEG 2021 included regulations for installations that have been operating for more than 20 years. While these installations will maintain their feed-in priority, they will be subject to a reduced feed-in tariff until the end of 2027 at the latest (§ 25).

Indeed, the EEG 2021 has faced criticism from various interest groups both during its development and after its implementation. One major point of criticism is that the proposed expansion paths for renewable energy set out in the amendment were not ambitious enough to meet necessary climate targets. Another concern is related to the surcharge system. Critics argue that the surcharge system for financing renewable energy expansion is inefficient, with some suggesting that this should be replaced by funding directly from the federal budget or switching to a carbon pricing mechanism. There are also concerns about the impacts of these surcharges on the competitiveness of German industry, with fears that they might encourage companies to relocate to EU member states or peripheral countries where energy costs are lower. The final view was that Germany could shift away from renewable energy promotion entirely and move towards direct market pricing. This perspective stemmed from concerns about maintaining the competitiveness of German industry and is indicative of broader debates about the best ways to transition to a low-carbon economy.

The EEG 2023 represents a pivotal amendment to the EEG 2021, enacted in July 2022. Some components of the amendment were promptly entered into force, with the remaining elements becoming effective as of 1 January 2023. This EEG 2023 ushers in a novel phase in the promotion of renewable energy, signaling a critical change in the trajectory of green electricity regulation. The EEG 2023 comprises a wide range of measures, strategically designed to alleviate the pressure on households and businesses. From a renewed parliamentary perspective, it was deemed essential to prioritize public interest and security considerations over private interests, thereby accelerating the expansion of renewables.

Projected increases in tender volumes for wind and solar energy are expected to persist until 2028/29 to achieve the novel expansion objective. The plan aims for at least 80% of Germany's electricity consumption to be derived from renewable energy by 2030, effectively doubling the current proportion of total consumption. This target is predicated on a proposed escalation in electricity production from 600 to 800 terawatts by the decade's end to support more electrified industrial processes, heat production, and electric mobility. Nevertheless, a focus on consumption targets, rather than generation targets, could be interpreted as a strategic maneuver to navigate the recent stagnation of renewable growth in Germany. This goal can be fulfilled through electricity imports complemented by acquiring guarantees of origin. In the same vein, the aspiration for nearly climate-neutral energy production by 2035 was removed during the legislative process. However, it is noteworthy that a new provision, § 1a EEG 2023, links greenhouse gas neutrality to the completion of the coal phase-out.

The EEG 2023 also makes provisions for innovative solutions that merge renewable energy sources with hydrogen and electricity storage. These solutions are eligible for funding under the EEG 2023, a strategy aimed at mitigating the unpredictable nature of electricity production using renewable energies. In the new legislative framework, generation plants using green hydrogen will be among the entities receiving financial support.

Substantially higher remuneration rates for new photovoltaic systems installed on rooftops from 30 July 2022 onwards have been ratified. This, in conjunction with the introduction of new regulations that facilitate a mix of systems with both full and partial feed-in, acts as a stimulus for comprehensive solar system installations on rooftops, including for private consumption.

The EEG 2023 also introduces new incentives aimed at enhancing local acceptance and implementation of the energy transition. Beginning in 2023, wind and solar projects operated by energy cooperatives will be exempt from tendering duties, fostering a less bureaucratic process. Furthermore, the provision for financial participation (i.e., paying levies to municipalities) is extended to onshore wind farms from 2023.

One of the most significant modifications in the EEG involves setting a definitive end date for the promotion of renewable energy sources. This timeline, expected to follow the coal phase-out in 2038, will presumably be influenced by market dynamics. It is important to note, however, that while this decision may act as a guiding principle, it does not confer any enforceable rights to individuals.

Lastly, the EEG 2023 maintains the principle of giving precedence to the development of renewables during the approval process. This accelerates the decision-making process and, as a novel feature of the amendment, now includes the planning and approval of hydropower plants.

In conclusion, the EEG 2023 marks a significant shift in the renewable energy landscape in Germany. It encapsulates ambitious targets, extensive legislative amendments, and innovative approaches to grid connection. Nonetheless, the full implications of this legislation will be unveiled with time, particularly concerning the phasing-out of green electricity promotion and the EU law implications following the abolishment of the green electricity surcharge, even though the Commission approved the EEG 2023 in September 2022 stating that the new state aid scheme is (1) necessary and appropriate to promote the production of renewable energy sources, reduce greenhouse gas emissions and contribute to better grid stability (2) proportionate as it is limited to the minimum necessary, and the positive effects of the scheme, in particular the positive environmental effects, outweigh its negative effects in terms of distortions to competition.[54]

The Energy Financing Act of 2022 (*Energiefinanzierungsgesetz*, EnFG), in this vein, was a considerable step toward altering the financing mechanism of green electricity. The EnFG effectively ended the EEG surcharge (*EEG Umlage*) regime and consolidated the financing requirements in the form of a fixed right for the TSOs from the Federal Government (§ 6). This means a reduction in electricity costs for consumers, which would necessitate an increase in tax income to promote existing and new renewable investments.

On another note, it is important to discuss the Combined Heat and Power Act (*Kraft-Wärme-Kopplungsgesetz*, KWKG 2023) within the context of renewable energy in Germany. The KWKG 2023 aims to increase net electricity generation from combined heat and power to promote energy savings and environmental and climate protection (§ 1). Electricity produced from CHP plants that are already supported under the EEG does not fall under the KWKG. According to the KWKG 2023, CHP installations have both grid access and feed-in priorities (§ 3(1)), which are at the same level as those outlined in the EEG 2023. This helps to ensure the consistent integration and promotion of CHP technology within Germany's broader energy system.

The KWKG, similar to the EEG, sets up a series of regulations to promote and facilitate the operation of CHP installations. As per the KWKG 2023, operators of CHP plants with an installed capacity exceeding 100 kW must directly market the electricity or use the co-generated electricity for their own consumption (§ 4(1)). For smaller operators of CHP installations with an installed capacity of up to 100 kW, they have multiple options: they can market the electricity directly, use the co-generated electricity themselves, or feed it into the grid (§ 4(2)).

Further incentives are provided for operators of new, modernized, or upgraded CHP plants. They are eligible for additional financial support (*Zuschlagzahlung*) per § 6–7. However, this eligibility is subject to tenders. Smaller new CHP plants (with up to 2 kW installed capacity) are exempt from the tendering scheme and are directly entitled to the financial support (§ 9). The financing of the KWKG promotion is also subject to EnFG regulation per § 26 KWKG.

The Wind Energy at Sea Act (*Gesetz zur Entwicklung und Förderung der Windenergie auf See*, WindSeeG 2023) was enacted to regulate and promote the

[54]European Commission State aid: SA.102084 EEG 2023. https://competition-cases.ec.europa.eu/cases/SA.102084.

development of offshore wind energy installations within Germany's exclusive economic zone and territorial waters. As stated in the first section of the act, the goal is to steadily increase the installed capacity of offshore wind energy installations to a total of 70 gigawatts between 2022 and 2045. This increase is to be achieved in a cost-efficient manner and must take into account the grid capacities needed for the purchase, transmission, and distribution of electricity. In addition to planning, preliminary investigation, approval, construction, and operation of offshore wind energy installations, the WindSeeG 2023 also oversees the process of decommissioning these sites when necessary (§ 2, § 68.1.3).

One of the key components of the WindSeeG is the regulation of the tendering process for new offshore wind energy capacity. According to the act, offshore wind energy installations that are commissioned after 31 December 2020 are only entitled to a market premium for the electricity they generate if they hold a funding award issued by the BNetzA as a result of the tendering process (§ 14). Beginning in 2021, the BNetzA is required to annually invite bids in line with the site development plan (§ 16). This approach aims to ensure a competitive and efficient expansion of Germany's offshore wind energy capacity while ensuring the stability and reliability of the electricity grid. The WindSeeG 2023 also includes provisions for the tendering of market premiums for existing offshore wind installations per § 26 of the act. For installations commissioned after 31 December 2020, the BNetzA is responsible for determining eligible parties and the value to be applied to the electricity they generate. This process is conducted through tenders in which only existing projects can participate.

On a broader scale, Germany has implemented emission control measures as a way to promote green electricity indirectly. While these measures do not directly incentivize the use of renewable energy sources, they aim to reduce the competitiveness of conventional carbon-intensive energy sources, thereby creating a more favorable environment for green electricity. A key component of Germany's emission control measures is the Greenhouse Gas Emissions Trading Act (*Treibhausgas-Emissionshandelsgesetz* or TEHG), which was first introduced in 2004 to transpose the EU emission trading law to the domestic level.[55] The act underwent several amendments over the years, with the latest version reflecting the 2018 amendment of the EU ETS directive. Under the TEHG, companies in industries included in the scheme are required to obtain permits for emitting greenhouse gases (currently, only carbon dioxide emissions are covered as per § 2 TEHG). Initially, some of these certificates were awarded free of charge at the beginning of the trading period (§ 9 TEHG), but the majority of permits have since been auctioned (§ 8 TEHG). The permits are traded on the German Emissions Trading Authority (*Deutsche Emissionshandelsstelle*, DEHSt), which also allows the trading of emission certificates awarded from cross-border emission reductions within the EU borders.

Regarding the compatibility of the EEG's special compensation mechanism with EU law, there have been a few legal debates that centered around whether it

---

[55] Rodi (2020), p. 225.

constituted the use of state resources and if so, whether it was justified. The Commission, in its assessment of EEG 2012, ruled that the special compensation scheme was a form of state aid that disproportionately favored energy-intensive industries, making it incompatible with EU state aid law. However, the ECJ disagreed, ruling instead that the special compensation scheme did not constitute the use of state resources, and thus was legally justified.

In the case of EEG 2014, the Commission again found that the special compensation mechanism constituted the use of state resources. Unlike the 2012 case, though, the Commission also found that its impact on trade was limited, and therefore, the scheme was justified. The Commission did not raise any objections to EEG 2017, EEG 2021 and EEG 2023. In conclusion, based on these decisions, it seems that the special compensation mechanism of the EEG is justified under EU law, as it does not constitute the use of state resources (as ruled by the ECJ), and any impact on trade is deemed to be minimal (as ruled by the Commission).

The question of compatibility with the WTO law and national law issues are separate matters. These debates focus on whether Germany's green energy promotion schemes violate the principles of non-discrimination and national treatment under the WTO law, and whether they are consistent with German constitutional law and administrative law principles. While the compatibility of Germany's EEG special compensation mechanism with the WTO law and its constitutionality has raised some debate, the current consensus seems to suggest that it does not violate either.[56] From a WTO law perspective, the mechanism may face scrutiny because it partially protects energy-intensive businesses from surcharges, possibly conferring an unfair advantage on downstream products. However, based on previous WTO Appellate Body decisions such as *Canada – RE*, it seems that the FIT schemes are not (in and of themselves) considered infringements of WTO law. Since the German green electricity promotion system does not contain LCRs as of yet, it is further protected against potential WTO law violations.

Although the surcharge scheme for installations falling under the EEG has been abolished by the EnFG, KWKG and WindSeeG surcharges continue to be applicable. Nevertheless, the "special compensation" exemption for energy-intensive enterprises, hydrogen producers, railways, electric bus operators, and maritime transportation is retained by the EnFG (§ 29), which could potentially pose challenges under WTO law if considered a fiscal subsidy.

From a constitutional law perspective, critics have argued that the EEG (or similarly KWKG and WindSeeG) surcharges might represent an unconstitutional special levy or a hidden tax.[57] However, the Federal Court of Justice of Germany (*Bundesgerichtshof*, BGH) has ruled that the EEG surcharge does not infringe the Constitution, particularly in terms of Article 105 and subsequent articles. The BGH categorized the EEG surcharge as a form of "price regulation" rather than a "special

[56] For the former view: Dröge et al. (2004).

[57] Manssen (2012).

levy", effectively safeguarding it from constitutional challenges.[58] However, the EnFG will necessitate renewed legal discussions, since it partially shifts the surcharge burdens from the consumers to taxpayers.

In conclusion, while the green electricity promotion schemes of the successive EEG amendments have sparked some legal controversy, current jurisprudence suggests they are largely compatible with the EU, WTO, and national law. However, as legal and policy landscapes evolve, it is always possible that new challenges or interpretations may arise in the future. However, addressing the complexities and potential shortcomings in future will require continuous assessment and adjustment. International coordination will also be essential to promote green electricity, prevent carbon leakage and ensure that efforts to reduce emissions are effective on a global scale.

References

Altenschmidt S (2015) Die Versorgungssicherheit im Lichte des Verfassungsrechts. Neue Zeitschrift für Verwaltungsrecht

Bahmer L, Loers S (2017) Ausschreibungswettbewerb im Erneuerbare-Energien-Gesetz (EEG) 2017: Vom Vergaberecht lernen? Gewerbearchiv

Bader C (2019) Germany - Getting the deal through: renewable energy 2019. Lexology Website 2019. https://www.lexology.com/gtdt

Beveridge R, Kern K (2013) The Energiewende in Germany: background, developments and future challenges. Renew Energy Law Policy Rev 4:3–12

Braaksma L, Fleming R (2020) Phasing out coal-fired power plants in the European Union: examples from the Netherlands and Germany. In: Roggenkamp MM, Banet C (eds) European energy law report. Intersentia, pp 261–287

Cassel S (2018) Stand und Perspektiven der Energiewende aus Sicht des Bundesministeriums für Wirtschaft und Energie. In: Ludwigs M (ed) Klimaschutz, Versorgungssicherheit und Wirtschaftlichkeit in der Energiewende. Duncker & Humblot GmbH, Berlin

Dröge S, Trabold H, Biermann F et al (2004) National climate change policies and WTO law: a case study of Germany's new policies. World Trade Rev 3:161–187. https://doi.org/10.1017/S1474745604001752

Dümke C (2015) Daseinsvorsorge, Wettbewerb und kommunale Selbstverwaltung im Bereich der liberalisierten Energiewirtschaft. Universitätsverlag Potsdam, Potsdam

Egerer J, Oei P-Y, Lorenz C (2018) Renewable energy sources as the cornerstone of the German Energiewende. In: Hirschhausen CV, Gerbaulet C, Kemfert C et al (eds) Energiewende 'Made in Germany': low carbon electricity sector reform in the European context. Springer International Publishing

Eichhammer W (2015) Europas Energie- und Klimapolitik als Instrumentenmix: Ergibt das Puzzle ein stimmiges Bild und wie können erneuerbare Energien gefördert werden? In: Müller T, Kahl H (eds) Erneuerbare Energien in Europa. Nomos, pp 23–38

Fehling M (2014) Neues Regulierungsrecht im Anschluss an die Energiewende. Die Verwaltung 47:313–349

Fischer K (2018) Umweltrecht. In: Steiner U, Brinktrine R (eds) Besonderes Verwaltungsrecht, 9th edn. C.F. Müller

[58] Modest (2014).

Fouquet D (2018) Germany. In: Fouquet D (ed) Renewable energy in the Member States of the EU, 2nd edn. Claeys & Casteels

Franke P (2018) Neue Steuerungsinstrumente für den Windkraftausbau? In: Rosin P, Uhle A (eds) Recht und Energie. De Gruyter, pp 201–214

Frondel M, Ritter N, Schmidt CM, Vance C (2010) Economic impacts from the promotion of renewable energy technologies: the German experience. Energy Policy 38:4048–4056. https://doi.org/10.1016/j.enpol.2010.03.029

Frondel M, Schmidt CM, Vance C (2014) Revisiting Germany's solar cell promotion: an unfolding disaster. Econ Anal Policy 44:3–13. https://doi.org/10.1016/j.eap.2014.02.001

Gentzsch A (2018) Der Gesetzgeber als Projektmanager der Energiewende?: Möglichkeiten und normative Grenzen am Beispiel des Smart Meter Rollouts. In: Rosin P, Uhle A (eds) Festschrift für Ulrich Büdenbender zum 70. De Gruyter, Geburtstag

Hazrat J (2017) Die Förderung Erneuerbarer Energien in Deutschland, dem Vereinigten Königreich und Frankreich: Eine vergleichende Untersuchung unter Einbeziehung europarechtlicher und ökonomischer Aspekte, 1st edn. Nomos

Held H (2021) Carbon Capture and Storage (CCS) or Re-Use in der Klimaforschung, 6. Bucerius Energy Law Day 2021. https://www.unibremen.de/fileadmin/user_upload/fachbereiche/fb6/feu/FEU/VIR/200216_BLS_VIR_Tagungsprogramm_Kompensationsmechanismen_im_KlimaschutzR_7.5.21.pdf

Hirschfeld M, Heidrich B (2013) Die Bedeutung regionaler Governance-Prozesse Für den Ausbau des Höchstspannungsnetzes. Akademie für Raumforschung und Landesplanung Report 2013. http://shop.arl-net.de/media/direct/pdf/ab/ab_005/ab_005_09.pdf

Jurca AM (2014) The Energiewende: Germany's transition to an economy fueled by renewables. Georgetown Int Environ Law Rev 27:38

Kelly R, Schmidt K (2019) Energieleitungsausbau auf der infrastrukturrechtlichen Überholspur: "NABEG 2.0": ohne Tempolimit zum Stromautobahnnetz der Energiewende. Archiv des öffentlichen Rechts 144:577–654. https://doi.org/10.1628/aoer-2019-0037

Kemfert C, Oei P-Y, von Hirschhausen C (2018) General conclusions: 15 lessons from the first phase of the Energiewende. In: Hirschhausen CV, Gerbaulet C, Kemfert C et al (eds) Energiewende 'Made in Germany': low carbon electricity sector reform in the European context. Springer International Publishing

Kloepfer M (2011) Umweltschutzrecht, 2nd edn. C.H. Beck, München

Koch H (2020) 20 Jahre Erneuerbare-Energien-Gesetz: Erstens Sonne, zweitens Wind. Die Tageszeitung 2020. https://taz.de/!5675757/

Kühling J (2019) Energieordnung im Wandel: Entwicklung von Wettbewerb und Regulierungsrecht. In: Franke P, Theobald C (eds) Energierecht im Wandel: Festschrift für Wolfgang Danner zum 80. Geburtstag, 1st edn. C.H. Beck

Manssen G (2012) Die EEG-Umlage als verfassungswidrige Sonderabgabe. Die öffentliche Verwaltung 13

Maubach K-D (2014) Energiewende: Wege zu einer bezahlbaren Energieversorgung, 2nd edn. VS Verlag für Sozialwissenschaften

Modest C (2014) BGH, Urteil vom 25.06.2014, Az. VIII ZR 169/13: EEG-Umlage nicht verfassungswidrig. EWeRK 5

Morey M, Kirsch L (2014) Germany's renewable energy experiment: a made-to-order catastrophe. Electr J 27:6–20. https://doi.org/10.1016/j.tej.2014.05.009

Morris C, Jungjohann A (2016) Energy democracy: Germany's Energiewende to renewables. Palgrave Macmillan

Müller D (2013) Germany: the Energiewende and its ramifications for the German support regime for renewable energies. Renew Energy Law Policy Rev 4:81–89

Müller H (2010) Zukunftsenergie für Deutschland – Vision 2050 – Perspektiven 2020. In: Ehricke U (ed) Energierecht im Wandel. Nomos, pp 59–69

Oei P-Y (2018) Greenhouse gas emission reductions and the phasing-out of coal in Germany. In: Hirschhausen CV, Gerbaulet C, Kemfert C et al (eds) Energiewende 'Made in Germany': low carbon electricity sector reform in the European context. Springer International Publishing

Ohlhorst D (2019) Biographie der Energiewende im Stromsektor. In: Radtke J, Canzler W (eds) Energiewende: Eine sozialwissenschaftliche Einführung. Springer

Oschmann V (2010) A success story – the German renewable energy act turns ten. Renew Energy Law Policy Rev 1:45–59

Petersen M, Thomas H (2014) Energy law in Germany, 2nd edn. Wolters Kluwer Law & Business, Den Haag

Pielow J-C, Benrath D, Hoff M, Schlegel K (2019) Energierecht. In: Ehlers D, Fehling M, Pünder H (eds) Besonderes Verwaltungsrecht: Band 1: Öffentliches Wirtschaftsrecht, 4th edn. C.F. Müller

Praetorius B (2020) Grundlagen der Energiepolitik. In: Radtke J, Canzler W (eds) Energiewende: Eine sozialwissenschaftliche Einführung, 1st edn. Springer

Pritzsche KU, Vacha V (2017) Energierecht: Einführung und Grundlagen. Beck C.H., München

Rodi M (2020) Das Recht der Energiewende. In: Radtke J, Canzler W (eds) Energiewende: Eine sozialwissenschaftliche Einführung, 1st edn. Springer VS, Place of publication not identified

Säcker J (2016) Die Aufgaben der Verteilnetzbetreiber bei zunehmender Erzeugung erneuerbarer Energien und der Digitalisierung der Energiemärkte. Zeitschrift für das gesamte Recht der Energiewirtschaft 294

Sattich T (2018) The international reverberations of Germany's Energiewende geoeconomic in the EU's geo-energy space. In: Scholten D (ed) The geopolitics of renewables. Springer International Publishing

Schafhausen F (2018) Die aktuellen Herausforderungen an die Klimaschutzpolitik. In: Hofmann E (ed) Die Zukunft der Energiewende: 32. Trierer Kolloquium zum Umwelt- und Technikrecht vom 28. bis 29. September 2017. Erich Schmidt Verlag

Schiffer H-W (2018) Energiemarkt Deutschland: Daten und Fakten zu konventionellen und erneuerbaren Energien. Springer

Schmidt CM (2018) Das Vernünftige vernünftig tun: Wege zu einer rationalen Energie- und Klimapolitik. In: Rosin P, Uhle A (eds) Festschrift für Ulrich Büdenbender zum 70. Geburtstag. De Gruyter

Schneider J-P, Theobald C, Albrecht M et al (2013) Recht der Energiewirtschaft: Praxishandbuch, 4th edn. C.H. Beck, München

Sopher P (2015) Lessons learned from Germany's Energiewende: the political, governance, economic, grid reliability, and grip optimization bedrock for a transition to renewables. Renew Resour J 29:6–13

Stecher M (2015) Das Prinzip der umweltverträglichen Energieversorgung in energiewirtschaftsrechtlichen Ausprägungen und umwelt(energie)rechtlichen Verzahnungen. Duncker & Humblot, Berlin

Theobald C, Danner W (2019) Energierecht, 103rd edn. C. H. Beck

von Danwitz T (2006) Regulation and liberalization of the European electricity market - a German view. Energy Law J 27:423

von Hirschhausen C (2018) German energy and climate policies: a historical overview. In: Hirschhausen CV, Gerbaulet C, Kemfert C, et al. (eds) Energiewende 'Made in Germany': low carbon electricity sector reform in the European context. Springer International Publishing

Chapter 7
Green Electricity Promotion in Turkey

The country selected as the second example in this book is Turkey. Despite a considerable similarity to Germany in terms of geographic and population size, Turkey nonetheless exhibits stark disparities in its stage of economic development. However, Turkey shares an analogous characteristic with Germany is the scarcity of petroleum and natural gas. The comparative examination of the policies and legislative frameworks of these two nations could elucidate the contrasting trajectories they have embarked upon toward the achievement of a sustainable, affordable, and secure energy mix.

This chapter will scrutinize the strategic objectives and the prevailing condition of Turkey's electricity infrastructure, thereby rendering the exploration of related legal complexities more comprehensible. The discourse will primarily center on matters of the electricity mix, considering their elevated significance in the context of this research. Following this, the fundamentals of Turkish energy law will be discussed, with special emphasis on the pivotal regulatory bodies and statutory provisions.

Ultimately, the strategies employed to promote green electricity production will be assessed. As indicated previously, an in-depth review of a country's policy landscape and legal systems serves to make a comparative analysis in the following chapter.

7.1 Policy Background

While Turkey and Germany share similarities in terms of territorial and population size, significant differences are observed in their economic and policy climates. Prior to starting a detailed comparative analysis, it is imperative to delineate these conditions. Germany and Turkey can be classified as nations with insubstantial petroleum and gas reserves. Around 1% of Turkey's domestic demand for these resources is met through indigenous production. Moreover, reserves of high-grade hard coal are

O. Cagdas Artantas, *Promotion of Green Electricity in Germany and Turkey*, EYIEL Monographs - Studies in European and International Economic Law 33,
https://doi.org/10.1007/978-3-031-44760-0_7

exceedingly limited within Turkish borders, in contrast with the German situation. The only abundant fossil fuel resource in Turkey is low-grade lignite, exploited predominantly for electricity generation and meeting household needs in rural regions. Consequently, Turkey has been compelled to depend on carbon imports to fulfill escalating energy demands over several decades.

This reliance on energy imports creates a multitude of vulnerabilities in Turkey's energy policy. Primarily, it engenders a geopolitical energy security dilemma. While Turkey has commenced efforts to diversify its carbon import sources, its dependence on natural gas from Iran and Russia and coal from the global market remains substantial. In 2018, imported natural gas contributed to 30.88% of Turkish electricity generation, while imported coal accounted for 21.31% of the same.[1] Therefore, nearly half of Turkey's electricity generation and associated financial liability can be attributed to imported carbon. The remainder is chiefly constituted by electricity generated from inferior-quality local lignite and renewable sources.

This situation precipitates a primary energy security risk, manifesting as the impact of imported gas price volatility on the energy supply. Furthermore, reliance on imported energy exerts a deleterious influence on Turkey's trade balance. The chronic trade deficit, in turn, negatively affects the strength of the local currency. The currency fluctuations witnessed since 2018 highlighted the risks associated with an import-dependent energy industry. Experiences analogous to the fallout of the 1970s Petroleum Crises in the West have stimulated Turkey to accelerate its risk mitigation measures.

Another facet of Turkish energy policy pertains to the nation's geopolitical positioning. Turkey serves as a bridge between the resource-rich Eastern powers and the industrially advanced, energy-demanding Western nations. The increasing number of natural gas pipeline connections further enhances Turkey's strategic importance in energy trading. For instance, the newly commissioned Trans-Anatolian Natural Gas Pipeline (TANAP) facilitates access to Azerbaijani gas, while the TurkStream pipeline bolsters connectivity to Russian reserves.

Five principal objectives can outline Turkey's energy policy, the foremost being the localization of energy resources. The term "localization" within the Turkish context encompasses a broad spectrum of elements. However, briefly, it encapsulates the nation's aspiration for energy self-sufficiency. Given Turkey's lack of hydrocarbons, swift exploration and exploitation of petroleum and natural gas resources are not viable strategies to achieve self-sufficiency. Consequently, dependency on imports is an "inescapable reality" in Turkish energy policy. However, long-term self-sufficiency hinges upon the implementation of three key components:

(1) The first component is capitalizing on renewable energy to its fullest potential. Turkey has substantial renewable energy resources. For instance, it has a considerable hydropower potential, built for electricity generation throughout the twentieth Century. In 2018, hydropower plants accounted for 13.86% of

[1] EPDK, Elektrik Piyasası 2018 Yılı Piyasa Gelişim Raporu, 2019.

licensed electricity generation. Additionally, Turkey experiences solar radiation levels equal to other Mediterranean and North African countries. Although its wind power potential falls short compared to Northern European countries, the solar potential remains largely untapped and presents significant opportunities for development. Additionally, Turkey has many geothermal sites, making it one of the leading actors in geothermal power production. Although it is in its infancy, biomass energy generation also holds promise. Therefore, strengthening its renewable energy infrastructure is a priority for Turkey.

(2) The second component involves nuclear power. Turkey aims to establish a minimum of three nuclear electricity plants. Nevertheless, it currently lacks the requisite technical expertise to construct, operate, and decommission these facilities and manage nuclear waste. Consequently, Turkey has to provide legal concessions to foreign companies to build its nuclear power plants. Turkey's first nuclear unit, the "Akkuyu Nuclear Power Plant," is currently under construction in Mersin, undertaken by Russia's Rosatom. The remaining two nuclear power plants are in the planning stages.

(3) The third component of Turkey's energy localization strategy is leveraging its indigenous lignite resources. Turkey seeks to expedite exploration and exploitation operations for lignite. A promotional scheme in the form of a market premium has been instituted to incentivize this process. This scheme rewards coal electricity plants for transitioning to local lignite, echoing the localization objective of Turkey's energy policy. However, this policy witnesses a backlash from local environmental groups. More importantly, this capacity experiences hardships in the face of the EU's Carbon Border Adjustment Mechanism, which makes lignite-sourced electricity a burden on industrial exports.

The second aim of the Turkish energy policy is to guarantee energy accessibility, which also consists of several elements. The foremost aspect of energy accessibility entails expanding and modernizing energy grids. Ongoing operations aim to extend natural gas supply to the furthest reaches of Turkey, while total electrification of rural areas is projected to be achieved imminently. Particular emphasis is placed on enhancing the energy grid, especially in the country's western regions, to accommodate additional installed capacity. Robust transmission lines are essential for conveying electricity generated in the hydropower plants in the east to the industrially advanced western regions. Enhancing the energy grid would also likely increase electricity transmission efficiency and curtail the frequency of blackouts.

Despite the emergence of innovative trends such as mini-grids and off-grid systems, these approaches currently hold minimal significance in Turkey. Predominant political and economic forces favor a unified, centralized electricity grid, perceived as pivotal for promoting economic growth and industrial expansion.

The second facet of accessibility is affordability, a concept intimately linked with energy pricing. Lower-income demographics may be marginalized from the energy market if prices are prohibitively high. The purchasing power parity (PPP) might provide a more accurate depiction of the situation than mere comparisons of electricity prices across the country. While energy prices in Turkey are either relatively low or comparable to European rates, the purchasing power of low-income groups within the country tends to be markedly limited. This economic disparity represents one of the vulnerabilities in Turkish energy policy, which successive governments have striven to address over recent decades by subsidizing household electricity consumption.

In the Turkish legislative framework, the government predominantly determines end-user electricity tariffs, and the state retains a monopoly over natural gas transmission. Given these regulatory prerogatives, governmental intervention in the energy industry is common in Turkey, primarily aimed at ensuring affordability. Additionally, the previously outlined localization objective indirectly supports the affordability goal by reducing energy costs, as locally generated energy is generally less expensive than imported energy. Initiatives to improve energy efficiency also contribute to energy accessibility, given their potential to reduce energy expenditures in low-income households.

Despite these efforts, energy prices in Turkey have steadily escalated due to the limited effectiveness thus far of localization and other policy objectives in curbing prices. This trend is primarily attributable to the depreciation of the Turkish Lira since 2018, which has adversely impacted energy affordability. Firstly, the weakened Turkish Lira has rendered imported energy less accessible to lower-income households. Secondly, the US-dollar-denominated power purchase agreements under YEKDEM (Turkish Feed-in Tariff system) have partially pegged the price of electricity to USD. Consequently, each downward fluctuation in the Turkish Lira's value diminishes energy affordability in Turkey. Even government-regulated prices in the energy sector have witnessed increases, even though consumption of electricity promotion via state sources.

The third energy objective of Turkey pertains to energy efficiency, a key factor in mitigating energy demand and GHG emissions. Despite considerable enhancements in industrial and household energy efficiencies since the 1980s, Turkey is not perceived as a particularly energy-efficient nation. Energy intensity (energy consumption per unit of national income) in Turkey slightly exceeds the OECD median, indicating areas of inefficiency.[2] Since Turkish energy demand tends to grow in tandem with economic expansion, one key goal is to uncouple energy demand from economic growth. In order to realize this, investments in efficiency initiatives from both the public and private sectors are anticipated.

Turkey's fourth energy policy aim is to position itself as an "energy trading hub" within its regional context. To this end, the development of the European Network of Transmission System Operators for Electricity (ENTSO-E), European Network of Transmission System Operators for Gas (ENTSO-G), and natural gas pipeline interconnectivity hold significant importance within the Turkish agenda. The expectation is that increased interconnectivity will not only decrease energy costs but also diversify the source portfolio of the Turkish energy trade.

[2]TMMOB Makina Mühendisleri Odası, Türkiye'nin Enerji Görünümü, 2020, p. 371.

Turkey's fifth and final energy policy objective is to establish itself as a natural gas producer. This objective has spurred extensive exploration activities within Turkey's Exclusive Economic Zone (EEZ) in the Black Sea and the Mediterranean, activities that also coincide with external political ambitions. Recently, promising discoveries have been made in the Black Sea EEZ. Successful exploitation of natural gas reserves within Turkey's EEZ would likely confer positive impacts upon the country's energy policy, potentially reducing dependency on natural gas imports, aiding in the mitigation of emissions by decreasing coal demand, and increasing accessibility by driving down energy prices.

7.2 Legal Background

In this subchapter, the focus is on the legal foundations of Turkey's green electricity promotion. The legislative framework and regulatory bodies involved are especially important to understanding the context for the various promotion schemes to be discussed later.

Firstly, it is crucial to understand some key characteristics of Turkey's legal system. Historically, the Republic of Turkey has been a highly centralized state. While there are municipalities with locally elected officials, their powers are limited mainly to public service procurement. Province governors, appointed by the President rather than elected locally, serve as the local representatives of the central government. As a result, even local decisions tend to be made in the capital city, Ankara, and then carried out by the governors. There are no federal equivalents to the central organs, and regulatory authorities hold universal jurisdiction across all of Turkey and on all relevant matters.

Another distinctive feature of Turkey's legal system is its ongoing "Europeanization" process. Although Westernization has been a significant historical trend in Turkey, the term "Europeanization" in the contemporary sense pertains to Turkey's ongoing accession process to join the European Union. This process is influenced primarily by two factors: negotiations with EU bodies and the independent impact of European policy and legislation.

The EU maintains a list of requirements on a broad range of issues, from economics to cultural policy, organized into chapters. At the time of writing, negotiations on 16 of these chapters are ongoing (e.g., Science and Research, Environment), with some chapters being blocked by either the EU itself or specific member states.[3] Despite the stagnation in Turkey's EU accession process since 2016, the potential for the EU to reopen closed chapters has compelled Turkish authorities to align their legislation with EU law. The accession process still serves as a reference point for the Turkish Parliament.

---

[3] Avrupa Birliği Bakanlığı (2016) Katılım Müzakerelerinde Mevcut Durum. https://www.ab.gov.tr/katilim-muzakerelerinde-mevcut-durum_65.html.

Moreover, Turkey is a party to the "European Union-Turkey Customs Union Agreement" and is thus required to periodically align its legislation with the Customs Union's requirements. The "EU-Turkey Association Council" oversees compliance with these requirements. As per the council's decision, Turkey was required to comply with Article 107 TFEU.[4] However, it is worth noting that Turkey has yet to fully adopt the TFEU's requirements for state aid monitoring.

The second impact of EU law on Turkish legislation, often referred to as the "Brussels Effect" in academic literature, is the influence of EU law and policy on non-member countries due to its perceived high quality and influence. Furthermore, the EU's market power encourages neighboring countries to align their laws and policies with the EU's. Turkey exemplifies such a country. The EU is Turkey's leading export partner, necessitating that Turkey consistently aligns itself with EU economic standards and policies. Additionally, the Turkish public often sees EU law and policy as universal standards, and EU examples frequently dominate Turkish reform debates.

Through these two influences, EU law is a significant resource for Turkish authorities when considering amendments to legislation or changes in economic policy. This influence also extends to energy law reforms, particularly in the field of green electricity promotion. Turkish energy law often emulates EU law and the examples set by member states. Germany, often considered a "green economy pioneer" in Turkey, has been a significant source of inspiration for new energy regulations. For instance, Germany served as a model for the Turkish Feed-in Tariff system and subsequent tendering models, albeit with numerous modifications.

Having outlined these two key characteristics of Turkish law and policy relevant to this discussion, the main authorities competent in the field of electricity can now be examined. The first such authority in Turkey is the Presidency (*Cumhurbaşkanlığı*). The power and scope of the "Presidential Decree" system adopted in 2017 is still a subject of debate within Turkey. However, it can be argued that the President, as the head of the executive branch, is responsible for setting the general direction of energy policy and overseeing and regulating the competent bodies. This excludes independent regulatory bodies, which are established by acts of Parliament. In practice, though, the implementation of energy policy is largely delegated to the relevant ministries.

The Presidency is supplemented by "Presidential Offices" (*Cumhurbaşkanlığı Ofisleri*) and "Policy Committees" (*Politika Kurulları*), which function as advisory bodies. However, none of these offices or committees directly address energy issues. The "Investments Office" (*Yatırım Ofisi*) may provide advice on energy matters within the context of investment. The President has the authority to freely establish and modify these offices and committees, allowing for the potential creation of an advisory office focused on energy issues in the future.

Ministers are appointed and dismissed at the discretion of the President, and they are not considered separate entities from the legal persona of the State, which the

[4]Decision 1/95 of the EC-Turkey Association Council, 22 December 1995, Article 34.

President represents. Nevertheless, they do have jurisdiction in their respective fields of duty. Two ministries have responsibilities related to energy issues. The first is the "Ministry of Energy and Natural Resources" (*Enerji ve Tabii Kaynaklar Bakanlığı*), and the second is the "Ministry of Environment, Urban Planning, and Climate Change" (*Çevre, Şehircilik ve İklim Değişikliği Bakanlığı*). As their names suggest, the former is more directly involved with the energy sector.

The Energy Ministry in Turkey is responsible for setting the policies for energy and natural resources, issuing various licenses, facilitating the exploration and exploitation of energy sources, and overseeing operations in the energy and mining sectors. According to the Act establishing the Ministry, it is tasked with developing strategies and policies to further utilize renewable energy sources.[5]

In practice, there are no significant overlaps of authority between the Parliament and the Energy Ministry. While the Parliament does have a committee that addresses energy issues (Commission on Industry, Trade, Energy, Natural Resources, Information, and Technology, "*Sanayi, Ticaret, Enerji, Tabii Kaynaklar, Bilgi ve Teknoloji Komisyonu*"), it typically follows the Energy Ministry's lead when enacting laws related to the energy sector. However, this balance between the Parliament and the government is subject to the realities of Turkish politics and could change in the event of a government and a parliamentary majority cohabitation with differing energy priorities.

The specialized branch dedicated to renewable energy expansion under the Energy Ministry (General Directorate of Renewable Energy, YEGM, *Yenilenebilir Enerji Genel Müdürlüğü*) was abolished in 2017. The Presidential decree that abolished the Renewables Directory tasked the General Directorate of Energy Affairs (EİGM, *Enerji İşleri Genel Müdürlüğü)* with handling renewable energy.[6] Another directorate, the General Directorate of Mineral Research and Exploration (MTA, *Maden Tetkik Arama Genel Müdürlüğü*), is responsible for exploring coal sources. Finally, the Directorate of Mining Affairs (*Maden İşleri Genel Müdürlüğü)* is tasked with the licensing procedures for geothermal energy installations.

On the other hand, the Ministry of Environment has a crucial role in the development of new energy installations. It evaluates the environmental impact reports, which are required by law for most new types of renewable energy installations. Finally, the Ministry of Environment's "Climate Change Department" (*İklim Değişikliği Başkanlığı*) is tasked with establishing the national green taxonomy criteria, which may prove to be pivotal for green electricity investments.

The Energy Market Regulatory Authority (EPDK, *Enerji Piyasası Düzenleme Kurulu)* in Turkey is another vital player in the energy sector, functioning as the independent energy regulator. Established in 2001, EPDK's role is to protect the interests of energy consumers and ensure the competitiveness of the energy market. It does this through its regulations, monitoring the energy market actors, and issuing various types of licenses and end-user tariffs. Furthermore, EPDK is responsible for

[5] 3154 sayılı Enerji ve Tabii Kaynaklar Bakanlığının Teşkilat ve Görevleri Hakkında Kanun 2/1-h.

[6] 1 sayılı Cumhurbaşkanlığı Kararnamesi (CBK) 168/1, 169.

issuing the origin certificates for renewables and conducting auctions for new green electricity capacity.

The Turkish energy sector comprises several companies, either owned by the State or tasked by the State under administrative or private law agreements. The forerunner of these companies was the Turkish Electricity Administration (TEK, *Türkiye Elektrik Kurumu*). Established in 1970, TEK operated as a state monopoly with a vertically integrated structure covering electricity generation, transmission, and distribution branches. Although the history of the electricity sector in Turkey dates back to 1902 with a small hydropower terminal, electricity provision was primarily the responsibility of municipalities and several local companies with long-term concessions before TEK's establishment.[7]

In 1993, with the wave of privatization in Turkey, TEK was split into two state companies: the State Electricity Generation and Transmission Corporation (TEAŞ, Türkiye Elektrik Üretim İletim A.Ş.) and the Turkish Electricity Distribution Corporation (TEDAŞ, Türkiye Elektrik Dağıtım A.Ş.). Then, in 2001, TEAŞ was further unbundled into three companies: the Electricity Generation Corporation (EÜAŞ, Elektrik Üretim A.Ş.), the Turkish Electricity Transmission Corporation (TEİAŞ, Türkiye Elektrik İletim A.Ş.), and the Turkish Electric Trade and Contracting Corporation (TETAŞ, Türkiye Elektrik Ticaret ve Taahhüt A.Ş.).

As the Turkish electricity sector evolved, the country embarked on a significant phase of privatization across all state sectors. The electricity distribution company, TEDAŞ, underwent geographic unbundling and was eventually privatized. Similarly, parts of the electricity generation installations owned by EÜAŞ were also privatized. TETAŞ was shut down in 2018 and re-incorporated into EÜAŞ, the electricity generation company. However, the electricity transmission monopoly, held by TEİAŞ, remained under state ownership. In 2015, another state company, the Energy Markets Operation Corporation (EPİAŞ, Enerji Piyasaları İşletme Anonim Şirketi), was established to facilitate energy trade at the Istanbul Energy Exchange (EXIST).

The sector's evolution has resulted in a "semi-privatized" legal structure in Turkey, and privatization remains an ongoing process. Gradually, the ownership of coal power plants and the "rights to operate" hydropower plants are auctioned off, leading to a diminishing generation portfolio for EÜAŞ. According to the Privatization Administration (*Özelleştirme İdaresi*), further privatizations in the electricity sector are planned. One such target for future privatization efforts could be TEİAŞ, preferably by an initial public offering.[8]

After assessing the authorities competent in the field of electricity, the constitutional rules and core legislation in Turkey should be elucidated. Several articles of the Turkish Constitution of 1982 indirectly govern the energy sector.

[7] See: Dilli B, Nyman KJ, Turkey's Energy Transition: Milestones and Challenges, 2015.

[8] Turkish Privatization Administration, 2019-2023 Dönemi Stratejik Planı, 2019.

(i) According to Article 2, the Republic of Turkey is classified as a social state. The term "social state" is understood in Turkey as a broad principle implying the State's economic obligations towards its citizens. For instance, the provision of electricity at an affordable, fair price would fall under this principle.
(ii) Article 56/1 asserts the "right to a healthy and balanced environment." Article 56/2 states that "It is the duty of the State and citizens to improve the natural environment, to protect environmental health and to prevent environmental pollution." These two paragraphs could be viewed as the constitutional foundation for green electricity promotion measures since green electricity investments contribute to a "healthier and more balanced" environment.
(iii) According to Article 168, "natural wealth and resources shall be under the authority and at the disposal of the State. The right to explore and exploit these belongs to the State. The State may delegate this right to individuals or corporate bodies for a certain period." This article is particularly crucial in the context of geothermal energy generation and coal mining.

The principal legislation during the era of TEK was known as the "TEK Act" (*TEK Kanunu*).[9] This act governed all electricity-related matters and the powers of the vertically integrated monopoly. Notably, in the early privatization era of the 80s in Turkey, an act enabled the government to appoint private companies with the local electricity monopoly.[10] As per the EU accession discussions, a landmark act was adopted in 2001 when TEK was unbundled into two state monopoly corporations: the Electricity Market Act (EPK 2001, *Elektrik Piyasası Kanunu*).[11]

EPK 2001 introduced the "licensing" model to the electricity generation sector. Before the licensing approach, three models were present in the Turkish electricity generation sector: "Build-Operate-Transfer" (BOT), "Transfer-of-Rights" (TOR), and "Build-Operate" (BO). The BOT and TOR models were active between 1984 and 2001.[12] In the BOT model, a private sector actor was granted permission to build an electricity generation installation and operate it for a specified period. After this period, the ownership of the installation was transferred to the State without any costs or debts incurred. The TOR model represented a partial privatization. In this model, the right to operate an electricity installation was transferred to a private entity for a period for a fee. After this duration, which allowed the investor to return a profit, the right to operate reverted to the State.[13]

The BO model was in use between 1997–2001, exclusively for coal thermal power plants. This model granted permission to build an electricity installation and,

[9] 1312 Sayılı Türkiye Elektrik Kurumu Kanunu.

[10] 3096 sayılı Türkiye Elektrik Kurumu Dışındaki Kuruluşların Elektrik Üretimi, İletimi, Dağıtımı ve Ticareti İle Görevlendirilmesi Hakkında Kanun.

[11] 4628 sayılı Elektrik Piyasası Kanunu.

[12] 3996 sayılı Bazı Yatırım ve Hizmetlerin Yap-İşlet-Devret Modeli Çerçevesinde Yaptırılması Hakkında Kanun, 4283 sayılı Elektrik Enerjisi Üretim Santrallerinin Kurulması ve İşletilmesi ve Enerjinin Yap İşlet Modeliyle Satılmasına Dair Kanun.

[13] Voyvoda and Voyvoda (2019).

in contrast to the BOT model, operate it for an indefinite period. The licensing model replaced these three models.

EPK 2001 served as the central electricity act until its amendment in 2013. It founded the EPDK, the independent energy regulator, unbundled the state monopoly (TEAŞ into three corporations), and facilitated the privatization of generation and supply sectors. The entrance of private corporations into the electricity field was subjected to a "licensing" system, by which the administration (Energy Ministry or EPDK) unilaterally allowed the operations of the investor. EPK 2001 did not contain any exceptions regarding the electricity sector, meaning the Turkish Competition Authority (RK, *Rekabet Kurumu*) has been monitoring this sector.

The Electricity Market Law of 2001 (EPK 2001) underwent significant amendments in 2013 (EPK 2013).[14] As delineated in Article 1, the primary objective of EPK 2013 is to facilitate the establishment of a financially robust, stable, and transparent electricity market. This market, governed by private law provisions, seeks to foster competition while guaranteeing the provision of electricity in a sufficient, high-quality, uninterrupted, affordable, and environmentally friendly manner. It also ensures independent regulation and surveillance within this market sphere.

EPK 2013 delineates a licensure system encompassing nearly all functions in the electricity market, as clarified in Article 4. These functions include electricity generation, transmission, distribution, wholesale, retail sale, market operation, import, and export. In order to execute these tasks, private entities are required to secure licenses from the Energy Market Regulatory Authority (EPDK). According to Turkish law, EPDK is a financially and administratively autonomous energy regulator with the responsibility of regulating and overseeing the energy market.[15] As an administrative body, any decisions made by the EPDK are subject to appeals through the administrative court system. The aforementioned licenses are permissible for a maximum period of 49 years and must be acquired separately for each installation. Nevertheless, the EPK 2013 concedes that separate installations utilizing the same connection point may be considered a single "virtual" installation.[16]

Entities may apply for a "preliminary generation license," which enables them to procure necessary land and other relevant permissions. Turkish law empowers administrative authorities to expropriate land for the advantage of private investors. According to Turkish expropriation law, a "public interest decision" is requisite for such land expropriation. However, as stated in Article 19/1-a of EPK 2013, any expropriation decisions made by the EPDK are exempt from this requirement.

A particularly pertinent element for green electricity is the potential for "unlicensed generation". This does not entail the removal of all permitting processes but does signify a substantial reduction in bureaucracy. Importantly, this model

[14] 6446 sayılı Elektrik Piyasası Kanunu.

[15] 4628 sayılı Enerji Piyasası Düzeleme Kurumunun Teşkilat ve Görevleri Hakkında Kanun, Article 4.

[16] 6446 sayılı Elektrik Piyasası Kanunu, Article 5/1-f.

enables smaller investors to construct new capacity without being constrained by nationwide or local capacity limits. Unlicensed green electricity generation is confined to 1 MW of installed capacity per project, a limitation that may be increased fivefold by the President, as per EPK 2013 Article 14/2. Additionally, off-grid projects, storage capacities under a specific threshold set by the Energy Ministry, and Combined Heat and Power (CHP) projects above a particular efficiency level are exempted from licensure requirements.

Article 7/4-ç of EPK 2013 stipulates that the Energy Market Regulatory Authority (EPDK) may organize auctions for new grid connection capacity in instances where more than one applicant vies for the same connection point. Such auctions bear significant relevance for green electricity investors given that connection points frequently become points of contention in areas where renewable resources are abundant.

The task of transmission grid expansion within Turkey is singularly managed by the state transmission company, TEİAŞ, as per Article 8 of EPK 2013. This consolidates considerable advantage for Turkey in terms of expanding and refurbishing its grid. Given the absence of federal structures and the transmission market's pre-unbundled situation, TEİAŞ can effortlessly undertake grid improvements. The financing of TEİAŞ operations is sourced from "system fees" collected from distributors and generators, with the rates for these fees set by the EPDK in a tariff. Moreover, TEİAŞ facilitates the integration of new green electricity capacity into the grid. In cases where TEİAŞ lacks the necessary funding to provide a new connection, green electricity investors are permitted to co-finance the connection. The costs incurred are subsequently recouped from the system fees over a maximum period of five years (Article 8/5). TEİAŞ also manages cross-border interconnections, operating, for example, the ENTSO-E connections of Turkey to Bulgaria and Greece. In addition to these duties, TEİAŞ is tasked with long-term supply security planning, preparing supply security projections for the subsequent 20 years (Article 20/1-a).

As stipulated in Article 9, distribution services in Turkey are unbundled and executed by local subsidiaries of major energy companies, holdings, or consortiums (for instance, the Başkent EDAŞ of EnerjiSA A.Ş, or the Boğaziçi EDAŞ of the Limak-Cengiz-Kolin Consortium). Distribution companies are responsible for expanding and refurbishing the distribution grid as needed. Similarly, wholesale and retail activities are unbundled and undertaken by supply companies. In contrast, the electricity market operator company, EPİAŞ, is charged with the task of resolving legal disputes within the electricity market (Article 11/14).

As outlined in EPK Provisional Article 13, no treasury guarantees shall be extended to electricity investments under the Build-Operate-Transfer, Transfer of Rights, or Build-Operate models. Historically, treasury guarantees were instrumental in concessional agreements within the electricity sector, effectively mitigating project risks associated with electricity generation, transmission, or distribution projects. However, green electricity generation projects do not necessitate treasury guarantees as they are supported by FITs.

A notable aspect of EPK 2013 is the "consumption tariff cross-subsidization mechanism" implemented towards the end of 2020. As stipulated by Provisional Article 1 of EPK 2013, an "equalization" process will be applied to consumption tariffs across Turkey until 2025. The President possesses the authority to extend this period by an additional five years. This mechanism aims to balance the profits of distribution companies operating under different market conditions. For instance, distribution companies in regions experiencing additional profit losses due to electricity theft can benefit from this mechanism, receiving payments from other companies. These payments are gathered and distributed by the state electricity generation company, EÜAŞ.[17] This model of cross-subsidization aligns with the perception of electricity provision in Turkey as a "public service".[18]

7.3 Promotion Schemes and Debates

This subchapter will elucidate the promotional schemes for green electricity and discussions surrounding these systems. The first scheme under scrutiny, the "General Investment Promotion Scheme", which also promotes green electricity investments, encompasses numerous fiscal incentives. This scheme has its roots in a Council of Ministers' decision from 2012 and has been subject to annual amendments since its inception.[19] According to Article 1 of the Decision, the scheme's objectives encompass directing savings towards high-added-value investments, boosting production and employment, fortifying the economy's competitiveness through research and development-centric or strategic investments, promoting foreign direct investments, mitigating regional development disparities, and encouraging industrial clustering, environmentally friendly investments, and research and development.

In its final iteration, the General Investment Promotion Scheme stratifies Turkey into six regions based on their levels of development. Measures to promote investments are amplified in less developed regions (Article 3). In order to qualify for the benefits offered by the scheme, investors are required to procure a "Promotion Certificate" from the Ministry of Industry and Investment (Article 7). The scheme primarily alleviates the tax obligations of the investor. Additionally, a portion of the public insurance expenditures for certified investors is covered by the State. The scheme further enables the Ministry of Industry and Investment to shoulder a certain proportion of the interest payments arising from the investors' debts (Article 11). Furthermore, the Ministry of Environment is permitted to provide land assistance to certified investors (Article 16). Lastly, the Ministry of Industry and Investment may

[17] Elektrik Piyasasında Uygulanacak Fiyat Eşitleme Mekanizması Hakkında Tebliğ, RG Yayın Tarihi: 6.03.2013, RG Sayısı: 28579.

[18] Çal (2007); Ergün (2010).

[19] 15/6/2012 Tarihli ve 2012/3305 Sayılı Yatırımlarda Devlet Yardımları Hakkında Karar.

issue direct grants to selected investors (Article 21). Of note, the scheme prioritizes investments in green electricity equipment production (Article 17/1-ö).

Regarding the promotion of green electricity, the central legislative instrument is the YEKK, the Renewables Act.[20] YEKK governs the application of renewable resources, encompassing everything from the certification process to licensing, promotional schemes to monitoring. The objectives of this Act, as stipulated in Article 1, are to encourage electricity generation from renewable energy sources, safely integrate these sources into the economy in an economical and qualified manner, diversify sources, reduce greenhouse gas emissions, utilize waste products, protect the environment, and foster the development of the industry necessary to achieve these goals.

Although YEKK is a short text, it is complemented by comprehensive secondary law in the form of administrative acts. The foremost piece of secondary law in this context is the "YEK Regulation".[21] Given the close relationship between these two texts, they will be explored collectively in this subchapter. Moreover, rather than scrutinizing the individual articles of the act and the regulation, the focus will be on the promotional schemes.

The second green electricity promotion scheme to be examined here is the certification system outlined in EPK 2013, YEKK, and the regulation. EPDK issues a certificate (YEK Belgesi) for electricity generated from green sources (EPK 2013 Article 7/6). This certificate can be used in domestic and international electricity trade and to fulfill quota obligations. Therefore, it is a prerequisite for benefiting from the primary support mechanism.

The third system that we will scrutinize here has been pivotal in supporting green electricity in Turkey since 2005: The Renewable Energy Sources Promotion Mechanism (YEKDEM, *Yenilenebilir Enerji Kaynakları Destekleme Mekanizması*). YEKDEM played a significant role in Turkey's rapid expansion of green electricity. In 2005, the proportion of green electricity in the energy mix was approximately 20%. This increased to 40% over the course of 15 years, largely due to the YEKDEM scheme. This scheme was in force until 2020, as stipulated in YEKK. In 2020, the system was extended for one year by a Presidential decree. In January 2021 and again in May 2023, the YEKDEM tariff was updated by Presidential decrees.[22] This latest tariff will be accessible for new installations until December 2030.

YEKDEM is, by nature, a FIT system. Electric producers are given compensation for the electricity supplied to the grid according to a fixed tariff (YEKK Article 6, YEKK Annex 1). Furthermore, YEKDEM is a technology-specific system. For

---

[20] 5356 sayılı Yenilenebilir Enerji Kaynaklarının Elektrik Enerjisi Üretimi Amaçlı Kullanımına İlişkin Kanun.

[21] Yenilenebilir Enerji Kaynaklarının Belgelendirilmesi ve Desteklenmesine İlişkin Yönetmelik, RG Yayın Tarihi: 01.10.2013. RG Sayısı: 28782.

[22] Cumhurbaşkanı'nın 17.09.2020 tarih ve 2949 sayılı kararı. RG Yayın Tarihi: 18.09.2020 RG Sayı: 31248.; Cumhurbaşkanı'nın 29.01.2021 tarih ve 3453 sayılı kararı. RG Yayın Tarihi: 30.01.2021 RG Sayı: 31380.

instance, during the first YEKDEM period, wind energy was compensated at 7.3 US cents per kWh, while the rate for solar energy was 13.3 cents per kWh. The remuneration rates in the YEKDEM were based on the US Dollar, which was intended to foster investment security by offering a guarantee in hard currency. After the update in 2021, this "dollarized guarantee" is discarded and replaced with a guarantee in Turkish Lira. However, the Turkish Lira-based FIT is updated based on an averaged basket comprising the Turkish wholesale price index, consumer price index, Euro increment value, and US Dollar increment value. Given the strong ties between the price indexes in Turkey and the USD valuation, this annual adjustment of the local content premium will be most influenced by hard foreign currencies (Euro and USD). Essentially, this "averaged basket" method equates to a USD guarantee. Perhaps to mitigate this issue, the Decree stipulates ceilings in US Dollars for the tariff rates based on each type of facility.

According to YEKDEM, electricity distributors are mandated to purchase electricity generated from renewable sources.[23] However, the FIT is confined to the licensed maximum installed capacity. Any quantity surpassing this threshold was subject to the market price. This threshold scheme could be attributed to two reasons. The first is to maintain the stability of the Turkish grid, and the second is to limit the expansion of green electricity to align generation with demand and keep electricity prices affordable.

YEKDEM guarantees the purchase of generated electricity at tariff rates for a period of ten years. Compared to other examples, this duration may seem short. However, YEKDEM attracted significant investment and facilitated the expansion of green electricity, almost to a point where it negatively impacted the affordability of electricity prices. As such, it can be argued that a ten-year feed-in tariff guarantee in USD has been sufficiently attractive for many investors in Turkey. However, YEKDEM's effectiveness has not yet been thoroughly tested. How investors will respond to a Turkish Lira-denominated FIT and "averaged basket" tariff updates remains to be seen. However, it is important to note that the annual tariff update ceilings in USD may deter investment or oblige investors to look for alternative promotion methods, suchlike via small-size unlicensed generation and micro-size net metering.

The cost of promotions through YEKDEM was passed onto end consumers in the form of a surcharge (YEKDEM *Birim Maliyeti*). This surcharge is collected from suppliers and transferred to generation companies by the market operator, EPİAŞ (EPK 2013 Article 6). One issue arises from the ever-increasing costs in the Turkish Lira due to currency fluctuations in Turkey, as YEKDEM guarantees are backed by a USD tariff. As the Turkish Lira depreciates against the USD, the YEKDEM surcharge increases accordingly. This puts pressure on low-income households and energy-intensive businesses. The absence of a rebate for energy-intensive businesses has made YEKDEM a target of criticism from the Turkish industry.

[23] YEKK Article 6/A.

Additionally, the rapid expansion of renewables in Turkey was seen as "too fast" by policymakers, fearing potential grid security issues. Turkish policymakers showed a preference for conventional energy sources like local lignite over intermittent renewable energy sources. The priority given to local coal over renewables in cases of grid access contests effectively reflects this stance. YEKDEM appeared to have been "too successful" in terms of expanding renewables. There was often more demand for renewable energy licenses than anticipated, indicating that the FIT rates were higher than necessary.

YEKDEM also includes LCRs. These requirements essentially promote the use of locally produced equipment as opposed to imported products, rather than being a precondition for benefitting from YEKDEM. The feed-in tariff remuneration is increased for each type of equipment specified in YEKK. For instance, using a locally produced solar energy inverter led to an additional payment of 0.6 USD cents/kWh.. For solar cells, it was 3.5 cents/kWh. Hypothetically, under YEKDEM, a solar energy installation fully equipped with local products could be remunerated at a rate of 20 USD cents/kWh instead of 13.3 cents/kWh.[24] The YEKDEM update in 2021 abolished the USD-based local content premium in favor of a Turkish Lira-based premium tariff. However, like the FIT updates, the Turkish Lira-based local content premium will be annually updated with an equally averaged basket of the Turkish wholesale price index, consumer price index, Euro increment value, and US Dollar increment value. Given that price indexes in Turkey are strongly linked to the US Dollar valuation, this annual update of the local content premium will essentially constitute a dollarized guarantee.

YEKDEM's local content requirements are technology-specific (such as hydropower, wind, photovoltaics, concentrated solar, biomass, and geothermal) and are predesignated in an annex table for 28 types of equipment. The local content premiums of YEKDEM are paid for five years, while the FIT continues for ten years.

The Turkish LCRs for green electricity equipment aim to replace imports partially rather than entirely. Given Turkey's technological capacity, completely replacing the import of green electricity equipment would not be realistic. However, in conjunction with the YEKA program described below, these local content requirements could potentially enhance the production capacity of the Turkish industry and support the development of the green industry in Turkey.

The fourth type of green electricity promotion in Turkey is the "Renewable Energy Resource Area" (YEKA, *Yenilenebilir Enerji Kaynak Alanları*) system.[25] This is a tender-based promotion scheme in which the Ministry designates zones of land or sea as highly efficient green electricity generation areas and auctions the new capacity to be built in these sites. Turkey adopted the YEKA model in 2016 to encourage large-scale green electricity generation projects. In the initial phase of

[24] YEKK Article 8/B.

[25] Yenilenebilir Enerji Kaynak Alanları Yönetmeliği, RG Yayın Tarihi: 09.10.2016. RG Sayısı: 29852.

YEKA, a tender occurs and the bidder offering the lowest remuneration rate is awarded the contract. The term of the YEKA contract is 15 years.

The YEKA operates under two models. In the first model, the project developer is granted the right to build and operate the facility at a guaranteed price determined by the tender, on the condition that they manufacture certain specified green electricity equipment in Turkey. In the second model, the obligation shifts from local equipment production to the utilization of local products. Therefore, both models involve some form of local content production or usage requirement. Additionally, in both models, the developer is required to establish a research and development division that will operate for at least ten years.

To date, three YEKA projects have been awarded: one 1000 MW solar project and one 1000 MW wind project with a local manufacturing obligation, and one 1000 MW solar project split among four developers, each responsible for 250 MW parts, with local content requirements. Subsequent large-scale solar and wind YEKA projects were canceled due to low bidder interest. The YEKA system is expected to continue with smaller projects, with an installed capacity of around 10 to 50 MW. Moreover, these new projects are anticipated to follow the second model of YEKA, which mandates the use of local content instead of local manufacturing.

One key characteristic of the YEKA system is its provision for land aid. As the Energy Ministry designates the land or sea area to be used as a YEKA zone, it transfers the right of land use according to the YEKA contract. The investor is responsible for paying the expropriation cost for the designated zone.

Turkish policymakers appear to favor maintaining the YEKA system to encourage substantial green electricity projects at state-designated sites, coupled with local content requirements. However, the YEKA system is not without its challenges. As previously noted, upcoming YEKA tenders will likely involve smaller projects than the initial ones. This is due in part to the limited interest from solar companies for large-scale projects, such as those at 1000 MW, in Turkey. Several factors contribute to this lack of interest, including economic difficulties in Turkey that make project financing unfeasible, the perceived low remuneration cap set by the EPDK, and the potential disincentive of the "manufacture in Turkey" requirement. Consequently, future YEKA projects are expected to be smaller, without the manufacturing condition. It is hoped that these "Mini-YEKA" projects with local content requirements will achieve more success in terms of obtaining better prices through tendering.

The YEKA projects in Turkey face the challenge that, as of 2023, tendering takes place in the Turkish Lira. This may dissuade investors who prefer the security of hard currency guarantees. The concept of "Turkish Lira-based mini-YEKAs" may act as a deterrent to investment in renewable energy in Turkey, thereby limiting the expansion of green electricity. This could potentially contradict the Turkish energy policy, which prioritizes local energy sources.

The fifth method of promoting green electricity in Turkey is through grid-related guarantees. According to the YEKK, green electricity sources are prioritized over conventional forms, except for local lignite.[26] In fact, the regulations state that if there are multiple applications for the same grid access point, local lignite power plants take precedence over renewables.[27]

The sixth regulatory promotion of green electricity involves easing the process for new capacity. This scheme allows installations to increase capacity if the expansion takes place on the same site and is approved by the transmission system operator, TEİAŞ. While this scheme simplifies capacity expansion without additional regulatory burdens, approval from TEİAŞ is still required. It is likely that if the new capacity could cause congestion on the grid, TEİAŞ would not approve the expansion.

Seventh, the "unlicensed generation" system encourages small green electricity projects. According to the EPK 2013, green electricity projects with an installed capacity of up to 1 MW, or those that generate electricity solely for self-use, are exempt from the requirement to obtain a license or establish a company.[28] This accelerates the project's timeline and makes it financially more feasible, as the license obligation typically requires the establishment of a private legal entity and the payment of various fees. The President has the authority to increase the maximum installed capacity threshold to 5 MW. The electricity produced by unlicensed production will be remunerated at YEKDEM tariff rates for a duration of ten years.[29]

Eighth, an amendment to the Unlicensed Generation Regulation in 2019 introduced net metering as an option for unlicensed electricity producers in Turkey. Unlicensed generators with a capacity of up to 5 MW and solar electricity generators installed on roofs or facades with a capacity of up to 10 kW can avail of the net metering system.[30] The net metering is subject to the consumption tariff set by the EPDK, with some reductions and rebates granted in favor of the distribution company.

Ninth, a 2020 amendment made it possible for Turkish electricity consumers to opt for green electricity. Consumers can be subjected to a special consumption tariff designed to promote green electricity upon request. The EPDK sets these "green tariffs". The electricity supplier transfers the additional income generated from these tariffs to the green electricity investors. This scheme effectively generates more revenue for green electricity and can be considered a regulatory promotion scheme.

To promote this scheme, a "green electricity consumption certificate" scheme was added to the YEK Regulation.[31] Licensed suppliers now can issue certificates for

[26] YEKK, Article 6/C. Elektrik Piyasası Bağlantı ve Sistem Kullanım Yönetmeliği, Article 10A/3, RG Yayın Tarihi: 28.01.2014, RG Sayısı: 28896.

[27] Elektrik Piyasası Bağlantı ve Sistem Kullanım Yönetmeliği, Article 6/3.

[28] EPK 2013 Article 14.

[29] Lisanssız Elektrik Üretim Yönetmeliği, RG Yayın Tarihi: 12.05.2019, RG Sayısı: 30772, Article 24/1-b.

[30] Lisanssız Elektrik Üretim Yönetmeliği, RG Yayın Tarihi: 12.05.2019, RG Sayısı: 30772, Article 26.

[31] YEK Regulation Article 24/A.

green electricity consumption. The aim of these certificates is to encourage the use of green tariffs by certifying and publicizing green electricity use. In practice, the use of the green tariff was minimal as of 2023. There is also a sectoral demand for a regulatory framework to enable corporate PPAs so as to provide income security for new projects.

Finally, as an indirect promotion scheme, the climate laws in Turkey should be considered. Compared to its European counterparts, climate law in Turkey is relatively limited and is regulated at the ordinance level. These ordinances are based on the "Environment Act", which does not explicitly mention climate.[32] Instead, the Environment Act mandates private entities to comply with government monitoring regarding their environmentally harmful activities. In 2014, the Ministry of Environment and Urbanization issued an ordinance and a notification concerning monitoring GHG emissions.[33] These texts, having equal legal effectiveness, dictate that the Ministry will monitor the GHG emissions resulting from economic activities. The Ministry categorizes emission-intensive activities and prepares a report on GHG emissions. Emissions from electricity generation are also monitored by the Ministry, per these regulations.

However, there is currently no GHG emissions limitation measure in force. As such, it would not be accurate to view this monitoring duty as an indirect promotion of green electricity. The closest measure to an emissions limitation system is the "Voluntary Carbon Market Mechanism", established by a notification issued by the Ministry of Environment and Urbanization in 2013.[34] The relevant notification refers to the UNFCCC and allows for the issuance of "voluntary certificates" for carbon emission reductions. Companies can trade these certificates voluntarily, and many companies participating in this voluntary carbon market are renewable energy investors. Green electricity generation companies, for instance, may sell these certificates to obtain additional income. Consequently, this mechanism can be seen as a minor indirect promotional tool for green electricity.

At the time of writing, the Turkish government is considering proposing a "Climate Act" as a regulatory response to imminent measures such as the Carbon Border Adjustment Mechanism (CBAM) under the European Green Deal. Until now, the Turkish economy has grown without significant consideration for emissions. The majority of Turkish export products carry a considerable carbon footprint. As such, a carbon footprint-based tariff on Turkish exports could have significant implications for the Turkish economy.

To avoid additional tariff impositions on its products, Turkey will need to reduce emissions across all sectors of its economy, from electricity generation to end-product manufacturing. In conclusion, the forthcoming "Climate Act" in Turkey

---

[32] Çevre Kanunu, No: 2872, RG Yayın Tarihi: 11.08.1983, RG Sayısı: 18132.

[33] Sera Gazı Emisyonlarının Takibi Hakkında Yönetmelik, RG Yayın Tarihi: 17.05.2014, RG Sayısı: 29003; Sera Gazı Emisyonlarının İzlenmesi ve Raporlanması Hakkında Tebliğ, RG Yayın Tarihi: 22.07.2014, RG Sayısı: 29068.

[34] Gönüllü Karbon Piyasası Proje Kayıt Tebliği, RG Yayın Tarihi: 9.09.2013, RG Sayısı: 28790.

will need to address this imminent trade obstruction. One can anticipate the establishment of a national cap-and-trade system for emissions and a national green taxonomy to handle this risk. These measures would help to align Turkey's environmental policies with international standards, potentially mitigating the economic impacts of external mechanisms like the CBAM. However, developing and implementing such systems will undoubtedly pose significant challenges. These might include the need for technological advancements, capacity building in various sectors, legislative modifications, and potentially substantial changes in the national energy mix and industrial practices. Despite these challenges, these measures could stimulate a more sustainable and resilient economy in the long term.

References

Çal S (2007) Türkiye'de Kamu Hizmeti ve İmtiyazın Dönüşüm Öyküsü. TOBB Yayınları

Ergün ÇE (2010) Elektrik Piyasasında Kamu Hizmeti, 1st edn. Çakmak Yayınevi

Voyvoda ÖK, Voyvoda E (2019) Türkiye'de Enerji Sektörünün Yeniden Yapılandırılması Sürecinde Hukuk Düzenlemeleri – Elektrik Sektörü. Çalışma ve Toplum 1

Chapter 8
Comparison of Models and Proposals

8.1 Comparison

This section is designed to compare German and Turkish green electricity promotion by focusing on three primary dimensions: the economic landscape, governmental policy, and the legal structure. Thereafter, policy and legislation suggestions will be provided for both countries.

8.1.1 Economic Comparison

From an economic perspective, there are numerous similarities and substantial differences between Germany and Turkey. Geographic considerations play a dominant role in shaping these economies. Germany, a country in Northern Europe, exhibits a higher wind potential, whereas Turkey, situated in the Mediterranean region, boasts greater solar potential. With a landmass nearly twice as large as Germany's, Turkey may leverage this size advantage for the deployment of solar energy installations.

The geographical orientations of the two nations differ significantly. Turkey has an east-west orientation, while Germany is oriented from north to south. This distinction in orientation is crucial for solar energy deployment and the siting of energy grids. Turkey's extensive southern region, with its high solar radiation, presents a distinct advantage for solar energy. The country's east-west alignment simplifies and reduces the cost of grid expansion in a north-south direction. Consequently, from a geographical standpoint, it is entirely feasible for Turkey to establish solar energy installations in its southern regions and transmit electricity northwards, towards populous cities such as Ankara and Istanbul.

O. Cagdas Artantas, *Promotion of Green Electricity in Germany and Turkey*, EYIEL Monographs - Studies in European and International Economic Law 33,
https://doi.org/10.1007/978-3-031-44760-0_8

However, Turkey's terrain is predominantly mountainous, which poses certain disadvantages. For instance, the Taurus Mountains, which separate the Mediterranean region from Inner Anatolia, can present complications for siting installations and expanding the grid. This mountainous terrain also obstructs Mediterranean winds, diminishing the performance of wind energy.[1] The seismically active geographical formation of Turkey implies greater geothermal activity. Lastly, Turkey's proximity to energy-rich countries in Western Asia affords it easier access to natural gas resources.

In contrast, Germany benefits from higher wind energy potential, which permeates the country's inner regions via its flatlands.[2] However, Germany experiences lower solar radiation. The highest solar radiation in Germany (found in South Bavaria) is only equivalent to the lowest solar radiation in Turkey (found in the Eastern Black Sea) for certain periods throughout the year. With low seismic activity, Germany's potential for geothermal power is correspondingly minimal. Additionally, Germany's north-south land orientation complicates and elevates the cost of grid expansion projects.

The disparity in economic development between Germany and Turkey significantly influences the policies and legal structures promoting green electricity. An appropriate comparison should take into account the distinct economic development levels of both countries. Germany is a highly industrialized, high-income nation, whereas Turkey is a moderately industrialized, middle-income country.[3] Generally, Germany experiences a positive trade balance, while Turkey tends towards a negative trade balance under normal conditions. This discrepancy leads to a weaker Turkish Lira, contrasted with Germany's hard currency, the Euro.

Turkish investors incur higher risk premiums when borrowing hard currencies like the USD or Euro. With its lower risk premium, Germany allows its investors to borrow Euros at minimal interest rates for extended periods. This disparity simplifies project financing in Germany while making it less viable in Turkey. As such, Turkey has consistently had to offer USD-based tariff remuneration to stimulate investment in the green electricity sector.

Though the populations of Germany and Turkey are comparable, approximately 80–85 million each, the difference in their levels of industrialization means that their energy demands vary substantially. German energy consumption lies between 275,000–300,000 ktoe (kiloton of oil equivalent), while Turkey's energy consumption approximates 150,000 ktoe.[4] Interestingly, German energy demand has been on a steady decline since 1990 due to decreasing energy density. Turkish energy demand, meanwhile, had been rising steadily until a marked reduction to near-zero

[1]Meteoroloji Genel Müdürlüğü (2021) Türkiye Rüzgar Atlası. https://mgm.gov.tr/genel/ruzgar-atlasi.aspx

[2]Global Wind Atlas (2021) Germany Wind Map. https://globalwindatlas.info

[3]World Bank (2021) Upper middle income countries data. https://data.worldbank.org/country/XT

[4]Enerdata (2021) Germany Energy Information. https://www.enerdata.net/estore/energy-market/germany/

growth after 2018. This slowdown resulted from the diminished economic growth, sinking energy density, impact of the COVID-19 pandemic and global recession risk. It can be deduced that Turkish energy demand may align with Germany's only in the long term, contingent upon a revitalization of economic growth. It should be noted that Turkey's population growth rate is significantly decreasing. The stagnation of Turkish energy demand due to slowing economic growth presents a lower incentive for investors without tariff guarantees. This likely prompted the reintroduction of the YEKDEM feed-in tariff scheme. The government's energy localization target could only be achieved through the continued implementation of the FIT.

The varying technological capacities of Germany and Turkey further impact the promotion of green electricity. Germany stands as a global leader in green technologies, while Turkey exhibits moderate capacities in this context. This discrepancy has necessitated Turkey's adoption of local content and production requirements to foster the development of its green electricity technology. This necessity becomes particularly crucial considering currency fluctuations. However, recently Turkey has presented an impetus in green industry, particularly following the cost increases in the EU after the Russian invasion of Ukraine. A considerable number of investors preferred Turkey as a manufacturing base to serve the demand in the EU.

In contrast, Germany has maintained proficiency in green technology for an extended period. However, over the past decade, a substantial portion of green energy equipment production has transitioned to China, Northern Africa, or partners like Turkey. As a result, Germany has effectively transitioned from a "green technology equipment exporter" to an importer.[5] Addressing this shift would necessitate a range of protectionist measures at the EU level. However, any such measures would likely be contested by China in the WTO dispute resolution system, as is the case with the recent consultations against CBAM. Therefore, it is not anticipated that Germany will adopt local content requirement measures to safeguard its green industry.

8.1.2 Policy Comparison

Having compared the economic dimensions of green electricity promotion in Germany and Turkey, the analysis now shifts to policy aspects. Initially, the political climate towards green energy in both nations warrants scrutiny. The political environments of both countries are generally favorable towards green electricity. However, Germany experiences more pronounced "Not in my backyard" sentiments, where local communities frequently oppose large-scale projects in their regions, particularly those involving wind energy, sometimes with successful outcomes. These oppositions in Germany partially stem from economic considerations

[5] Arzt (2019).

associated with the Energiewende, the country's energy transition policy. Locals often object to green electricity projects that they perceive as imposing an unjust burden on the local environment and economy.[6]

In contrast, "Not in my backyard" responses are relatively new in Turkey. Both grid expansion and green electricity generation projects typically proceed in Turkey with minimal opposition from local populations. Public reaction is usually reserved for projects with significant environmental impact, such as those requiring extensive woodland logging, open pit mining, or geothermal drilling potentially posing pollution risks. The anticipated employment opportunities and economic growth arising from green electricity projects help to ease public reaction in Turkey. However, the public is becoming increasingly active due to social media campaigns and successful cases of project cancellations.

Among different types of green electricity sources, solar energy is viewed most favorably in both nations. This constitutes an additional advantage given Turkey's abundant solar radiation, as Germany will need to rely on onshore wind power to compensate for low solar radiation levels. The German grid expansion plans are often politically and legally challenged, which poses a notable disadvantage for Germany's energy transition.

The political climates in both Germany and Turkey are significantly influenced by their international legal obligations. As an EU member state, Germany is integral to the EU Green Deal policy. Conversely, Turkey, a candidate country with currently suspended negotiations, will be indirectly impacted by the European Green Deal through what is termed the "Brussels Effect". For instance, trade with the EU constitutes nearly half of Turkey's exports, thereby necessitating (at least a partial) alignment with EU Green Deal policies. Under the EU law, Germany is subject to binding long-term green electricity targets, whereas Turkish targets are short-term and less stringent. These targeting contrasts are essential when examining green electricity promotion policies and legislation in Germany and Turkey.

As previously noted, the green electricity policies of Germany and Turkey diverge considerably, each occupying opposite poles of climate policy. A key comparison can be made between these countries' decarbonization approaches.

Germany has established a robust climate policy aimed at significantly reducing GHG emissions. To achieve this, a broad range of policies is employed, such as promoting green electricity, energy efficiency, and electro-mobility. A pivotal policy tool for decarbonizing Germany is the coal phase-out plan. This ambitious project carries substantial costs, but the prevailing political will in Germany appears resolute that the German economy can sustain such a plan. Policymakers anticipate that the German economy can benefit from this shift and transform its conventional industry into a green, digitized, decentralized structure that is competitive in the twenty-first century.

[6]Clean Energy Wire (2021) Germany between citizens' energy and Nimbyism. https://www.cleanenergywire.org/dossiers/peoples-energiewende

Contrary to Germany, Turkey has not set ambitious climate protection and decarbonization targets. Several reasons underlie this, many of which were previously mentioned. In essence, Turkey is a developing economy with inherent vulnerabilities, such as trade and public budget deficits, currency shocks, and slowing growth. The cost of decarbonization might be prohibitive for Turkey, leading to a distinct path being followed. Turkey consciously carbonizes its energy mix, favoring local lignite, in alignment with its economic situation and the aim of "localization". It can be argued that further energy localization might mitigate some of Turkey's economic issues, particularly the trade deficit. Although economic objectives alone may not justify the absence of a Turkish climate policy—given that climate change is a global concern requiring collective action—understandably, some nations will pioneer decarbonization while others adopt alternative paths. Thus, Turkish "Net-Zero" status may be postponed a decade compared to Germany.

The second notable distinction between the two nations in terms of energy policies is their position on the "Nuclearization - Denuclearization" dichotomy. Germany denuclearized its electricity mix in 2023, while Turkey is planning the development of at least three nuclear power plants in total, with one currently under construction. The swift phase-out of Germany's nuclear power capacity might appear contradictory to its climate policy, given that nuclear power plants emit negligible or no GHG emissions. Nonetheless, both the public and policymakers seem to leave this contradiction in the past.

The question concerning Turkey's nuclearization is whether an energy policy path featuring nuclear power is viable, contrasting Germany's approach. Given that energy storage technology is still emerging and developing countries like Turkey will likely be late adopters, there is a need for a balancing energy capacity to counter the intermittency of expanding renewables. Local lignite appears to be only a short-term solution to this challenge in Turkey, and a long-term substitute like nuclear power fits into the national strategy. Turkey could deviate from Germany's path, develop substantial nuclear capacity, and reduce the need for local lignite use. This could assist in curbing GHG emissions considerably in Turkey. Undoubtedly, establishing nuclear capacity is a costly endeavor. As Turkey lacks experience with nuclear technology, it is inevitable that foreign companies will be tasked with building, operating, and decommissioning this capacity, rendering nuclear power more expensive for Turkey. A "Turkish Nuclear Program" to commence technology transfer or R&D was not planned as of the date of writing.

In conclusion, Turkey faces a complex dilemma: an affordable but climate-harming option or a costly but climate-friendly one. Turkey's current energy policy demonstrates an ambition to follow both paths; however, economic factors suggest a greater likelihood of pursuing the latter. The most evident indicator of Turkey's trajectory is the prioritization of the EU markets as an export target. This preference will require substantial emission reduction and legal alignment.

The third distinction between the two countries in the context of green electricity expansion is the presence or absence of local content requirements (LCRs) in their promotional schemes. Turkey seeks to develop a local "green" industrial capacity, whereas Germany does not share this objective. Germany's decision to forgo LCRs could be attributed to several reasons. First, there is a legal dimension: as a member of the EU, Germany is held accountable for actions that impact trade within the Union, making it challenging to impose local content usage or manufacturing requirements without violating EU and WTO laws. Second, being a substantial trading power, Germany is more likely to face WTO inquiries from other trading nations, such as the US or China. LCRs of smaller countries often go overlooked by these trade powerhouses. Beyond these considerations, Germany might not require such conditions since it already has a competitive "green" industrial capacity. Naturally, even Germany has room to expand its industry as green technology rapidly evolves. Still, localizing green technology might not be an urgent policy issue due to Germany's trade surplus. Conversely, Turkey may need to cultivate its industrial capacity to offset its trade deficit.

The fourth policy distinction between Germany and Turkey is intimately connected to their geographical locations. Turkey aims to become an energy hub in its region, engaging in numerous regional projects for natural gas trade. To further solidify its trade position, Turkey aspires to become an active partner of ENTSO-E and ENTSO-G. Meanwhile, Germany views energy trade as a means to facilitate its energy transition goals. Germany does not harbor ambitions of becoming a regional energy hub but expects the TEN-E strategy's success to make electricity affordable and cleaner across the country. This is because electricity trade balances countries' electricity generation capacities, reducing storage needs.

The fifth policy divergence between Germany and Turkey exposes the economic disparities between these two nations further. Turkey is strongly committed to becoming a natural gas producer in the short term, a goal which might be achievable considering Turkey's proximity to natural gas-rich territories and recent exploration discoveries. On the other hand, Germany refrains from natural gas exploration and exploitation initiatives, as its potential for natural gas production is extremely limited. Instead, Germany has a "green hydrogen policy" aimed at alleviating reliance on natural gas imports in the medium-to-long term. This policy is closely tied to green electricity promotion, as hydrogen is considered a "storage technology". By utilizing excess green electricity, Germany could reduce its dependence on imported natural gas through hydrogen technologies.

Despite their divergences, Germany and Turkey also share certain common interests and objectives in the realm of green electricity policy. Both nations aim to maximize the utilization of green electricity within their natural and grid limitations. However, they approach this common goal with differing motivations. Germany's pursuit is rooted in environmental and climate concerns, while Turkey's aim is more aligned with energy localization. For Germany, energy localization might only be a secondary objective.

Another shared policy aim is to maximize energy efficiency, particularly in their respective industrial sectors. Energy efficiency is a crucial component in both countries' energy policies to reduce energy intensity and limit energy demand. Nevertheless, again, the underlying primary motivations differ. Germany views energy efficiency as a pathway to achieving its climate and energy goals, while Turkey perceives it as a strategy to amend its trade balance and realize energy localization. Naturally, improved energy efficiency would undoubtedly aid Germany in reducing its dependence on imported natural gas.

Lastly, Germany and Turkey share a similar approach to energy affordability and accessibility. Both nations strive to maintain energy affordability for lower-income households and energy-intensive industries. As noted earlier, Turkey attempts to keep energy affordable by setting consumption tariffs, while Germany provides industry rebates. However, the truth remains that energy costs have risen significantly in both countries over the past decade.

8.1.3 Legal Comparison

Having concluded the analysis of economic and political comparisons, attention can now be directed toward contrasting the laws promoting green electricity in Germany and Turkey. This legal scrutiny finds its roots in the previously outlined economic and policy comparisons, given that the topic in question—the promotion of green electricity—cannot be judiciously inspected without assigning due importance to its economic and policy dimensions.

The preliminary point of comparison necessitates addressing the constitutional status of green electricity. Neither constitutional regime presents a direct constitutional guideline regarding the promotion of green electricity. Nevertheless, both countries, by their constitutions, are recognized as social states committed to environmental preservation. The social state feature of Germany and Turkey, as previously discussed, exhibits a strong association with the affordability and accessibility of energy. A persuasive argument can be constructed that energy prices must remain affordable and accessible to uphold the "social state criterion" of both constitutional frameworks. Concurrently, the environmental preservation criterion tasks both states with the responsibility of providing energy in the most environmentally and climatically benign manner feasible. This premise prompts a crucial question: the allowance of new coal power plants in Germany and Turkey. This issue has lost significant relevance for Germany owing to its "coal phase-out plan". However, the question remains pertinent for Turkey, given the absence of a coal phase-out plan in its policy framework.

The most straightforward response to the coal power plant inquiry is that the environmental protection clauses within the Turkish and German constitutions have not historically obstructed the authorization of new coal power plants. For instance, Turkey continues to grant new permits for local lignite power plants. These permits are not contested on the basis of unconstitutionality but rather due to violations of environmental statutes, such as zoning infringements or violations of natural life preservation. Hence, it can be contended that the constitutional frameworks of both nations do not act as barriers to carbon-intensive investments. This argument gives rise to a subsequent claim: the promotion of green electricity falls under the purview of international law and domestic policy in Germany and Turkey. These two states establish the groundwork for the promotion of green electricity through international commitments and domestic policy decisions.

The obligations under international law diverge for Germany and Turkey. Germany is an existing member of the European Union, whereas Turkey remains a candidate for EU membership. Nevertheless, under its Customs Union Agreement with the EU, Turkey is subject to the same state aid regulations as Germany. However, the Customs Union Agreement enforcement mechanisms are notably limited, leading to Turkey's divergence from its obligations under TFEU Article 107. This deviation has profound implications for the promotion of green electricity in these two countries.

Primarily, Germany possesses limited policy leeway to endorse green electricity through state resources. As previously indicated, the rulings of the ECJ in *PreussenElektra*, *Vent de Colere*, and *EEG 2012* were particularly stringent about the use of state resources. Consequently, Germany is compelled to depend on transmission system operators for the collection of the green electricity surcharge and payment of feed-in tariffs and premiums.

In contrast, Turkey relies on a state enterprise, EPİAŞ, to administer these operations. The dependence on a state company to execute the aforementioned tasks could prove to be significantly problematic within the EU system for a critical reason: promotion through a state company bestows the State with supreme control over the resources in question. This scenario could be scarcely different from funding the feed-in tariff from the state treasury, an argument that derives its basis from the *Vent de Colere* decision.

An additional concern regarding Turkey's compliance with TFEU Article 107 arises from the potential distortion of competition through the preferential treatment of certain actors and sectors. To qualify for the Turkish General Investment Promotion Scheme, which incorporates fiscal aid for green electricity investments, investors are required to secure a "Promotion Certificate" from the Ministry of Industry. This requirement could easily be interpreted as favoring specific actors, thus *prima facie* selective per EU law. Furthermore, the Turkish General Investment Promotion Scheme determines sectors and regions eligible for more flexible fiscal promotion. This approach could likewise be used to substantiate the selectivity of the system. For Germany, the adoption of a comparable system would be infeasible as the ECJ would inevitably annul such a system, unless allowed by EU law with a regional development exception.

The final concern regarding compliance with TFEU Article 107 relates to its effect on inter-state trade. As previously indicated, electricity trade remains relatively limited. However, the trend leans towards a more substantial electricity trade at the continental level. Turkey is not excluded from this system; it is interconnected to the ENTSO-E grid. Consequently, it is reasonable to anticipate that the volume of electricity trade between the EU and Turkey will increase in the future. While the promotion of green electricity currently exerts a marginal influence on inter-state trade, the further development of the interconnection between the EU and Turkey will undoubtedly augment this effect. This scenario is likely to transpire even more rapidly for Germany, given its enhanced interconnectivity with the other EU

Member States. Therefore, both countries will need to carefully consider the trade effects of their respective green electricity promotion schemes.

The compliance of Germany and Turkey with the WTO law also presents distinct differences. Germany is a global trade power, while Turkey is considered a developing country in this respect. Consequently, German trade measures are more likely to be targeted than their Turkish counterparts, placing Germany in a more rigid position, particularly concerning industrial promotion. As such, Germany does not have a public program to promote green industrial development beyond Research and Development grants.

Conversely, Turkey has implemented several measures to bolster its green industry. Firstly, the General Investment Promotion Scheme offers fiscal aid to investments in the production of green energy equipment. Secondly, the FIT scheme provides a higher tariff for the utilization of locally produced energy equipment. Additionally, the Turkish green electricity tendering system, YEKA, provides more relaxed conditions for either the use or manufacture of green electricity equipment. Such measures would pose significant challenges per EU and WTO law for Germany.

At the international level, Germany and Turkey exhibit significant differences in terms of compliance with the UNFCCC law. Germany actively participates in the Paris Agreement; conversely, Turkey has ratified it with a long delay. This discrepancy has implications for their respective emission control regulations. As previously noted, Germany is bound by an ambitious emission reduction target, whereas the Turkish emission reduction strategy is less ambitious and more flexible. Consequently, the promotion of green electricity is an evident necessity for Germany in line with the mandates of the Paris Agreement. To meet the emission targets, Germany is required to facilitate an energy transition with a high degree of success. The establishment of emission targets affords Germany a more comprehensive range of measures. While both countries employ emission monitoring, emission reduction measures such as emission trading are solely accessible in Germany. Implementing the coal phase-out plan has significantly complicated the construction of new coal power plants in Germany. On the other hand, building such units in Turkey is comparatively straightforward.

Furthermore, the Paris Agreement obligates Germany to contribute to the "Green Climate Fund". Due to its categorization as an upper-middle-income economy, Turkey is exempt from such a requirement, but it is also not eligible to benefit from the Fund.

Having addressed the international law obligations of Germany and Turkey relating to the promotion of green electricity, a comparison can now be drawn between the domestic legal structures in both countries that oversee this issue.

Firstly, it is essential to acknowledge the constitutional differences between these two countries. Germany operates as a federal republic, whereas Turkey is a unitary and highly centralized state. This disparity influences every aspect of their energy governance. In Germany, as discussed in the context of grid expansion issues, numerous policy matters are administered at the state level. Conversely, in Turkey, the central government manages nearly all energy-related matters. This dynamic makes the promotion of green electricity more challenging in Germany due to federal restrictions on new capacity and grid expansion.

Secondly, the energy regulators in Germany and Turkey, BNetzA and EPDK, respectively, share similar competencies concerning the promotion of green electricity. Both regulators oversee and supervise the promotion processes, including the issuance of new capacity permits and tendering procedures. However, due to federal restrictions in Germany, the policy space of BNetzA is considerably constrained. These limitations imposed on BNetzA complicate the monitoring, supervision, and regulation of green electricity promotion in Germany. Nonetheless, over the past decade, Germany has progressed towards more centralized control of the Energiewende under the auspices of BNetzA, resulting in the regulatory landscapes of the two countries becoming more similar.

Thirdly, Germany and Turkey diverge in their levels of electricity sector unbundling and privatization. The German electricity market, in accordance with EU law, is entirely unbundled, save for a few public supply companies at the local level. Conversely, the Turkish electricity market is predominantly privatized and semi-unbundled. As mentioned above, electricity transmission in Turkey is overseen by a state company, TEİAŞ. Furthermore, several coal power plants and hydroelectric dams remain the property of the state-owned electricity generation company EÜAŞ. The privatization process of the remaining EÜAŞ assets is ongoing. However, a minor segment of these assets is approaching the end of their lifecycles, meaning that they will likely remain under EÜAŞ's ownership. The privatization of TEİAŞ, on the other hand, is expected to occur in the following years.[7]

TEİAŞ manages electricity transmission across all of Turkey, representing a distinct advantage over Germany, where four separate private companies oversee transmission. This advantage for Turkey is particularly evident in the context of grid expansion. TEİAŞ benefits from "urgent expropriation" rules that expedite grid expansion projects. The lower population density of rural Turkey further benefits these projects. Conversely, due to its rural population density and highly unbundled electricity transmission market, Germany faces lagging development of the electricity grid. However, it should be noted that should Turkey's EU membership process progress, it will be required to unbundle its transmission sector, nullifying its advantage in grid expansion.

After the legal structures governing green electricity promotion in Germany and Turkey, we can now progress to the core of this section, comparing the specific green electricity promotion schemes of both countries.

As discussed previously, both Germany and Turkey initiated their green electricity promotion endeavors with a feed-in tariff scheme. However, Germany's primary promotion scheme has evolved with each successive amendment to the EEG. Germany transitioned from a FIT to FIP and subsequently to tendering processes.

[7] Anadolu Ajansı (2021) TEİAŞ özelleştirme kapsamına alındı. https://www.aa.com.tr/tr/ekonomi/teias-ozellestirme-kapsamina-alindi/2293109

This evolution can be perceived as a shift from a fixed tariff system to a market price-oriented, competitive model.

Conversely, Turkey maintains the feed-in tariff mechanism as its primary promotional measure, only establishing a tendering system for a portion of new capacity in highly efficient zones (YEKA). Consequently, Turkey has not experienced a transition to a market price-oriented system that relies on tendering for FIP. In the Turkish context, tenders for new capacity represent the exception rather than the norm, with the primary system for promotion remaining the FIT. This dependence on FIT implies price rigidity in the electricity market and imposes a greater financial burden on consumers. As will be proposed in the subsequent section, a transition to a market price-oriented competitive system could potentially aid Turkey in overcoming these challenges.

The innovative "South Quota" feature of the German tendering system, introduced in the Renewable Energy Sources Act (EEG) of 2021, ensured a specific quantity of new capacity was established in southern states. This quota was dropped by the amendment in 2022. Contrarily, Turkey has not implemented such a scheme for regional development. However, Turkey's "General Investment Promotion Scheme" provides fiscal incentives for investments in underdeveloped regions, thereby making invesments in these areas more viable for green electricity investors.

The German EEG system categorizes solar energy installations into two segments, further incentivizing roof-installed and similar systems. Turkey, on the other hand, has not developed such a segmentation system. Nonetheless, Turkey offers "unlicensed generation" options, which encourage the proliferation of micro installations. Thus, segmentation and unlicensed generation can be seen as two distinct systems aiming toward the same goal.

Turkey does not possess a specific promotion scheme for combined heat and power (CHP) installations. Instead, these installations are promoted via the FIT, YEKDEM. In contrast, Germany has enacted specific legislation for CHP installations, the Combined Heat and Power Act (KWKG), highlighting Germany's focus on emerging green technologies. Similarly, Turkey lacks a separate act for offshore wind power, while German legislation has addressed this issue through the Offshore Wind Energy Act (WindSeeG). This discrepancy can be attributed to the limited offshore wind capacity in Turkey, a source of energy that is a crucial part of the German electricity mix.

Germany and Turkey have provisions for the certification of green electricity generation and consumption, although this scheme is a newer development in Turkey. Quota schemes are not in place in either country, suggesting that green electricity generation certificates primarily serve as a legal foundation for the main promotion schemes: FIP in Germany and FIT in Turkey. However, the future may see the introduction of green electricity quotas as an additional or alternative promotion system in both nations. Consumption certificates, while voluntary, also contribute to the promotion of green electricity.

A significant point of divergence between Germany and Turkey's green electricity promotion laws is their approach to local content and manufacturing requirements. Turkey offers extra tariff payments for the use of locally sourced materials or the local manufacture of green electricity equipment, without making these practices obligatory. Conversely, Germany has chosen not to adopt such a protective mechanism. The reasons for this decision, as discussed previously, can be condensed into a simple summary: such protective measures in Germany could quickly become the target of scrutiny from the EU organs and WTO dispute settlement body. Turkey, however, employs these mechanisms as a way of promoting its own green industry.

Both nations also offer grid-related guarantees, reflecting a shared ambition to incorporate a large amount of green electricity capacity into their respective grids. However, these guarantees are restricted by the regulations governing new capacity in both Germany and Turkey. Germany conducts tenders for new capacity, with the exception of micro installations, while the Turkish transmission company TEİAŞ is responsible for deciding on capacity expansion connected to its grid points.

In terms of energy accessibility and affordability, Germany and Turkey pursue distinct strategies. Germany offers rebates on the green electricity surcharge for energy-intensive businesses but provides no such rebates for low-income households. In contrast, Turkey employs a more holistic approach by directly regulating the electricity price via electricity consumption tariffs. These tariffs are set at different rates for industry and households, with industrial electricity tariffs typically higher than those for households.

In conclusion, Turkey and Germany's different economic factors, environmental priorities, and political landscapes naturally result in different approaches to promoting green electricity. However, given the global imperative to address climate change, drawing from best practices across countries is essential. With this in mind, the following section will propose a way forward for both countries, drawing on lessons from their experiences.

8.2 Obstacles and Policy Proposals

The disparities between Germany and Turkey's green energy promotion models are undeniable, mirroring the variations in their economic, political, and legal landscapes. Previously, the shared aspects of these systems have been highlighted. In the ensuing discussion, the aim is firstly to outline the principal issues of the green electricity promotion schemes operating in these nations. Subsequently, policy proposals, predominantly derived from a comparative analysis of these two models, will be put forward.

8.2.1 Germany

Despite the success of German green electricity promotion schemes in galvanizing new investments in green electricity, several pressing concerns call for the attention of legislators and regulators. Firstly, the current German model extends renewable energy surcharge rebates to energy-intensive industries. Economically, this strategy is justifiable as it curtails the "industrial migration" to nations offering cheaper, carbon-intensive energy. However, this system starkly contradicts Germany's environmental and climate policies. Enterprises benefitting from this rebate demonstrate diminished motivation to invest in energy efficiency and green electricity generation. Further exacerbating the situation, the surcharge rebate model shifts the burden of green electricity promotion onto households, leading to escalated electricity prices for low-income households and consequently undermining public support for the EEG system. To rectify this, a two-fold proposal is suggested. Initially, the green electricity surcharge rebates (which are still applicable for electricity from plants under the KWKG and WindSeeG) for energy-intensive businesses should be terminated. In its place, these rebates ought to be allocated to businesses that invest in new energy efficiency and emission reduction. This approach aligns more harmoniously with German energy and climate policy. The EnFG 2022 was a milestone for Germany to implement a similar strategy. Subsequently, a new category of consumption promotion scheme should be introduced for low-consumption households. This second step would enhance energy affordability in Germany and restore public support in Energiewende.

The second concern surrounding Germany's green electricity promotion pertains to expanding the electricity grid. The completion of the energy transition in Germany is contingent on the presence of a robust and intelligent grid. Given the current pace of grid expansion in Germany, which is insufficient, there is an urgent need for acceleration. The unbundled transmission service market presents a significant impediment to this goal. However, due to EU law, the unbundling of this sector cannot be reversed. Instead, Germany should focus on simplifying and expediting its permitting processes for expansion. The enactment of a "rapid expropriation act," akin to the Turkish model, could potentially address this issue. Germany could speed up the grid expansion and the construction of "smart grids" through a comprehensive federal act on swift land acquisition. However, it is imperative to bear in mind that rapid expropriation in Germany could potentially undermine public acceptance of the Energiewende.

Lastly, despite Germany's advocacy for green electricity, this book highlights the necessity of strengthening local production of equipment, a strategy that aligns with the EU Green Deal Industrial Plan. Germany will need to step up its protective measures per the Green Deal Industrial Plan. Furthermore, diversifying energy resources remains critical until a significant storage capacity, facilitated by batteries and hydrogen, becomes operational. It may also be necessary for Germany to reconsider its nuclear energy phase-out, make provisions for smaller nuclear entities like modular reactors. After recent changes to the EU Taxonomy system, nuclear energy is now considered a "green investment". This could help improve the image of SMRs in German public discussion. Additionally, initiating a final surge of high-efficiency coal electricity capacity supplemented by carbon-capture processes should be evaluated so as to cope with geopolitical risks.

8.2.2 Turkey

Comparable to the German scenario, Turkish green electricity promotion schemes have proven successful regarding the expansion of installed capacity. Nevertheless, compared to Germany, Turkey's experience in promoting green electricity is relatively nascent. Consequently, a range of issues can be identified within the Turkish model, leading to the formulation of several policy proposals.

A broad policy recommendation for Turkey involves initiating emission targeting and implementing measures for emission reduction. The motivation behind these proposals extends beyond environmental concerns and is also economically driven. The CBAM's entry into force will likely impose an additional burden on Turkish exports to the EU economic area. Consequently, Turkey stands to benefit from reducing the carbon footprint of its products. Ratifying the Paris Agreement and pledging a substantial long-term carbon emission reduction target constituted an initial step. Emphasis should be placed on Turkey's efforts to mitigate emissions, establish a well-rounded carbon pricing mechanism, and bolster its promotion of green electricity. The importance of Turkey's integration into the EU market through its national ETS and taxonomy must be highlighted, requiring the development of tailored national legislation that addresses domestic necessities. These schemes should extend to and target conventional electricity generation installations in order to discourage new carbon-intensive investments.

Furthermore, it should be proposed that improved collaboration between the EU and Turkey in the realms of sustainability finance, electricity trade, green hydrogen, and local equipment production could potentially offer mutual benefits.

While FITs serve as suitable launching points for promoting green electricity, they become insufficient in responding to price signals as the energy market matures. Essentially, feed-in tariffs do not operate competitively and fail to incentivize price reductions. Given Turkey's short-term need for energy price reductions, the initial policy recommendation should entail abolishing the FIT mechanism, YEKDEM, before 2030. The subsequent green electricity promotion regime in Turkey should incorporate competitive mechanisms. The most suitable alternative to substitute would be a system of "tendering for FIP". This model would stimulate competition for lower prices and supply the Turkish energy mix with affordable green electricity, a much-needed element. Consequently, the current "Tendering for specific zones" system (YEKA) should be amalgamated with this primary system. A unified, singular tendering regime would offer investors in Turkey a more facilitative investment climate. However, during the amendment of the YEKDEM system, the FIT should be preserved for small or micro installations. Imposing tendering requirements on such installations could impede the expansion of green electricity, given that tendering processes tend to be expensive and bureaucratic.

Turkey must also confront the issue of energy affordability. The FIT surcharges are increasingly burdensome for low-income households, as the support is (more or less) pegged to the USD. Consequently, with each devaluation of the Turkish Lira, these surcharges rise in a manner disconnected from Turkey's real income growth, making electricity increasingly unaffordable over time. The main policy recommendation for Turkey for this issue aligns with the one proposed for Germany: consumption promotion for low-consumption households. Without such a scheme, a significant portion of the population risks exclusion from electricity provision, although it is legally designated a public service in Turkey. As a social state, Turkey cannot afford to exclude such a large segment of its population from a public service. Introducing a consumption promotion represents the most direct means of reinstating energy affordability.

References

Anadolu Ajansı (2021) TEİAŞ özelleştirme kapsamına alındı. https://www.aa.com.tr/tr/ekonomi/teias-ozellestirme-kapsamina-alindi/2293109

Arzt I (2019) Nix mit Solarenergie made in Germany: Gute Zelle, schlechte Zelle. Die Tageszeitung: taz

Clean Energy Wire (2021) Germany between citizens' energy and Nimbyism. https://www.cleanenergywire.org/dossiers/peoples-energiewende

Enerdata (2021) Germany Energy Information. https://www.enerdata.net/estore/energy-market/germany/

Global Wind Atlas (2021) Germany Wind Map. https://globalwindatlas.info

Meteoroloji Genel Müdürlüğü (2021) Türkiye Rüzgar Atlası. https://mgm.gov.tr/genel/ruzgar-atlasi.aspx

World Bank (2021) Upper middle income countries data. https://data.worldbank.org/country/XT

Chapter 9
Conclusion

This book, as outlined in the introduction, was guided by several objectives. The initial goal was to define the overarching term "promotion" to establish a foundation for subsequent discussions. However, defining promotion presents challenges. This work endeavored to construct a definition of promotion from economic and legal perspectives. In essence, the following definition can be proposed: Promotion is a process that confers a better position upon recipients compared to their market counterparts. This definition may seem overly simplistic for many scenarios. States and their promotion schemes represent complex mechanisms; thus, this definition may require adaptation to intricate economic relationships.

However, when one attempts to apply the aforementioned definition to the green electricity market, another complication arises: The green electricity market does not adhere to the traditional definition of a "market." This sector is heavily regulated, and to a significant extent, manufactured by the State. Consequently, how can we identify market equivalents for comparison with the promotion recipient? This issue was at the heart of Canada – RE. However, the Appellate Body refrained from offering a solution to this question. Instead, they evaluated the issue from a different angle: The local content requirements. Therefore, we must seek insight elsewhere. The "Market Economy Investor Test" employed by the ECJ could provide some guidance here. In determining promotion, it will be essential to ascertain whether the recipient gains an economic advantage that it would not have obtained under normal market conditions. This secondary step also presents challenges as it necessitates accepting a "hypothetical green electricity market" as the reference point. The construction of a hypothetical green electricity market is inherently error-prone, given that such a market is non-existent. Consequently, dispute resolution bodies may need to rely on a "case-by-case" analysis when determining whether promotion is present in a given scenario.

Conversely, energy authorities have duties extending beyond simply identifying whether a measure constitutes promotion. They often aim to encourage the generation of green electricity. The absence of a "free green electricity market" does not

O. Cagdas Artantas, *Promotion of Green Electricity in Germany and Turkey*, EYIEL Monographs - Studies in European and International Economic Law 33,
https://doi.org/10.1007/978-3-031-44760-0_9

preclude authorities from promoting these activities. However, they encounter a specific dilemma: How to determine the extent of promotion? Germany initially implemented a straightforward feed-in tariff system, offering promotion for 20 years to green electricity installations. Over time, it became evident that the level of promotion within this model could impose a significant burden on the overall electricity market. Turkey faced a similar predicament. The "best practice" developed in Germany was the introduction of measures that simulate free-market competition. As such, the "Tendering for Feed-in Premia" and "Tendering for new capacity" schemes were recommended for Turkey. These methods are more adept at determining the total volume of promotion, as they exhibit greater price sensitivity. Conversely, feed-in tariffs are particularly advantageous for micro-installations (like rooftop-mounted solar panels). Consequently, an efficient scheme should incorporate both competitive elements and tariffs to accommodate varying volumes and applications.

This study draws on economic and political data but largely constitutes a legal examination of green electricity promotion regimes. Four legal frameworks have been scrutinized in this work: The WTO, EU, Germany, and Turkey. These entities have been investigated within their own contexts and in comparison to each other. Among these, the "largest" framework is the WTO, considering its nearly global coverage. However, the WTO's legal stipulations regarding green electricity promotion are minimal, primarily due to the limited trade of electricity in substantial volumes. Consequently, the WTO's dispute resolution arm has primarily addressed promotion of green electricity equipment production, given the larger trade volumes involved.

EU law provides detailed regulation for green electricity promotion. The RED II is an example of such a comprehensive approach. The case law of the ECJ further clarifies the legal aspects of green electricity promotion. The *PreussenElektra* line of cases opens up policy space for green electricity promotion measures, provided the transmission system operator oversees the collection and payment of surcharges. Conversely, the *Vent de Colere* case establishes the legal status of public collection and payment of surcharges, concluding that such a measure is incompatible with the single market. Therefore, ECJ decisions underscore the role of transmission system operators. However, issues relating to EU law and green electricity promotion are likely to increase over time due to the growth of continent-wide electricity trade. Ensuring the cross-border validity of promotion schemes will prove challenging, and the success of joint promotion schemes per RED II will also remain uncertain.

The compatibility of the EU emission trading system and green electricity promotion schemes is a contentious issue in Germany. The argument presented here suggests that these two measures can function simultaneously due to their distinct goals. A similar proposition was made for Turkey, recommending the establishment of a concrete emission target and emission trading system, along with a revamped green electricity promotion system.

Germany and Turkey are distinct countries in geography, economy, politics, and law. However, there is no reason not to identify and adopt "best practices" from each country. The central thesis of this book suggests that competitive and tariff elements, along with carbon pricing schemes, should be part of the energy transition in Germany and Turkey. This is one of many suggestions. However, it is essential to acknowledge that domestic energy transitions alone will not suffice to reverse or slow down climate change. Regional and international collaboration is needed to address today's climate and environment-related issues. Cooperation at the EU level, although crucial, is not sufficient. The EU and Germany should foster "climate and energy partnerships" across Eastern Europe, the Middle East, and North Africa. Consequently, it is proposed that Germany and Turkey could establish such a partnership in climate and energy issues.